EAST CENTRAL EUROPE
AFTER THE WARSAW PACT

EAST CENTRAL EUROPE AFTER THE WARSAW PACT

Security Dilemmas in the 1990s

Andrew A. Michta

Foreword by
VOJTECH MASTNY

Contributions in Political Science, Number 296
Global Perspectives in History and Politics

George Schwab, Series Adviser

GREENWOOD PRESS
NEW YORK • WESTPORT, CONNECTICUT • LONDON

Library of Congress Cataloging-in-Publication Data

Michta, Andrew A.
    East Central Europe after the Warsaw Pact : security dilemmas in
the 1990s / Andrew A. Michta ; foreword by Vojtech Mastny.
       p.   cm. — (Contributions in political science, ISSN 0147–1066
; no. 296)
    Includes bibliographical references and index.
    ISBN 0–313–27886–5 (alk. paper)
    1. Europe, Eastern—National security. 2. Warsaw Treaty
Organization. 3. Poland—National security. 4. Czechoslovakia—
National security. 5. Hungary—National security. I. Title.
II. Series.
UA646.8.M53   1992
355′.033047—dc20   91–33126

British Library Cataloguing in Publication Data is available.

Library of Congress Catalog Card Number: 91–33126
ISBN: 0–313–27886–5
ISSN: 0147–1066

First published in 1992

Greenwood Press, 88 Post Road West, Westport, CT 06881
An imprint of Greenwood Publishing Group, Inc.

Printed in the United States of America

The paper used in this book complies with the
Permanent Paper Standard issued by the National
Information Standards Organization (Z39.48–1984).

10 9 8 7 6 5 4 3 2 1

To Cristina and Chelsea

CONTENTS

ACKNOWLEDGMENTS

I would like to express my sincere thanks to the administration of Rhodes College for its support throughout this project, most of all for granting me a leave of absence to complete the book.

I am very much indebted to Tadeusz K. Zachurski of the Radio Free Europe Polish Section in Washington, D.C., and to P. Hartley Walsh of the Library of Congress for their patient assistance in my research. Professors Vojtech Mastny of the Johns Hopkins University Bologna Center and George Schwab of the CUNY Graduate Center read an early version of the manuscript and gave me the benefit of their critical comments and suggestions. A word of appreciation goes to Professor Ilya Prizel of the Johns Hopkins School of Advanced International Studies for his friendship and encouragement as I worked my way through the maze of East Central European politics and security issues.

Special thanks go to Jon Thompson of Defense Orientation Conference Association in Arlington, Virginia, for his friendship and his help in arranging my field work in Europe, and to Mertie and Robert Buckman of Memphis, Tennessee, for their generous commitment to the International Studies program at Rhodes College. I am grateful to Colonels Glenn Bailey and Ruth Anderson, who took the time out of their busy schedules as U.S. military attachés in Warsaw and Budapest, respectively, to assist me in my research. I also want to thank Sejm Deputy Henryk Michalak, Polish Deputy Defense Minister Janusz Onyszkiewicz, General Tadeusz Cepak of the Polish Army Foreign Liaison Office, General Jiri Divis of the Czechoslovak General Staff, Svatopluk Buchlovsky of the Czechoslovak Foreign Ministry, Colonel Tibor Koeszegvari of the Defense Research Institute of the Hungarian Defense Ministry, and Colonel Endre Javor of the Hungarian Defense Ministry for their introduction to civilian and military government officials in their countries. In addition, I would like to thank Deborah Klaum of Greenwood Press for her excellent work in the production of this book.

Most of all, I want to thank my wife, Cristina, for her patience, her understanding, and her unswerving support during the two years this book has been in the making.

FOREWORD

Collapsing frontiers, strife of nationalities, threatening streams of refugees—all these alarming events in Eastern Europe may deceive us into forgetting how dramatically security has improved in that area and beyond. It is well to remember that none too distant time when the region harbored the largest concentration of military power history had ever seen—all poised to annihilate Western Europe at a moment's notice. How recently has it been that experts agonized about such scary possibilities as the "grab of Hamburg" by a lightning thrust through West Germany by the Warsaw Pact's crack forces?

Nor were the countries of the region from which such perils emanated themselves secure in any sense of the word. They had been repeatedly targets of military coercion by their nominal Soviet ally, providing most of the drama in the otherwise uneventful history of European warfare since World War II. What is more, their military structures had been deliberately shaped so as to make them indefensible in case of a repetition of such operations. Can greater insecurity be imagined?

Today, when the Warsaw Pact, the Soviet empire, and, indeed, the Soviet Union itself are here no more, the prevailing concern among its successor states is about a "security limbo"—not a bad alternative to the sort of security certitudes they had experienced before. The allusion is to a feeling of insecurity that is general rather than specific and whose sources are difficult or even impossible to identify. When the Hungarian parliament, struggling to elaborate a new military doctrine for the nation, proposed an "all-around" or "concentric" defense, it dropped these terms on second thought, lest the wrong impression be created that the country was surrounded by enemies—as it had been for the previous thousand years but was no more.

To be sure, East Central Europe's postcommunist states face a host of very severe problems, old and new: economic decline, political discord, social dislocation. Yet all such problems were not even considered under the rubric of security in the past. Now they most appropriately are, and this, too, is an indication of how much the situation has changed for the better. For example, the mass hatred of Czechoslovakians or Hungarians for the hundreds of thousands of Gypsies in their midst—with a crime rate several times the national average—is certainly part of a formidable security problem. But it is simply not of the same order of magnitude as was the problem of how to avoid being obliterated in a nuclear exchange started by one of the many thousands of missiles in the neighborhood.

Lest the comforting picture be overdrawn, however, a clear difference should be made between the north of the region and the areas farther south and east, separated today by a line that has replaced the old Iron Curtain as marking the most important division on the Continent. It is, in the last analysis, the line between hope and fear, and this book is only about the lands of hope—the northern "Triangle." This is not the "iron triangle" of East Germany, Poland, and Czechoslovakia, which not so long ago was regarded as the Warsaw Pact's hard core—until it was exposed as being merely made of breakable plastic. The softer and more durable one unites Poland, Czechoslovakia, and Hungary—for the first time in history.

These are very different countries, inhabited by very different peoples, whose historical and geopolitical predicament is explored on the following pages in some detail. Only once before in modern times have these nations had an opportunity to develop free from outside interference—in the aftermath of World War I, when both of their overbearing Great Power neighbors, Germany and Russia, had been simultaneously weakened by defeat. The opportunity had not been used well and had ended in the double catastrophe of subjugation first by one and then by the other of the neighbors, in each case under two of the most monstrous regimes twentieth-century Europe has produced, Hitler's and Stalin's.

Now the opportunity for a new start is on hand for a second time, as both Germany and Russia are turning inward simultaneously and the countries between them are again capable of shaping their own destinies. But today's situation is not the same as seventy years ago; it is more promising. This time, Germany and Russia are not nations recently embittered by defeats by foreign enemies and susceptible to the appeal of tyranny. One is Europe's model democracy, wealthy, and reluctant to use power almost to the point of complacency, while the other has just emerged from tyranny and chooses the path of democracy for the first time in its history.

Nor is the wider Europe farther West than it used to be. It is not the vengeful, exhausted, and neurotic Europe that had been the product of the shambles of World War I; it is a tolerant, self-confident, and benign one—benevolent almost to the benign neglect of its less fortunate Eastern part. It is a Europe that has found new ways of transnational cooperation, and it has made them work. Indeed, much of the problem of the security limbo is in the difficulty of deciding which, if any, of several available models—NATO, Western European Union, Conference on Security and Cooperation in Europe, to name but a few—ought to be chosen for the foundation of the Continent's new security architecture. It is an important task, but not an urgent one, for there is no security crisis, only a plethora of serious problems, thus providing valuable time for discerning choice.

Finally, the peoples of the Triangle are not the same as they were. They and their governments have already proved a willingness to collaborate that was not evidenced before. There is not much love lost among them; however, sounder political links are based on self-interest rather than on love. It is the mutual recognition of the complementarity of fundamental interests, regardless of disagreement on the less fundamental ones, that propels the collaboration. There is no grand vision of an institutionalized union—a precept for making secondary disagreements primary—but otherwise little doubt about the direction in which all three are moving. It is the direction of democracy and integration with the rest of Europe, regardless of how long the road might be. That alone is already a remarkable security accomplishment.

Since the first draft of this book was completed in August 1991, the Soviet Union's collapse that month disposed of one of the potentially disturbing factors that had until then defined the security environment of the countries of the Triangle. It is a special tribute to the author—who not only asks the right questions but is also prepared to answer them even when speculation and prediction are required—that no substantive revision was necessary as a result of the dramatic August events. The book is as reliable a guide to the dilemmas of East Central European security after those events as it had been before them—only more topical. It is likely to remain so for a long time until the dust in the troubled region has settled.

Vojtech Mastny
Bologna, Italy

EAST CENTRAL EUROPE
AFTER THE WARSAW PACT

INTRODUCTION

Political geography is an obvious challenge to anyone choosing to write about Poland, Czechoslovakia, and Hungary, the three countries that constitute today's East Central Europe. Historically, the region's boundaries have shifted several times, defying the skills of cartographers and ethnographers alike and often making the clear delineation of national frontiers impossible. The peoples of these countries evolved within multinational empires, and their national identity developed later than in Western Europe. They emerged in the early twentieth century as "successor states," carved out of what once had been the domains of the Romanovs and the Habsburgs. They were pawns in World War II, saw their borders altered by the 1945 Yalta settlement, and again disappeared for four decades behind the Iron Curtain of Soviet communism. Today, since the 1989 collapse of the Soviet empire, Poland, Czechoslovakia, and Hungary have been reclaiming their sovereignty and their place in Europe. For the first time in their history they are acting jointly as a region committed to remaking itself in the image of the West. Since 1989 Poland, Czechoslovakia, and Hungary have been referred to both in the West and in the former Soviet Union as the "Triangle." The term is another name for East Central Europe.

The geopolitical concept of East Central Europe has endured, even if before 1945 it was impossible to chart the region's political map based on the Western notion of the ethnically cohesive nation-state. Prior to the destruction of the European Jewry and the dramatic population transfers of 1945, this "other Europe" was a rich collection of nationalities intermingled and interspersed to a degree that made the traditional nation-state criteria difficult to apply. The consolidation of these states was further retarded by the outbreak of World War II. As a result of the war, the nascent diversity of East Central Europe and Central Europe vanished for forty-five years, obliterated by the all-encompassing uniform idea of a communist Eastern Europe and Stalin's vision of the Moscow-dominated Soviet bloc. Still, during the communist rule, Poland, Czechoslovakia, and Hungary resisted as best they could the Soviet efforts to deny them their distinct national and cultural identity.

In the end, the disappearance of East Central Europe as a separate area of study in Western scholarship proved temporary—a testimony to its viability, notwithstanding the inexactness of the frontiers. In the aftermath of the 1989 anticommunist revolutions, the question of political geography resurfaced once again, driven by both the regional and the pan-European political transformation. The resurgence of East Central Europe has brought back with it a number of unresolved territorial and ethnic questions. At the same time, the region's political, economic, and security dilemmas of today reflect the radical change in international politics of the end of this century. The collapse of communism, the implosion of the Soviet empire, and the December 1991 demise of the Soviet Union itself have created an unprecedented opportunity for East Central Europe to overcome its geopolitical legacy. At the same time, the very scope of change now under way in Europe has brought with it a degree of uncertainty unprecedented since the end of World War II. This book seeks to rediscover East Central Europe as a historical region and, possibly, to redefine it as an important structure in the new European architecture, in light of both the opportunities and the uncertainties of post-1989 Europe. It concentrates on key security dilemmas East Central Europe faces today as it stands on the threshold of the next century.

Over the past two years, Poland, Czechoslovakia, and Hungary have been evolving into a distinct geopolitical region. They played a pivotal role in the 1989 revolutions, worked jointly in 1990 and 1991 to bring about an end to the Warsaw Pact, and have undertaken democratic and market reforms to take the Triangle into the European Community. For different reasons they are individually strategically important to the future of pan-European security: Poland and Czechoslovakia because they are a natural "bridge" between Russia and the West; Hungary because it is bordering on the Balkan tinderbox.

Prior to the Soviet domination of the region, it was customary for Western scholarship to combine Poland, Czechoslovakia, and Hungary together with Germany and Austria into a larger notion of Central Europe.[1] Likewise, Southeastern Europe included the Balkan states, while Eastern Europe proper consisted of the European portion of Russia as well as the Baltic states of Lithuania, Latvia, and Estonia. World War II imposed a new political map on the region, severing the historical and economic linkages that the original classification sought to capture. The war also retarded the economic and political development of Poland, Czechoslovakia, and Hungary relative to their West German and Austrian neighbors. It is too early, therefore, to view the collapse of communism in the East as synonymous with the restoration of the prewar Central Europe. While Poland, Czechoslovakia, and Hungary continue to share a strong cultural affinity with Central and Western Europe, at least a decade of economic reform and political consolidation is necessary before they can claim a place among developed European nations and become Central European not only in a geographic sense, but also in a political one. To do so, the Triangle must shake off completely the legacy of the forty-five years of Soviet imperial control.[2]

The outcome of World War II gave the idea of Eastern Europe a political meaning par excellence. Stalin's territorial gains in Europe after 1945, and the ensuing Cold War, compelled the West to regard the entire area as Eastern Europe—an implicit recognition by the West that, regardless of the region's historical and cultural ties to Western Europe, it had found itself on the other side of the East-West political divide. The forty-five years of Soviet imperial domination never made the arbitrary distinction appear any more justified, even if the notion of Eastern Europe was eventually accepted by the West as a political expedient. It took the upheaval of the 1989 revolutions to remake the communist-imposed political map of the region. In the two years between 1989 and 1991 the region's traditional pro-Western orientation and its old regional problems and conflicts, some reaching back to the turn of the century, have reemerged with a new force. At the same time, the 1991 collapse of the Warsaw Pact and the rapid Soviet withdrawal from Europe have left East Central Europe in a security vacuum.

Irrespective of how successful or unsuccessful the postcommunist democracies will ultimately be in their efforts to rejoin the West, the term *Eastern Europe* no longer describes the geopolitical reality. Rapid change in the region after 1989 has revealed that the East-West divide of the Cold War era has been replaced by a growing division between the northern and central European countries on the one hand and those lying to their south and east on the other. The Triangle of postcommunist successor democracies—Poland, Czechoslovakia, and Hungary—is moving virtually in unison to become a part of the West. The record of the past two years suggests that, among the former Soviet satellites, only Poland, Czechoslovakia, and Hungary have at present good long-term prospects for integrating themselves into the new Europe.

By contrast, the Balkans (with the possible exception of the Yugoslav republics of Slovenia and Croatia) have shown little promise of becoming a part of the West any time soon, inasmuch as reform in southeastern Europe has been stalled by volatile and potentially explosive nationalism. The same appears to be true of the Soviet successor states, where the nationalities crisis has been compounded by the legacy of communist dictatorship. Whatever the outcome of the current crisis in the former Soviet Union—that is, whether the country will ultimately fragment or whether the "commonwealth" formula negotiated by Russia, Byelorussia, and the Ukraine after the failed August 1991 hard-line coup, holds the Slavic core of the state together—the Soviet successor states may not be ready either politically or economically to claim a place in the European Community until well into the next century. In systemic terms, for the rest of the 1990s Russia will remain a distinctly "un-European" country and a great regional power still capable of threatening its neighbors. If the current trend continues, the new division in Europe will run between the core of its northern and central states on the one hand and their periphery to the east and southeast of the Continent on the other. In practical geopolitical terms, by the end of the decade Europe's eastern frontier will have shifted from the western border of the now defunct German Democratic Republic to the Bug River and the Carpatho-Ukraine—the eastern border lines of Poland, Czechoslovakia, and Hungary.

The new pattern of geopolitical divisions in Europe necessitates that Poland, Czechoslovakia, and Hungary be considered separately from the Balkan states, as well as from the western republics of the former Soviet Union.[3] East Central Europe is moving toward democracy and market capitalism, while the Balkans remain mired in nationalism and the remnants of communist dictatorship. In the coming years, the Triangle's historical experience combined with the policies pursued by Warsaw, Prague, and Budapest will further deepen the North-South division between East Central Europe on the one hand and Romania, Bulgaria, Yugoslavia (or what remains of the Serbian-led Yugoslav federation), and the reconstituted Soviet successor states on the other hand. This is particularly true when the question of national and regional security is concerned.

This book looks at key security issues confronting Poland, Czecho-slovakia, and Hungary in the last decade of the twentieth century. It describes policies that the three governments have already implemented and the blueprints for national and European security they have come to support. It views security as a function of politics and economics and pays special attention to military reforms undertaken by the three countries in response to the new international situation. It also tries to project the direction of future change in light of potential threats to the Triangle's security position.

The questions discussed here are ultimately about issues much larger than the regional security of East Central Europe. The future security framework of East Central Europe is of vital importance to the stability and security of the Continent as a whole. Throughout the Cold War period, East Central Europe constituted a critical area in the military strategy of the Soviet bloc, and on several occasions Moscow demonstrated its willingness to use military force to retain control over it. The disintegration of the Warsaw Pact after 1989 has not diminished the region's geopolitical and strategic importance. Defense planners of the North Atlantic Treaty Organization (NATO) have long recognized the region's military significance. In an eloquent testimony to the region's importance to Europe's security, as well as to the vital strategic linkage between Poland, Czechoslovakia, and Hungary, the Treaty on Conventional Armed Forces in Europe, signed in 1990, includes the Triangle in the key Central Area in Europe, with Germany, and the Benelux countries constituting its Western equivalent.[4]

Poland, Czechoslovakia, and Hungary are the fastest-changing postcommunist societies, determined to shed the remaining vestiges of Soviet-style collectivism and to become full-fledged members of the European Community. Their political elites share a general commitment to democracy and market capitalism as the only viable option in their quest to join Western Europe. The Triangle states also share analogous social, political, and economic problems bequeathed to them by forty-five years of communism and Soviet control. Their armies are organized in a similar fashion and use standard Soviet equipment. Until very recently they also shared the same joint Warsaw Pact coalition warfare doctrine, which had defined their military training and the putative conditions under which these armies would have been employed. Finally, all three were host countries to sizable Soviet army contingents, stationed in Poland since World War II, in Hungary since 1956, and in Czechoslovakia after the Prague Spring of 1968. They all have a common border with the former Soviet Union, while Poland and Czechoslovakia also border on Germany.

The recent history of the East Central European postcommunist states has been shaped to a varying degree by the political and cultural influence of their powerful neighbors. Russian influence was particularly strong in the case of Poland, while Hungary and Czechoslovakia developed within the orbit of German-Austrian culture and politics. Ethnic and religious divisions run differently in each of the three countries. Poland and Hungary are largely one-nation states, while Czechoslovakia is a federation of the

Czech and Slovak nations. Poland is overwhelmingly Catholic; Czechoslovakia is 50 percent Catholic and has a sizable Protestant minority constituting about 20 percent of the population; Hungary is about 50 percent Catholic and 25 percent Protestant. In terms of population size, Poland is the largest of the three, with 38.5 million people and the highest birthrate in the region; Czechoslovakia is about half the size of Poland, with over 15 million people; Hungary is the smallest of the three, with a population of barely over 10 million.[5]

The three countries command certain distinct cultural and political features that set them apart from the rest of the former Soviet bloc. Poland, Czechoslovakia, and Hungary are decidedly oriented toward the West in terms of their national aspirations. They are better prepared than the Balkan states, the Baltics, or Russia to become effective democracies and working market economies. The middle class, although not particularly strong in the region outside of Czechoslovakia, has survived in East Central Europe to a much greater degree than in other communist states. Poland, Czechoslovakia, and Hungary developed a strong national identity in the postwar period predominantly in opposition to Soviet-style communism; this has attenuated the national divisions and irredentist claims among the three. Moreover, as exemplified by the 1956 eruption of opposition to Moscow's domination in Hungary, by the Prague Spring of 1968 in Czechoslovakia, and by the periodic outbursts of national discontent in Poland, Stalinism had never managed to take root in these societies.

This book explores the limits of change in East Central European security in light of the disintegration of the Yalta system, the implosion of the Soviet empire, and the reemergence of reunified Germany as a great power in Europe. The dramatic changes on the Continent in 1989 have left its security system unglued: the anticommunist revolutions that began in Poland and then, pushed by a massive exodus of the East Germans, spilled south throughout the Soviet outer empire to culminate in a bloody outbreak of fratricide in Nicolae Ceausescu's Romania, have already remade Europe's political map. In the process they have changed our axioms about Soviet power. The remarkable "Autumn of the Peoples of Eastern Europe," crowned by West Germany's push for immediate reunification and the December 1991 demise of the Soviet Union, has shattered the postwar European order.

The revolutionary transformation of what had once been the Soviet bloc rests on an ill-fated effort by the Soviet Union to redefine its security position in Europe. At the core of the current flux in East Central European security lies the failure of *perestroika* reforms in the Soviet Union, a revolution from above which has by far exceeded the boundaries of

Moscow's original plan. The implosion of the Soviet empire has left an effective vacuum of power at the center of Europe. At the same time, the demise of Mikhail Gorbachev's reforms in the late 1980s has given an impetus to an anticommunist revolution throughout Eastern Europe and ultimately in the Soviet Union itself. The remainder of the 1990s will show whether the end of bipolarity in Europe can lead to a stable new political order for the postcommunist societies or whether it will bring about a repetition of the region's turbulent history.

The future of Poland, Czechoslovakia, and Hungary will ultimately depend on their successful transition from the Soviet-dominated Warsaw Pact to a new security framework capable of providing the requisite regional stability. This has been a particularly urgent task after the 1991 dissolution of the military structures of the Warsaw Pact and the organization's final collapse. The new conditions in the region demand that the Triangle develop a new relationship with the West as well as with the Soviet Union's successor states. It would be indeed a tragic repetition of interwar history if East Central Europe, caught up in domestic problems and old national hostilities, were to become once again a pawn in Great Power competition. If reforms were to fail and instability were to spread, another chance for bringing the "other Europeans" into Europe might not reappear any time soon. Failure to bring the region closer to Western Europe would also impact on the progress of European integration. If chaos were to mark the future of East Central Europe, it might eventually lead to a state of perpetual crisis, which could only encourage irredentism. In this broader sense, the future of Poland, Czechoslovakia, and Hungary—the three former Soviet satellites striving for democratic reform and market capitalism—has a clear pan-European dimension, inasmuch as instability in the region would inevitably affect the security of the entire continent.

Finding a solution to the East Central European security dilemma in the 1990s is also of concern to the North Atlantic alliance. As the leader of NATO, the United States has a vital interest in the Triangle's security, as it affects the stability of the rest of Europe. Today, more than at any time since 1945, regional security in the East poses a challenge to American diplomacy. Paradoxically, the very rapidity of the Soviet empire's collapse and the disintegration of the Warsaw Pact have left the West without an operational policy for the future in place. During the Cold War, NATO attempted to loosen the Soviet grip on Eastern Europe, first through direct subversion, then through selective engagement, then through détente. Today, after the goal of the past four decades has been accomplished, the West finds itself reluctant to move into the breach created by the implosion of Soviet power. In fact, uncertainty and hesitation as to the future of regional security in East Central Europe appear even more pervasive in the West than within the Triangle itself. Only recently has NATO begun to address the urgent security needs of the postcommunist states—witness its June and November 1991 official expressions of interest in the region's stability and continued independence.

The 1989–1990 revolutionary upheaval in Soviet-controlled Eastern Europe began in Poland with the installation of the Solidarity-controlled government of Tadeusz Mazowiecki in late August 1989 and culminated with the formal reunification of the German Democratic Republic with the Federal Republic of Germany in October 1990. A new security framework to replace the now largely defunct bipolar division of Europe is only beginning to take shape, and it is hoped that it will crystallize after the process of European integration in 1992 has been completed. The final shape of the new security regimen depends to a considerable degree on the successful reconstruction of eastern Germany, as well as on the resolution of the crisis that has brought about the disintegration of the Soviet Union. The ongoing domestic turmoil in the former USSR, as its successor states define the new commonwealth formula, remains a source of potential political upheaval the severity of which could exceed anything Europe has seen since 1945. Civil war in the former Soviet Union and, consequently, the waves of refugees crossing Europe to escape the destruction at home would dwarf the 1991 Yugoslav imbroglio and could precipitate an international crisis the magnitude of which the West still cannot fully appreciate. Among the former USSR's neighbors, the Triangle states are the most immediately concerned about the shape of the future Russian state, as the outcome of the Soviet internal crisis will inevitably impact on their own chances to complete the transition from communism to democracy.

At the same time, postcommunist East Central Europe is quickly reclaiming its independence. Together with the reinvigoration of interstate relations, the region is experiencing a renewal of autonomous domestic politics. Regional balance of power issues and possible territorial questions confronting Poland, Czechoslovakia, and Hungary from the East and the South today constitute a rapidly fluctuating self-contained diplomatic world embedded in pan-European politics. The reemerging East Central Europe is in itself a radical rejection of the postwar settlement in the East, including the complete elimination of the region's former ties to Moscow. This fundamental change is only the beginning of a long-term transformation, embarked upon by the Triangle in 1990–1991. The severance of the old linkages between the USSR and Eastern Europe, exemplified by the disintegration of the Warsaw Pact Supreme Joint Command, combined with NATO's inability to bring the postcommunist countries decisively into its own security system, is at the heart of the region's security dilemma. Since 1991 East Central Europe has found itself in a "grey zone" of the European balance of power.

Today the new successor states of East Central Europe are making independent decisions that will impact on their security in the years to come. Therefore, it matters to the West whether the governments of Poland, Czechoslovakia, and Hungary are fervently committed to regional tripartite cooperation or whether they opt for individual choices in foreign and defense policies. It also matters if the uncertainty about the region's future leaves the postcommunist democracies in perpetual isolation or if it will be replaced by a new security framework where the Triangle can find its place. For the rest of the decade, East Central Europe will continue to grapple with the question of security not only as a problem of defense policies and alliances but also as a question of overall regional stability. It will continue to search for ways to improve its chances for rapid economic growth and for ways to resolve the long-dormant ethnic and territorial problems facing postcommunist Europe as a whole. It will strive to transform the grey zone left by the Soviet withdrawal into a viable periphery of Europe's developed northwestern region, while doing its utmost to join Western Europe. While it is impossible to foresee how successful these policies will ultimately be, one can nevertheless already detect distinct trends and make reasonable predictions. With this in mind, this book reviews the Triangle's record to date in the area of national security policy, as well as several possible scenarios for change in the region during the remainder of the decade.

This book examines the emerging national security environment in East Central Europe based on the following propositions. First, changes in the region's security framework are directly a function of the Soviet Union's rethinking of the very concept of war in Europe, including the size and structure of Soviet forces; hence, a chapter is devoted to a discussion of the 1987–1989 Warsaw Pact reforms and their impact on Poland, Czechoslovakia, and Hungary. Second, small-scale, low-intensity military conflict along the East Central European periphery is today and will remain for the rest of the decade a distinct possibility, pending the final resolution of the nationalities crisis in the former Soviet Union and in the Balkans. The restructuring and redeployment of the Triangle's armies, as well as bilateral military cooperation treaties such as the one signed on January 22, 1991, by Hungary and Czechoslovakia,[6] constitute a clear recognition by Warsaw, Prague, and Budapest that the collapse of the Soviet empire may lead to irredentist claims against their national territory. Third, the

Western European and ultimately the pan-European orientation of the three East Central European states is dictated by the need for economic modernization and development and is an expression of the general consensus among the three governments that the real security threat in the immediate decade can come only from the East.

Although the 1990s began with a radical change in the balance of power in Europe, the old realities of geography and the historical record remain. The future of East Central Europe will inevitably be influenced by the region's past and by the collective memory of its people. In order to place the discussion of the current issues in a broader historical context, this book opens in chapter 1 with a general survey of the region's geopolitics and its history, from the creation of the successor states of 1918 until the 1987 reform of the Warsaw Pact. Chapter 1 also reviews the post–World War II Soviet vision of regional and bloc security, as symbolized by Stalin's choice of imperial expansion over diplomatic solutions and the 1955 creation of the Warsaw Treaty Organization (WTO). Finally, the chapter outlines the changes in the Warsaw Pact's military doctrine leading to the decision to restructure the WTO in the late 1980s.

Chapter 2 discusses the 1987 Warsaw Pact reform in the context of Soviet long-term military strategy in Europe, including its architects and its long-term objectives. It outlines the stages of Soviet and WTO military restructuring and the responses to the Soviet initiatives from individual East Central European countries. The discussion concludes with the collapse of the Soviet-dominated security zone in East Central Europe and a review of Moscow's security policies introduced in 1991 after the demise of the Eastern bloc.

Chapters 3, 4, and 5 constitute the core of the book. They are a country-by-country discussion of the national and regional security policies as well as the military reform programs adopted by Poland, Czechoslovakia, and Hungary in 1990 and 1991. Each chapter identifies the similarities and differences in their approach to the generally accepted pan-European security agenda, as determined by each state's specific needs and its historical experience. It addresses the most pressing current problems and possible challenges for the future facing individual Triangle states as they struggle to maintain their sovereignty and reform their political and economic systems. The concluding chapter discusses possible alternative security arrangements in East Central Europe in the 1990s, depending on the modalities of European politics of the post–Cold War era.

The material for the discussion of the new military doctrine and force deployment has been assembled from open Polish, Czechoslovak, and

Hungarian publications, from Western sources, and from a series of interviews conducted by the author in the course of researching this book. All the translations from Russian, Polish, and Czech have been done by the author, unless indicated otherwise.

The reader should keep in mind that as of this writing the military of the three successor democracies are still engaged in a lively debate about the structure and size of their armed forces, as well as the conditions under which they may operate. Nevertheless, it is already possible to discern the basic changes in the organizational structure, the deployment patterns, and the operational doctrines of those armies. These are likely to remain in place during the current phase of the security-building process after the disintegration of the Warsaw Pact and the collapse of the Soviet Union, and they may endure well into the 1990s.

This book's ultimate goal is to define the region's future security status in the context of a new European order. In the final analysis, East Central European security will derive from the outline of Europe's changed geopolitics. The Triangle's search for security in the 1990s forces the question whether Poland, Czechoslovakia, and Hungary will eventually become a bridge linking the West to Russia or whether they will remain "eastern frontier states" on the Continent's periphery, where Europe's boundary will be delineated by the end of this century. An answer to this question will define not only the regional but ultimately the all-European security of the future.

NOTES

1. Some authors writing on the interwar period have also included Switzerland and Italy as part of Central Europe. See, for example, R. V. Burks, *East European History: An Ethnic Approach* (Washington, D.C.: American Historical Association, 425 AHA Pamphlets, 1973), p. 3. The terms *Central Europe* and *East Central Europe*, referring to Poland, Czechoslovakia, and Hungary, increasingly have been in circulation as an analytical shortcut among experts in the field. See, for example, J. M. C. Rollo, *The New Eastern Europe: Western Responses* (New York: Council on Foreign Relations Press, 1990), pp. 1–2.

2. Over the past two years several leading government officials in Poland, Czechoslovakia, and Hungary have frequently used the term *Central Europe* to describe their countries as well as Germany, Austria, and possibly Italy. It is my view that for the time being such a broad classification reflects more their future aspirations than the current political reality.

3. Geography in the region has been more a question of history and politics than territorial landmarks. For example, Joseph Rothschild in his *Return to Diversity: A Political History of East Central Europe since World War II* (New York and Oxford: Oxford University Press, 1989) uses the term *East Central Europe* more comprehensively

to include the Balkans. It is even more common to speak of *Eastern Europe* to denote simply former Soviet satellites in the region.

4. Douglas L. Clarke, "The Conventional Armed Forces in Europe Treaty: Limits and Zones," *Report on Eastern Europe*, vol. 2, no. 2 (Munich: RFE/RL, January 11, 1991), p. 35.

5. *Atlas of Eastern Europe* (Washington, D.C.: Central Intelligence Agency, August 1990), pp. 18–24.

6. *RFE/RL Daily Report* (Munich: Radio Free Europe/Radio Liberty Research Institute, January 22, 1991).

1

THE LEGACY OF GEOPOLITICS, 1918–1985

THE REGION

It is a simple matter of geography that East Central Europe lies between two great powers which for a century have vied for primacy in the region. Poland, Czechoslovakia, and Hungary are sandwiched between Germany and Russia—two states whose resources cannot be matched by any of these three small states, either individually or collectively.

Geography has made the region a pawn in the struggle for supremacy between the two great powers. East Central Europe is extremely vulnerable to outside aggression. The most direct invasion route from West to East and East to West leads across the North European Plain through Poland. The North European Plain extends across Germany and Poland and then widens eastward into Russia, becoming a natural funnel through which European armies have marched in both directions.

The Carpathian Mountains adjoin Poland's southern border in the High Tatra range, a part of the country's frontier. The Carpathians cut through Slovakia and extend into the Balkans, reaching into Romania. Since most of the Carpathian elevations are small, they could never block access to the region from the open plains of southern Russia. In eastern Bohemia in Czechoslovakia the Bohemian-Moravian Uplands connect to the Moravian Plain, with the Sudeten Mountains forming its boundary in the northwest. Like the North European Plain, the Moravian Plain has been a major historical access route from northern Europe to the Danubian basin. Although most of Czechoslovakia's territory is mountainous and hilly, the mountains can hardly be considered an impassable barrier to invasion, and the country's geography has never been a defensive asset. The Hungarian state, which sits on the open plains of Panonia, in an area sometimes referred to as the Mid-Danube or the Hungarian basin, shares with Poland and Czechoslovakia similar vulnerability to invasion. The territory east of the Danube River is flat, while the region west of the Danube consists mostly of low, hilly terrain.[1] Hungary, landlocked and small, can be easily overrun by a determined invader.

Historically, this geographic vulnerability has influenced the region's politics. East Central Europe has evolved in the context of a distinct security disadvantage compared to Central and Western Europe. Modern nation-states emerged here much later than in the rest of Europe. Between the Congress of Vienna in 1815 and the collapse of Europe's multinational empires in 1918, the region was a part of the German, Russian, and Austrian dominions. The power of Germany and Russia in particular kept a tight lid on the region's national aspirations. A chance for the development of independent states came to East Central Europe only after World War I had undermined Europe's imperial order.

THE IMPACT OF WORLD WAR I

Poland, Czechoslovakia, and Hungary owe their modern-day existence to the unsettling results of World War I. They emerged as independent nation-states principally because of the collapse of the Russian, German, and Austro-Hungarian monarchies. The defeat of Russia by Germany and the subsequent 1917 Bolshevik Revolution, as well as the 1918 collapse of the Central Powers—the German Reich, Austria-Hungary, and Turkey—produced a new map of Europe in which national aspirations, ethnicity, and economic considerations were not always balanced. Ultimately, the interwar political settlement proved unstable, as Germany and Russia were only temporarily weakened while the United States chose to remain disengaged. Thus, the successor states developed and became consolidated in a vacuum of power.

The early 1920s was a period of brief respite for the successor states, because at the time Germany and Russia were unable to engage in active foreign policy in the region. The regional security system of the interwar period, which had rested on the guarantees of western Great Powers, became upset as soon as Russia and Germany were once more ready to exercise their influence.[2] The Rapallo Treaty of 1922, which brought the two pariah states out of political isolation and caused considerable concern in Western Europe over the future intentions of the two avowedly revisionist states, had begun to undermine the regional security system even before the arrival on the political scene of Adolf Hitler's National

Socialist German Workers' Party (*Nationalsozialistische Deutsche Arbeiterpartei*; NSDAP) and the Soviet-German alliance of 1939. The Ribbentrop-Molotov Pact marked the final disintegration of the European security system, spelling out an end to the successor states' brief independence.

The demise of the successor states with the onset of World War II does not mean, however, that they had been doomed from the start and could do nothing to influence their destiny. In light of the West's indecisiveness, a possible answer to their security needs might have consisted in regional cooperation. During the brief period of Germany and Russia's weakness and isolation, from the Treaty of Versailles of 1919 until the Rapallo Treaty of 1922 and the Locarno Treaty shortly thereafter, East Central Europe had an opportunity to strengthen the foundations of its security through regional cooperation, instead of relying solely on the French and British guarantees. East Central Europe needed to augment the Great Power security commitments with a workable regional security system that would bring together its population and economic resources in common defense against an outside threat. Although successor states would still need outside assistance to repel aggression, a regional alliance would have made them less vulnerable to pressure and political blackmail. It also would have served to stiffen the French and British resolve to live up to their military commitments in the East. It was to be the tragedy of the region in the interwar period that ethnic conflict and irredentism torpedoed all hopes for regional security cooperation.

SUCCESSOR STATES IN EAST CENTRAL EUROPE

Poland was the largest and most important state among the so-called successor states, that is, states created in Eastern and Central Europe by the post–World War I settlement of the Paris Peace Conference of January 1919. The new territorial settlement was dictated by the United States, France, Great Britain, and Italy.[3] Based on the principle of self-determination and the consent of the governed, Woodrow Wilson's original vision of a Polish state included all areas inhabited by ethnic Poles, which would have put Poland back on the map within the boundaries corresponding to those of the Polish-Lithuanian Commonwealth from before the country's first partition. In the course of the Paris negotiations Poland's eastern border became an intractable problem, which in the end was settled outside the conference table by the Polish-Soviet War of 1919–1920. In the process, Poland rejected the so-called Curzon line, which would have separated the Polish and Byelorussian ethnic areas. It exerted considerable pressure to acquire a portion of Upper Silesia, a portion of Lithuania including the city of Wilno/Vilnius to which claims were laid by the Poles as well as the Lithuanians, and Eastern Galicia with the city of Lwow/Lvov, contested by the Poles and the Ukrainians. In the end, by the early 1920s Poland emerged as an independent country about twice as large as the Paris conference had originally envisioned.

The interwar Poland was a poor agricultural state, which on account of the size of its population and its central location was driven into Great Power politics for which it was woefully unprepared. It was a multiethnic state, with the Poles constituting the majority population: 68 percent of the population was Polish, 14 percent West Ukrainian, 10 percent Jewish, 3.7 percent Byelorussian, 3.7 percent German.[4] Throughout the interwar period the minority question remained a central domestic issue, with Poland's treatment of its minorities deteriorating especially in the 1930s.

Czechoslovakia as a federation of both Czechs and Slovaks and including German, Magyar, Ukrainian, and Polish minorities was a much more artificial creation than Poland. The absence of ethnic, cultural, and historical unity, the country's strong economy not-withstanding, would prove to be a formidable challenge for the Czechoslovak republic to overcome. While a linguistic and a historical link existed between the Czechs and the Slovaks, the two peoples differed substantially as far as their economies, their geographic environment, and their historical experience were concerned. Tomas Masaryk, Czechoslovakia's founding father, considered the creation of a common republic for both the Czechs and the Slovaks as a way to fulfill the growing national consciousness of the two. Still, the problem of how to keep the two peoples within one nation-state while preventing the competing national interests from generating paralyzing internal tension would haunt Czechoslovakia between the two world wars, and it remains an important concern to this day.

The Czechoslovak Republic was created by the 1919 Treaty of St. Germain. The treaty established the Czechoslovak state, but it failed to address adequately the ethnic minority problem that would bedevil the federation for years to come. At the time, close to 35 percent of the fourteen million Czechoslovak citizens were neither Czech nor Slovak. Czechs constituted about 53 percent of the total, Slovaks about 17 percent. In addition, the new state included 3.2 million Germans, of whom 1.7 million lived in Bohemia, approximately 750,000 Magyars living in Slovakia, 460,000 Ukrainians (Ruthenians) in the country's eastern corner, and 75,000 Poles living close to the border with Poland.[5] Despite Prague's liberal minority policy in the interwar period, which was by far more tolerant than those of Poland and Hungary, the relations between the Czechoslovaks and the German and Magyar minorities remained strained. Consequently, the central government's task of maintaining a cohesive two-nation republic became progressively more difficult as the relations between the Czechs and Slovaks themselves deteriorated.

In addition to domestic problems, throughout the interwar period Czechoslovakia struggled to cope with hostility from neighboring states and with the perpetual threat of political isolation. Territorial disputes arose with Czechoslovakia's neighbors, notably with Poland over the Duchy of Teschen (Tesin/Cieszyn). Poland also claimed all of the Orava and Spis districts in the Carpathians, where the Polish-Czechoslovak frontier had been set by the Ambassadors' Conference of the Great Powers in July 1920. In addition to constant tension in relations with Poland, generated by the Polish border dispute, the Czechoslovak government never successfully addressed the nationalist claims of the western Ukrainians in the Carpatho-Ukrainian region. Relations with Hungary remained strained over the Magyar ethnic minority issue as well as a disagreement over territory. Hungary repeatedly questioned Czechoslovakia's southern border; Bratislava, Slovakia's capital, was at the time predominantly a German and Magyar town. In addition to Hungarian irredentism, Czechoslovakia was pressured by Germany over the German minority in the Sudetenland and by Austria over disagreements (subsequently resolved through negotiations) concerning the Czechoslovak-Austrian border demarcation. The combination of the ethnic and territorial problems gave Prague a deep sense of uncertainty, political isolation, and an overall tenuousness over the country's position.

Economically, however, Czechoslovakia was the strongest of the successor states. It was largely undamaged by war, and it contained over two-thirds of the industry but only one-fourth of the population and one-fifth of the area of the Habsburg Empire.[6] The country's population was relatively well educated, with very high literacy rates among the Czechs and Germans. Even with the loss of the traditional imperial markets, Czechoslovakia enjoyed considerable economic advantages over its neighbors, and its industry could have provided the necessary economic base for a regional security system in East Central Europe, had such a system successfully emerged.

From among the three newly created East Central European successor states Hungary was unquestionably one of the losers of the war. The country's borders were settled only after the territorial claims against it by

Czechoslovakia, Romania, Yugoslavia, and Austria had been met.[7] In 1914 the population of Hungary had been about twenty million, including ten million Magyars. After the peace settlement imposed on Hungary by the victorious allies in a treaty signed on June 4, 1920, in the Trianon Palace in Versailles, Hungary's population was reduced to slightly over eight million, of whom 7.2 million were Magyars. Consequently, close to three million ethnic Hungarians were left outside the new state's territory in two principal groups, including 750,000 Magyars in southern Slovakia, mostly in the plains between Bratislava and Mukacevo, and a large group of Magyars and related Szeklers in Romania's Transylvania region.[8] In effect, in the aftermath of the Treaty of Trianon, Hungary lost two-thirds of its prewar territory and three-fifths of its population.[9] In the process, portions of formerly Hungarian territory went to Austria, Czechoslovakia, Poland, Romania, Yugoslavia, and Italy; Czechoslovakia and Romania were the two principal beneficiaries of Hungary's territorial losses, and hence the two became automatically a target of Hungarian irredentism. The result of the settlement was confusing at best. The Treaty of Trianon effectively destroyed Hungary's historical integrity, but it restored the country's complete independence. Paradoxically, the newly acquired sovereignty would in the interwar period only further aggravate the Magyar sense of historical injustice, symbolized by the loss of national territory.

Trianon also brought about an utter devastation of Hungary's economic base. Hungary lost 58 percent of its railroads, 60 percent of its road mileage, 84 percent of its timber, 43 percent of its arable land, 83 percent of its iron ore, 29 percent of its lignite, and 27 percent of its bituminous coal resources.[10] In addition, Hungarian industry was cut off from its traditional sources of raw materials and from its traditional markets. Having its territory truncated and its economy destroyed, Hungary emerged from the postwar settlement as a staunchly revisionist power.

THE ETHNIC DILEMMA

The perceived injustices of the territorial settlement agreed upon by the Great Powers at the Paris conference effectively precluded regional security cooperation in East Central Europe. The ethnic minority issue proved even more damaging. Considering the region's historical legacy, it was virtually impossible to create successor states around their ethnic cores without substantial population transfers. Because the various nationalities in the region had developed within multinational empires, the creation of the new states left a number of ethnic minorities separated from their national states and surrounded by other nationalities. In addition, German towns and German settlements were scattered throughout the region, and they found themselves in newly established Poland, Hungary, and Czechoslovakia. About half a million Magyar-speaking Szeklers lived in southeastern Transylvania, and the postwar territorial settlement left them outside Hungary. The same was true of the Byelorussians and the Ukrainians in Poland and Czechoslovakia who found themselves cut off from the rest of their people.

The ethnic legacy of the postwar settlement made the successor states of East Central Europe inherently unstable because of their real and imagined vulnerability to outside influence on their national minorities. The profound sense of insecurity generated by the ethnic question often impelled the new governments to pursue repressive policies vis-à-vis their minority populations (with Czechoslovakia being the most restrained in this respect), thus fueling the preexisting resentments. Most important, the ethnic issue made friendly cooperative relations in the region impossible, weakening the overall security position of the successor states.

The class structure inherited by Poland, Czechoslovakia, and Hungary was another factor hampering cooperation, especially between Czechoslovakia and its northern and southern neighbors. The interwar conflicts among the countries of East Central Europe—such as the one between Poland and Czechoslovakia over the Teschen region or between Hungary and Czechoslovakia over the Magyar minority in Slovakia—were aggravated by the differing social stratifications and national traditions of the three states. The ruling elite in Poland, which emphasized its aristocratic past, felt drawn to the Magyar aristocratic ethos and displayed unmitigated contempt for the largely middle-class character of Czechoslovakia. The Poles' traditional affinity for Hungary and Hungary's hostility toward Czechoslovakia exacerbated the Polish-Czechoslovak animosity. Foreign policy differences followed. The Polish fears of Russia were clearly at odds with the Czechoslovak attempts to draw closer to the Soviet Union as a counterweight to the ever-present threat of German domination. The Poles would never forget that during the Polish-Soviet War of 1919–1920 the Czechoslovak government did not allow for military supplies desperately needed by the Polish army to cross Czechoslovakia's territory. Instead of seeking better relations with Czechoslovakia, Poland shared Hungary's position that Czechoslovakia was an artificial creation and a state that should eventually disappear from the map of Europe. From the outset, the ethnic settlement in East Central Europe carried in it the seeds of international conflict and it eventually precluded any meaningful security cooperation in this critical region of Europe.

SECURITY COOPERATION IN THE INTERWAR PERIOD

Although regional security cooperation among Poland, Czechoslovakia, and Hungary could never defuse the German and Russian threats, it could have gone a long way to ameliorate them. The tragedy of the interwar period in East Central Europe was that in light of the growing paralysis of French foreign policy and the progressive weakness of Great Britain, regional security cooperation among successor states aimed at containing Russia and Germany was never seriously attempted. Regionalism in thinking about East Central European security in the interwar period was out of the question largely because of the intractable ethnic problems and the festering border issues. Poland, Czechoslovakia, and, to some degree, Hungary were multinational states. The three had missed out on the process of nation-state formation in the nineteenth century, although Hungary more than Czechoslovakia and Poland saw its identity defined within the context of the Habsburg Empire.

Immediate political concerns were also a factor limiting regionalism. Collective regional security was not seriously considered because it might have provoked the Germans or, if one were to accept the Litvinov formula, it could have resulted in growing Soviet influence. The Poles and Czechoslovaks in particular hoped that their security could be ensured by bringing into the region the interests and influence of England and France. These plans hinged on the expectation that the Great Powers would regard the preservation of the status quo in East Central Europe as their vital national security interest. The 1938 Munich settlement demonstrated that this expectation was misplaced.

Regionalism as a solution to the threat posed by Russia and Germany failed not only in East Central Europe but in the northeast and the Balkans as well. The very multiplicity of the successor states made for their fundamental vulnerability to outside pressure. While taken en bloc the 115 million "liberated people"[11] east of the Polish-German border constituted potentially a sufficient force to repel any aggression, in reality those countries lacked a common agenda and were mired in the nationalities and economic problems inherited from the past. As a result, throughout the interwar period the successor states had only a marginal ability to affect their destiny. Their security and their continuing independence depended primarily on their ability to prevent either Germany or Russia from dominating the region. This was the only broadly shared common national security interest that Poland, Czechoslovakia, and Hungary could regard as a source for compromise and agreement. In most other respects, the three had distinctly different foreign policy agendas, which often conflicted with one another. Poland and Czechoslovakia were engaged in a dispute over Teschen, which in the end led to the 1938 Polish invasion, while Hungary and Czechoslovakia were in conflict over the Magyar minority in Slovakia and Carpatho-Ruthenia.[12] In addition to ethnic tensions, economic nationalism in the form of high tariffs, in particular during the economic depression of the 1930s, fueled mutual hostility and aggravated conflict.

For Poland the unresolved issue of Danzig and Upper Silesia in its relations with Germany would ultimately come to constitute a mortal danger to its national existence. Poland, which was the largest and the most populous of the successor states, with a territory larger than that of Italy and with a population of twenty-seven million that was growing rapidly, was by virtue of its geographic position impelled to play Great Power politics. Squeezed between Germany and Russia, both of which had territorial grievances against it, Poland had little room to maneuver. The only workable solution to its national security dilemma would have been a strong regional alliance backed up by a territorial guarantee from France and Great Britain. Still, because of ethnic animosities and competing territorial claims, Poland developed virtually from the start a hostile relationship with Lithuania and Czechoslovakia, its northern and southern neighbors. Poland entered the interwar period isolated in the region, with a still largely agricultural economy, a weak industry, and a myriad of ethnic and political problems at home. In this perspective, the foreign policy that Poland followed between 1918 and 1939 was more a product of the circumstances than an autonomous choice. Throughout the interwar period Poland was, in effect, as isolated as it had been in 1920.

In contrast to Poland, Czechoslovakia emerged from the Paris conference as an economically strong state with the makings of a flourishing modern economy. Still, Czechoslovakia was ethnically the least homogeneous of the successor states in East Central Europe. Slovak separatism and the pressure from the German and Magyar minorities were compounded by the irredentist claims against the Czechoslovak state pressed throughout the interwar period by Poland and Hungary, its northern and southern neighbors. The very shape of the state made it vulnerable to attack on the North-South axis, and the prospects of German and Austrian unification constituted a nightmare scenario, which when it came to pass made Czechoslovakia's security position untenable. By 1938 the country was surrounded by enemies, with the possible, if irrelevant, exception of Romania. In order to survive as an independent state, Czechoslovakia desperately needed both Great Power guarantees and a collective regional security alliance with Poland and, if possible, with Hungary. The geopolitical realities of the interwar period made such a regional security arrangement unattainable. Czechoslovakia remained isolated, with Great Power support, notably from the French and the British, quickly disappearing.

The interwar Hungary was economically weak, with 64 percent of the population still engaged in agriculture.[13] With the disintegration of the Habsburg Empire, Hungarian industry found itself cut off from its traditional sources of raw materials and markets, as well as losing the protection of past high tariffs against foreign competition. Hungary also lacked a Magyar middle class. The difficult domestic economic situation was compounded by the ethnic problem of the large Magyar minorities living outside the state's territory. By leaving sizable Magyar minority groups outside Hungary, the Paris conference in effect had set Hungary's foreign policy agenda and made regional security cooperation (especially with Czechoslovakia) impossible. Hungary, which had been in the camp of the Central Powers during World War I, remained a revisionist state throughout the interwar period and was distinctly pro-German in its foreign policy. While also a successor state, Hungary emerged from the war as a defeated power. When in June 1920 it was forced to sign the Treaty of Trianon, it not only lost 67 percent of its prewar area and 58.3 percent of its population,[14] but it also had to limit the size of its army to 35,000.[15] Hungary would openly repudiate that restriction in 1938 as part of its war preparations. In the interwar period, rather than search for regional alliances, Hungary harbored a strong and largely justified grievance against the existing territorial settlement in East Central Europe and the Danubian basin. Its foreign policy behavior prior to and during most of World War II was driven primarily by revisionism and an opposition to the Versailles settlement. Throughout the interwar period Hungary remained a vociferous critic of the Treaty of Trianon and it displayed an unswerving hostility toward Czechoslovakia. Under the circumstances, a regional security cooperation agreement in East Central Europe that would include Hungary was simply not possible. With the benefit of hindsight, it proved to be a misguided policy, as Hungary had to contend with the same Great Power equation in Central Europe that bedeviled Poland and Czechoslovakia and ultimately led to Hungary's domination by the Soviet Union.

IRRELEVANT ALLIANCES: A DIFFERENT KIND OF REGIONALISM

In the interwar period the successor states could hope to preserve their independence through (1) an alignment with the victors of World War I, in hope of obtaining their territorial and security guarantees, combined with (2) a regional security framework that would harness their collective strength. They failed on both counts due to political myopia as well as reasons beyond their control. The failure of the first option was due to the United States' withdrawal from the European political scene; Great Britain's unwillingness to involve itself actively in the region's politics until 1939; and France's confused foreign policy of developing relations with the small states, negotiating directly with Germany, and after 1934 looking to the Soviet Union as a counterweight to German power.[16] Neither a French-German rapprochement nor a French-Soviet alliance could constitute a viable security guarantee to the successor states, as it would address only half of their national security concerns. In the end, while France remained interested in preserving the territorial status quo in East Central Europe, it could do little by itself to guarantee a durable security arrangement for Poland and Czechoslovakia. For its part, Hungary regarded France as one of the principal enforcers of the Trianon dictate.

Regionalism did play a role in East Central Europe in the interwar period, but cooperation focused on secondary threats. The attempt to build a regional security framework around the Little Entente, established through a series of treaty agreements among Czechoslovakia, Romania, and Yugoslavia in 1920–1921, failed in its implicit goal of bringing about a "great entente" from the Baltic to the Aegean as a counterweight to the power of Russia and Germany.[17] The paradox of the Little Entente was that it aimed to protect its members against a secondary danger—that is, Hungary—while remaining inoperative against the primary threat of German or Russian Great Power designs. In addition, because it ostracized Hungary, the Little Entente made Budapest more prone to collaborate with Germany and Italy.[18] Even though the Little Entente's near-term objective of defending the territorial settlement of the Treaty of Trianon against Hungarian irredentism was accomplished, the value of this achievement remained questionable. Czechoslovakia's Prime Minister and later President Eduard Benes argued in 1924 that, whatever the shortcoming of the Little Entente, "it has preserved peace of Central Europe . . . and acted as a moderating influence in the series of conflicts."[19] Nevertheless, this "other kind of regionalism" was ultimately irrelevant as it failed to address the German and Russian threats.

The Little Entente was an ardent supporter of the League of Nations, seeing itself as an element in a larger mosaic of Europe's collective security arrangements. It established strong ties to France, and over the years it even developed an arbitration process. In 1933–1934 the Little Entente created a Permanent Council, an Economic Council, and a permanent Secretariat with an eye to coordinating foreign and national security policies. However, because of its preoccupation with Hungarian, and later Bulgarian, irredentism, the Little Entente failed to affect Europe's larger security needs. It was probably so because each of the members was preoccupied with a different Great Power threat: Czechoslovakia from Germany, Romania from Soviet Russia, and Yugoslavia from Italy.[20] Finally, the Little Entente was ineffective because it failed to bring Poland into its structure, and by design it left Hungary on the outside. Largely because of its territorial quarrel with Czechoslovakia, Poland expressed no interest in joining the alliance on the grounds that it was primarily directed against Hungary, Poland's traditional friend. Instead, Poland opted for a useless mutual defense agreement with Romania, its southern neighbor, to counter the growing Soviet threat. As far as the Polish government was concerned, the Polish-Romanian axis directed against Russia would buttress the French guarantees against Germany, thus providing for security against the country's two enemies. The Warsaw-Bucharest axis was another ultimately irrelevant attempt at regionalism.

The Polish-Lithuanian hostility over the issue of Wilno/Vilnius, to which both countries had laid claims, made the value of regional security arrangements in the north marginal. Poland had no diplomatic relations with Lithuania until 1938. Latvia and Estonia signed a bilateral security agreement in 1923, which was then expanded in 1934 into the Baltic Entente to include Lithuania. But with Poland remaining on the outside, the alliance had no real defensive value. Finland expressed no interest in joining it, orienting itself instead toward Scandinavia. In sum, the Baltic Entente contained no security guarantees against the growing threat of resurgent Russian power—the error for which the member states would pay dearly in 1940.

In comparison to the Little Entente and the Baltic Entente, the Balkan Entente, formally established in 1934, was even less effective. It included Greece, Turkey, Romania, and Yugoslavia, but not Bulgaria, which refused to renounce its territorial claims. The very terms of the Balkan Entente made it irrelevant as a solution to the region's security dilemma. The agreement provided for defense only against a Balkan aggressor, not against a Great Power. In reality it was directed against Bulgarian irredentism. While Romania and Yugoslavia were members in both the Little Entente and the Balkan Entente, they failed to forge a comprehensive regional security framework by linking the two agreements together.

Other attempts at regional cooperation proved equally chimeric and misguided. In 1927 Hungary signed a friendship and alliance treaty with Italy.[21] Through the 1934 Rome Protocols, Hungary and Austria sought security guarantees from Italy, which Mussolini's Fascist government was only too eager to provide as a counterweight to French influence in the region. Because of their common fear of Russia, Poland and Romania cooperated on a limited basis, including the signing of a limited military convention in 1919, but the treaty was not a mutual security commitment. In the 1930s Poland toyed with the idea of creating a Baltic confederation with Scandinavian countries to serve as a direct bridge to the Western powers, but the project collapsed when Scandinavia expressed no interest. Finally, in 1938 the Poles turned to the Italians with the idea of building a Rome-Belgrade-Budapest-Warsaw axis as a check on German expansionism to the east. The plan never went beyond the preliminary discussions between the Polish and Italian foreign ministers. In the end, in 1939 the French and British guarantees were all Poland had to ensure its sovereignty.

Overall, the security framework in the East in the interwar period rested on weak and largely irrelevant regional alliances, of which the Little Entente was the most prominent one, and on a French security guarantee that was only as good as the French foreign policy would make it. The French guarantee was exposed as hollow already in 1934–1935 when Paris failed to bring about an "Eastern Locarno" as a guarantee of the territorial arrangement in the East. The "Eastern Locarno" was to bring about a border settlement among Germany, Russia, Poland, Czechoslovakia, Latvia, Lithuania, and Estonia, with France underwriting the settlement. The French plan collapsed when Germany flatly refused to participate. Subsequently, Poland declined to sign the treaty without German participation, as without Germany the convention would then become simply an anti-German pact. In 1934 Poland signed a nonaggression treaty with Germany. With the collapse of the "Eastern Locarno" idea, the French settled for the unimplementable French-Soviet-Czechoslovak mutual assistance treaty of 1935. Within only one year this treaty in turn became eclipsed by events. The remilitarization of the Rhineland in March 1936 made it virtually impossible for France to meet its military treaty obligations to all its East European allies.[22]

The final disassembling of the interwar security system began in earnest with Hitler's gamble, in March 1936, to remilitarize the Rhineland. As the event went unchallenged by France, it effectively nullified the value of French security guarantees to Eastern Europe. With no viable regional alternatives present, the East Central European security framework lay in shambles. In the event, Czechoslovakia became quickly isolated and pushed down the road leading to the Munich settlement, with Poland coming up next on Hitler's agenda.

In the end, East Central Europe received the worst possible combination of unimplementable Great Power guarantees and irrelevant regional security agreements. Both the Polish-German Treaty and the French-Soviet-Czechoslovak Treaty upset the balance in regional politics, as they moved Poland closer to Germany, while Czechoslovakia shifted its attention to Russia. The final bankruptcy of the interwar security system was revealed in 1938 when Poland and Hungary participated in the dismemberment of Czechoslovakia after Munich. Poland claimed Teschen while Hungary received parts of southern Slovakia, as well as sub-Carpathian Ruthenia after the incorporation of Bohemia and Moravia into the Third Reich.

The collapse of East Central European security on the eve of World War II was indirectly a result of the successor states' inability to forge a regional alliance. Ultimately, however, it was a consequence of the inherent unreliability of Western Great Power security guarantees to the region. It is probable that regional cooperation in the 1920s and 1930s backed by mutual defense alliances could have stiffened the French resolve to resist Germany's resurgence in Europe. A workable ultimatum to Hitler in March 1936, backed by a credible threat of force by France and joint Polish-Czechoslovak operations, could have stopped Germany from remilitarizing the Rhineland. The lack of regional security cooperation and incessant hostility among neighboring successor states made the French security commitment to East Central Europe untenable.

THE IMPACT OF WORLD WAR II

The legacy of the interwar period in East Central Europe was only one factor that defined the security framework of the region after 1945; the second major influence was the war itself. The lessons of World War II differed for each country. Czechoslovakia succumbed to Hitler's political pressure on the West, symbolized in the betrayal of Munich in 1938. A year later, Poland chose to defend its independence, vesting its trust in the promises of French and British assistance. Despite the formal declaration of war on Germany, the French and the British did nothing to assist Poland directly. The sitzkrieg in the West made Hitler's blitzkrieg in the East that much faster. The Soviet invasion of Poland three weeks into the war completed the country's demise. In contrast to Poland and Czechoslovakia, Hungary entered the war as a satellite of Nazi Germany. By 1945, however, the three shared the same fate. Even though the Poles and the Czechoslovaks were nominally among the victors and Hungary was once again among the vanquished, the three countries became Soviet satellites, with their internal and foreign policies transformed to conform to the Soviet national interest.

World War II visited utter devastation on Poland as well as on portions of Czechoslovakia and Hungary. The horror of the Nazi occupation cost Poland over six million of its citizens, of whom half were Jews; between 1939 and 1945 Poland lost 22 percent of its prewar population.[23] The Soviet Union's joint participation with the Third Reich in the 1939 partition of Poland resulted in the deportations and death of thousands of Poles. The February 1945 territorial settlement at Yalta, which confirmed the Soviet territorial gains in the West and compensated Poland for the loss of its eastern provinces with German territory, led to mass population transfers, effectively eliminating the German minority in Poland and considerably reducing the Ukrainian and Byelorussian groups. The eight million Germans living in the territories awarded to Poland at Yalta were expelled.[24] This process, coupled with the virtual destruction of the Eastern and Central European Jews during the Nazi holocaust, altered dramatically Poland's ethnic composition. Poland, which had entered the war as a multinational commonwealth, emerged as a homogeneous nation-state, with ethnic Poles constituting 98 percent of its population.[25]

World War II strengthened the traditional Polish antagonism against both Germans and Russians. The German occupation in particular was the worst Poland had endured in its entire history. The Polish-German and the Polish-Russian national conflicts, both dating back several hundred years, were reinforced as a result of the national humiliation Poland suffered after the subjugation by Germany and Russia, respectively. The Ribbentrop-Molotov Pact of 1939, which had been the precondition of the German and Russian military action against Poland, became to the Poles a symbol of the duplicitous intentions of their western and eastern neighbors.

In terms of national frontiers, Poland emerged from the war with even more questionable borders than those which it had established in 1921. Poland was compensated for the territory lost in the east with areas taken from Germany to which its historical claims were quite tenuous. Although Warsaw presented the provinces east of the Oder-Neisse line as "regained territories," in fact they had been German areas for several centuries before the victorious powers awarded them to Poland in 1945. The acceptance of the Oder-Neisse line meant that Poland after the war would remain vulnerable to German irredentism, as about one-third of the postwar Polish territory had once belonged to the Reich.[26] Therefore, Soviet power alone could guarantee Poland's western borders. As long as Germany refused to renounce its claims to the territories east of the Oder-Neisse line, Poland's security and territorial integrity translated into its complete dependence on

Moscow. Finally, the postwar territorial settlement had implications for Poland's relations with the West as well. The most immediate reaction of the majority of the Poles after the war was a powerful anti-Soviet sentiment combined with a sense of their country's betrayal by the West, with Yalta becoming a symbol of the American and British appeasement of the Soviet Union.

In contrast to Poland, Czechoslovakia emerged in 1945 both humiliated and with the ethnic conflict between the Czechs and the Slovaks further exacerbated by the experience of the war. Slovak nationalism and separatism flourished during the German occupation, as Czechoslovakia had ceased to exist as a nation-state. After the war, Prague reaffirmed its control over all of Czechoslovakia, treating the country as a unitary nation-state and rejecting, until 1968, all calls for Slovak autonomy.[27] The question of the German minority was resolved immediately after the war by the wholesale expulsion of the three million Sudetic and Carpathian Germans.[28] The small Jewish population of Bohemia and Moravia had been virtually eliminated by the Nazis during the war, with the Tiso regime in Slovakia actively assisting the Germans in the rounding up of Jews.[29]

The key lesson learned by Czechoslovakia from 1938 and World War II was that Germany was its main enemy, that Western guarantees did not amount to much in a crisis, and that for better or worse the Soviet Union constituted the only power capable of protecting Czechoslovakia against German revanchism.[30] It is debatable whether after the total defeat of Germany such an assessment was justified. It may very well be that Prague was trying to make the best of a bad situation. However, the country's dismemberment in 1938 left deep emotional scars on Czechoslovakia's national psyche. Already during the war the Czechoslovaks shifted their foreign policy markedly toward the Soviet Union. In 1943 in Moscow, Czechoslovakia's President Eduard Benes signed a Soviet-Czechoslovak treaty of friendship, cooperation, and mutual assistance. Apparently, the Czechoslovak government-in-exile had reconciled itself to the idea that after the war it would have to work closely with the Soviet Union, including coming to terms with Czechoslovakia's communists.

Immediately after the war, Czechoslovakia's President Benes established a pro-Soviet government with popular support and attempted to transform Czechoslovakia into the most favored Soviet ally on the Continent. Soviet supremacy in Central Europe was considered by Prague to be a positive development, inasmuch as it would check any future pressure from Germany. Benes courted Soviet support and cooperated with Czechoslovakia's communists. The goal of his immediate postwar policy was to get the Sudetic Germans out of the country and to turn Czechoslovakia into a bridge for cooperation between the East and the West. In effect, the Czechoslovak government-in-exile posed as Stalin's obedient tool. It believed that the Soviets would maintain a moderate degree of interest in Czechoslovakia after the war and that Stalin would let Prague play a leading role in the region. At the same time, Czechoslovakia hoped to balance its Soviet policy with strong ties to the West. In June 1946, Foreign Minister Jan Masaryk approached France with a draft of an alliance treaty, and in 1947 Czechoslovakia announced its readiness to participate in the Marshall Plan. Stalin vetoed both initiatives.[31]

Like Poland, Czechoslovakia lost territory to the Soviet Union. The Carpatho-Ukraine became part of the USSR, and in the process Czechoslovakia acquired a border with the Soviet Union, which it had not had before the war. Still, in contrast to Poland, Czechoslovakia was not burdened by a history of anti-Russian sentiments; it was possible for Prague, save for Moscow's heavy-handedness, to build a strong working relationship with the Soviet Union. On the other hand, German occupation had never been as harsh in Czechoslovakia as it had been in Poland. As a result, the Czechoslovak-German relationship was not damaged beyond repair and, if given a chance, working relations with Germany could have been reestablished.

Hungary, which had based its prewar policies on the premise that its national and territorial grievances had to be addressed, once again emerged from the conflict as a defeated power. As a former Nazi satellite and the country that had formally declared war on the Soviet Union three days after the 1941 German attack on the USSR, Hungary was occupied by the Red Army and left by the British and the Americans to the Soviets to deal with at will. Western indifference was in part justified by the fact that in the final phase of the war Hungary had been governed by the Fascist Arrowcross regime installed by the Germans in place of deposed Regent Miklos Horthy. The wartime destruction and the subsequent Soviet domination of Hungary meant that the prewar goals of reclaiming the "ancient historical heritage" and restoring the "sacred lands" to Hungary had to be abandoned once and for all.[32] Hungary dealt with its own minority problems through the brutal and forcible expulsion of 170,000 ethnic Germans and 73,273 Slovaks.[33] The remnants of the Hungarian Jewish community that had managed to survive the war emigrated shortly thereafter.

In 1945 Hungary suffered additional territorial losses, and after the war it emerged with even less territory than it had held in 1937.[34] Despite the wartime devastation, however, the Hungarian population preserved its traditional sense of cultural fellowship with the Austrians and, indirectly, the Germans. The country's history, combined with its traditional element of alleged Magyar cultural superiority over the Slavs, contributed to an unyielding popular hostility toward Soviet occupation. While before the war Hungary had no common frontier with the Soviet Union and the anti-Russian sentiment in Hungary had never been as strong as in Poland, after 1945 anti-Russian feelings grew quickly among the population.

The Hungarians had initially hoped to remain outside the sphere of direct Soviet influence. They were encouraged in their expectations by Stalin's apparent willingness during the war to negotiate with Admiral Miklos Horthy, the Hungarian regent. It was also uncertain until 1944 whether the Red Army would get as far as Hungary; it was only after Romania switched sides in the fall of 1944 that Stalin saw an opening to move into the Balkans, occupying Hungary along the way. For military reasons, the British and the Americans gave Stalin a free hand in Hungary, and the Red Army conquered the country singlehandedly. While the Soviet army of occupation encouraged Hungarian communists, who had been more than willing to seize power, Stalin initially allowed three other Hungarian political parties to exist. At the end of 1945, the Hungarians were even allowed to hold free elections, which the communists resoundingly lost, getting only 18 percent of the vote. In 1947, however, Stalin's policy changed and the Soviets took full control of Hungary.

The economic devastation of East Central Europe was staggering, with Poland and Hungary suffering relatively greater damage than Czechoslovakia. More than half of the Polish livestock had been destroyed, while its transport and factories had been made inoperable. Poland's loss in terms of material resources was estimated at $18.2 billion.[35] Most of the railroads and bridges in Hungary were gone, the industrial base badly damaged, and the country ravaged by inflation. In the course of the war, the Polish, Czechoslovak, and Hungarian societies lost a large percentage of their professional classes, and the impending communist takeover after the war led to a wave of emigration of East Central European intelligentsia. Finally, the collapse of the interwar security system and the West's unwillingness to defend the small states' right to self-determination, as symbolized by both the 1938 Munich agreements and the 1945 Yalta territorial settlement, brought about a sense of profound disillusionment and betrayal.

In one fundamental respect, Poland, Czechoslovakia, and Hungary in 1945 came to share a common fate: they became Soviet clients, differences in their respective domestic political and economic conditions notwithstanding. Their links to the West were severed by Moscow's fiat, and their national aspirations became suppressed by Soviet power. The countries were taken over by Moscow-controlled local communist parties. Next, their domestic and foreign policies were aligned with those of the Soviet Union, and their armies developed to accommodate the military requirements set up by the Soviet General Staff. In 1955 the Warsaw Treaty Organization was established to harness the resources of what was now the Eastern bloc to the Soviet vision of security based on imperial expansion.

The paramount legacy of World War II for East Central Europe was the resolution of the seemingly intractable ethnic and territorial grievances. In the process, the communist socioeconomic experiment, dictated by Moscow, removed the question of regional security from the immediate policy agenda of Poland, Czechoslovakia, and Hungary. Concern for national security became synonymous with the implementation of the Soviet coalition warfare strategy and with the adoption of Soviet field manuals. Thinking about national security and military strategy became the sole prerogative of the Warsaw Pact.

THE WARSAW PACT UNDER KHRUSHCHEV

The Warsaw Treaty Organization, created by the Soviets in 1955, provided an institutional framework for the continued stationing of Soviet troops in Eastern Europe and was a first step by Moscow to utilize the resources of its satellites against NATO. In addition, for thirty-five years it perpetuated the Stalinist concept of Soviet national security based on imperial expansion and control over satellite regimes in Eastern Europe. The move by the Soviets to formalize their security relationship with the East Europeans reflected Moscow's basic security policy principle that continued presence in East Central Europe was a foundation of its defense against the West. In addition, the pact allowed the Soviets to tap the economic base and military capabilities of their clients to fit in their overall defense strategy. The military potential of Eastern Europe became important to Moscow after the 1949 creation of NATO and the subsequent remilitarization of the Federal Republic of Germany, which to the Soviets symbolized the United States' full-force return into European politics. Finally, Nikita Khrushchev's decision to create the WTO had a domestic policy dimension to it. Through its institutional structures the Pact compensated in part for the absence of Stalin's personal leadership, acutely felt since the dictator's death in 1953.

The WTO increased the overall value to Moscow of the military potential of Eastern Europe by consolidating the satellite armies under the unified Soviet command structure. Shortly after the creation of NATO, conscription was reintroduced in all Soviet satellite countries, and by 1953 the East Europeans were able to field sixty-five divisions, totaling approximately 1.5 million men (excluding East Germany, where conscription was reintroduced only in 1962).[36] The WTO non-Soviet military forces were restructured with an emphasis on the creation of a reliable and obedient new "proletarian officer class"; the process was accompanied by extensive purges of prewar officers who were charged with crimes ranging from cooperation with the old regime to high treason. The non-Soviet armies were reorganized and reequipped to conform with the Soviet model, while their national uniforms were either modified or completely replaced with designs conforming to the Soviet pattern. Political control in the 1950s was strengthened by the introduction in the structure of the armed forces of Main Political Administrations supervised by the Central Committees of East European ruling communist parties.

Soviet officers and security agents were detailed to serve in East European armies as advisers and commanders; they were the most immediate means of Moscow's control over its empire through 1956. This practice was most widely applied in Poland and Hungary; in Poland, Marshal Konstantin Rokossovsky, a famous Soviet World War II commander, became the country's defense minister and a member of the Polish communist party politburo. Soviet advisers were assigned to each satellite army as an independent channel of Soviet control; they reported directly to their superiors in Moscow and were exempt from East European criminal laws. In effect, until 1956 the East European armies were administered as if they were branches of the Soviet army. As such, the senior military establishments of non-Soviet WTO members became an alternative channel of Soviet control over the satellite countries—over their armies as well as their ruling communist parties.

The primary mission of the Warsaw Pact armies was defined in ideological as well as traditional military terms. They were committed to the protection of both their national territory and the communist system. Throughout the three decades of the evolution of the WTO strategy, the threat of an overthrow of the communist system was viewed as synonymous with military defeat. In strictly military terms, the strategy required that the Soviets and the Warsaw Pact not be defeated in a European conflict, because such a loss would likely lead to an overthrow of the communist system at home.[37] Because of this ideological dimension, the Warsaw Treaty Organization was by definition a means of policing the empire in addition to its role as a military pact. The WTO's military doctrine was based on the premise that in a war with the West a preemptive attack against NATO and offensive operations in Western Europe were the best way to ensure the survival of communism. The WTO defense strategy called for an attack against the West if and when the political leadership in Moscow determined that war had become unavoidable.

Change in the structure and the operational doctrine of the East European armed forces began shortly after Stalin's death in 1953 and reached a crescendo in the aftermath of the 1956 "thaw" following Khrushchev's de-Stalinization campaign. In addition to the move away from traditional infantry divisions, favored by Stalin, and a new emphasis on mechanized units, the East Europeans were now trained to fight on a nuclear battlefield. In 1956 the Pact's joint military command was established in Moscow. Still, the WTO remained largely a paper organization until the early 1960s. The Political Consultative Committee, the WTO's highest political body, met only four times between 1955 and 1961.[38] In fact, the Pact's primary role in the late 1950s was to legitimize the continued Soviet military deployment in Hungary and Romania after the ratification of the 1955 Austrian State Treaty. The Warsaw Pact structures served to contain the growing nationalism in Eastern Europe, especially in the aftermath of Stalin's death and the growing pressures for de-Stalinization following Khrushchev's "secret speech" to the twentieth Communist Party of the Soviet Union (CPSU) congress in which he had denounced Stalin's crimes.

The year 1956 was pivotal in the history of the non-Soviet militaries within the WTO. After the anti-Stalinist rebellion of 1956, including the "Polish October" and the Hungarian revolution, the Soviet "advisers" were sent home en bloc. National military uniforms were reintroduced and the local communist parties reasserted control over their armed forces. In addition, because of Chinese pressure and Romania's economic concessions, in 1958 the Soviets agreed to withdraw their troops from Romania. Moscow also concluded "status of forces" agreements with its clients, which for the first time spelled out the conditions under which the Soviet army would be stationed in Eastern Europe.

The partial relaxation of Soviet controls after 1956 was indirectly a function of East-West relations. In broad strategic terms, the inaction of the West during the Hungarian revolution reduced the Soviet fears that, given the opportunity, the West might launch a preemptive attack against the Pact. The lack of NATO's military response to the 1956 crisis, and especially to the precedent-setting use of the Soviet army to invade Hungary, symbolized to Moscow the growing Western acceptance of the Soviet sphere of domination in Eastern Europe. The WTO became the principal guardian of the status quo in the region. Despite its declared external-defensive mission, the Warsaw Pact's primary purpose was to keep in check the national aspirations of the satellites.

The importance of the East European troops to Moscow grew as Soviet strategy in Europe gradually changed. Two factors played a role: (1) the American buildup of nuclear weapons and (2) the growing Sino-Soviet split, which after 1957 threatened to erupt into an all-out confrontation. In order to match the Americans and to ensure that in a global war the communist system would be preserved, the Soviets launched a massive effort to develop their own nuclear weapons and delivery systems. In 1960 the Soviet Union established the Strategic Rocket Forces in a move indicative of a shift away from the traditional reliance on conventional weapons and toward a military strategy of which nuclear weapons would be an integral part. In turn, the growing Soviet nuclear capability and the emphasis on the WTO's offensive operations drove the Pact's military doctrine in the direction of a blitzkrieg strategy for operations in Europe. The Soviets attempted at first to reduce their defense expenditures in the area of conventional forces, as Khrushchev expected to compensate for the reductions in the Soviet forces by imposing an additional burden on the East Europeans.

The 1960s saw the development of the WTO's coalition warfare strategy, which rested on the assumption that the East Europeans would plan to fight as an integral part of an overall Soviet military offensive operation against NATO. The 1961 meeting of the Political Consultative Committee initiated the modernization process of the non-Soviet Warsaw Pact armies and launched the first joint military exercise, "Brotherhood-in-Arms '61."[39] More important, in the early 1960s the air defense systems of individual East European countries were integrated in the overall Soviet system of national air defense. Throughout the decade, the WTO military doctrine stipulated that the Pact's forces would drive into Western Europe, defeat NATO, and overthrow the existing governments while seeking to preserve the West's industrial base as a source of postwar economic reconstruction of the East.[40] The blitzkrieg offensive operations against NATO, planned for by the Warsaw Pact in the 1960s, were to ensure control over Western Europe before the United States had the opportunity to resupply its allies. If successful, this strategy would deny the Americans a beachhead on the Continent and, consequently (so it was hoped), would force Washington to negotiate with Moscow under conditions of stalemate following the WTO's victory.

In the 1960s the only Warsaw Pact country that presented problems for the Soviets was Ceausescu's Romania. In 1964 Ceausescu reduced the term of conscription from two years to sixteen months and cut the overall size of his army by 40,000 men. In 1966 Ceausescu caused a minor sensation when he openly suggested that Soviet troops be withdrawn from

Eastern Europe altogether. In addition, Ceausescu argued that the position of the WTO commander-in-chief should become a rotating appointment so that the East Europeans would also be given the opportunity to lead. Shortly thereafter, Romania refused to allow for joint WTO maneuvers on its territory and itself refrained from sending troops to participate in joint WTO maneuvers in other countries. Romania's participation in WTO exercises was henceforth limited to sending observers.[41]

Bucharest's pressure for greater independence in dealing with Moscow within the Warsaw Pact had some impact on Poland and Czechoslovakia. In the 1960s Poland entertained the idea of creating a "national front" within the WTO coalition strategy; it would allow for a Polish contingent within the Pact to be controlled by Polish officers.[42] In 1968 Czechoslovakia briefly entertained the idea of modifying its security arrangement by possibly signing bilateral treaties in addition to the security guarantee within the Warsaw Pact.[43] Both attempts, which were an expression of the yearning by the East Europeans for greater independence within the WTO, ended in failure.

WARSAW PACT REFORMS UNDER BREZHNEV

The invasion of Czechoslovakia in 1968 was a watershed in the Pact's history, because the Soviets demonstrated that they could use non-Soviet coalition forces to enforce compliance in the region. Troops from Poland, Hungary, Bulgaria, and East Germany participated in the operation; Romania was the only country within the Warsaw Pact to object to it. In the aftermath of the 1968 invasion, five Soviet divisions remained in Czechoslovakia as the newly constituted Soviet Central Group of Forces. In addition, the Soviets continued to station four divisions in Hungary and two divisions in Poland.

The organization of the Warsaw Pact underwent a major reform in 1969, in part to bring about the badly needed modernization of the non-Soviet forces and in part as a result of the growing Sino-Soviet split. The 1969 clash along the Ussuri River between the Soviet and the Chinese units forced Moscow to increase rapidly its deployment in the Far East; the number of Soviet troops stationed along the border with China went up from fifteen divisions in 1969 to forty-five divisions in 1973. Such a major new commitment of military power required that the non-Soviet WTO units in the European theater be modernized and made an integral part of Soviet strategic planning.

The WTO reform program was announced during the 1969 Budapest meeting of the Pact's Political Consultative Committee. The 1969 reform

(1) established the Committee of Defense Ministers as the highest consultative body of the WTO, (2) restructured the WTO Joint High Command, (3) created a Permanent Staff under the Joint High Command, (4) established the Military Council in charge of planning and quality control, (5) created the Technical Committee on Science and Technology responsible for weapons research and development, and (6) adopted a new statute for the Joint Armed Forces whereby the non-Soviet WTO deputy defense minister automatically became a deputy commander-in-chief of the WTO Joint High Command.[44] As part of the reform, the Northern Tier of the Warsaw Pact, which included Poland, East Germany, and Czechoslovakia, was assigned to and trained for rapid offensive operations against NATO forces to ensure that the war was conducted on Western European territory. The WTO coalition warfare strategy called for the creation of an "external front" deep inside NATO defenses. The strategy stipulated that a future war would take place in a nuclear environment, and the Warsaw Pact troops trained accordingly.

The 1969 reform of the WTO structure and strategy reflected deeper changes in Soviet security policy, introduced in 1967–1968 as the USSR was approaching the condition of rough parity with the United States in strategic nuclear weapons systems. The new Soviet security policy had an important political dimension: by 1968–1969 the Soviet Union was moving toward détente with the United States, in part the result of Washington's recognition of Moscow's formidable military power. Trouble in Eastern Europe, sparked by the Prague Spring of 1968, and the 1969 military confrontation with the Chinese induced the Kremlin to accelerate the process of détente.

The modernization of the non-Soviet WTO forces in the 1970s notwithstanding, the Soviet army remained the core of the Pact's offensive forces and it grew both in numbers and in technological sophistication. The decade also witnessed a renewed interest on the part of the Soviet military in the utility of limited military force applied for narrowly defined political objectives. Already in the late 1960s the Soviets were no longer unequivocal in their insistence that a global war between NATO and the Warsaw Pact would involve massive nuclear strikes by both sides. The change in the Warsaw Pact's strategy was in part a response to the United States' shift to the "flexible response" strategy in Europe and to Charles de Gaulle's decision to pull France out of NATO's military organization. The renewed emphasis on conventional forces was augmented by the Soviets in 1973 with the "no first use" policy, which declared that, if a conflict between NATO and the Warsaw Pact did take place, the Soviet side would not be the first to resort to the use of nuclear weapons. The "no first use" formula became a part of an elaborate propaganda campaign directed at NATO's public opinion to force the Western alliance to reciprocate with a "no first use" commitment of its own.

The Soviet Union's preoccupation in the 1970s with the modalities of conventional war in Europe reflected a changed global balance of power. By 1980 the Soviet armed forces numbered about five million men and were without a doubt the largest military establishment in the world. This force was supplemented by fifty-five non-Soviet Warsaw Pact divisions. The Soviet Union's nuclear parity with the United States had given Moscow's unquestionable numerical superiority in conventional weapons a decidedly new military significance; in the 1970s the direction of military planning was beginning to reflect this shift in the balance of power in Europe.[45] The prospect of a massive conventional operation in the West, which would knock NATO out before it could resort to a nuclear response, was from Moscow's point of view an attractive option. If implemented successfully, it would limit the damage to WTO territory and might prevent the escalation to nuclear war altogether.[46] While reformulating the Warsaw Pact's military doctrine, the Soviet military had an opportunity to test its views on limited war outside the European theater in the 1979 invasion of Afghanistan.

The overall number of Soviet troops notwithstanding, the size of the Soviet and the combined Warsaw Pact forces masked deep problems present within the Soviet force structure. By 1980 the crisis of efficiency, which for years had pervaded the Soviet economy as well as every facet of Soviet life, began to paralyze the defense industry as well. In comparison to the developed Western countries, the Soviet manpower base had a low technical-cultural level when measured against the requirements of modern warfare. In addition, the Soviet industrial base was insufficiently developed to provide modern high-technology weaponry. By 1980 it was becoming increasingly apparent that new technologies, in particular computer-based weapons systems, would change the face of modern warfare, leaving the Soviet army behind.

By 1980 a crisis in the WTO defense industries began to surface. The decade of the 1970s saw a rapid growth in the defense sectors of both Soviet and non-Soviet WTO member countries. The military industries of the Northern Tier countries, in particular those of Czechoslovakia and Poland, had become important additions to the Warsaw Pact's overall defense potential. Weapons exports to the Third World were now an important source of hard currency earnings for the Soviet bloc. By the mid-1980s the East Europeans ranked among the top five weapons exporters in the world. In 1987 Czechoslovakia ranked fourth in the world as a weapons exporter, after the USSR, the United States, and France; Poland ranked fifth. In terms of the percentage of arms exports to the country's total value of exports, Czechoslovakia ranked third in the world (7.86%), immediately after the Soviet Union and North Korea, and Poland ranked fourth (6.21%).[47] But the numbers told only one side of the story. Most of the weapons produced and exported were inferior compared with their NATO counterparts. The volume of production and the investment it had required of the two Soviet clients became an unsustainable burden on their economies and contributed to the East European economic crisis of the 1980s.

In the late 1970s the Soviets began another cycle of evolution in their defense doctrine, which would take them into Gorbachev's *perestroika* reforms. The technological requirements of the modern battlefield and the inadequacy of the Soviet industrial base were key factors stimulating the change. In 1987 the average growth rate for the non-Soviet Warsaw Pact economies was barely 2 percent, compared to the average 2 to 3 percent for 1986.[48] In addition, the economies of the Warsaw Pact countries proved increasingly incapable of providing high-technology items that became components of state-of-the-art weapons in the 1980s.

Changes in U.S.-Soviet global competition were the underlying reasons for the Soviet military restructuring in the 1980s. By 1979 the Soviet Union faced a new situation in the Middle East, where the ongoing conflict and America's commitment to defend access to Gulf oil could put Moscow and Washington on a collision course. If indeed such a conflict were to remain local, the Warsaw Pact's plan for a preemptive offensive into Western Europe had to be modified to allow the Soviets to fight a limited war in the South. In short, this new requirement placed the Warsaw Pact for the first time since World War II in a situation where defense rather than offense in the Western theater of operations against NATO had to be emphasized. In addition, changes in NATO's tactics between 1979 and 1982—including the plan to hit Soviet second- and third-echelon forces in the rear, as evidenced by the modernization of NATO intermediate nuclear forces—raised the real possibility that a WTO offensive into Europe might in fact be stopped.[49]

The fundamental shift in Soviet strategic planning from strictly offensive defense in the West to an emphasis on defensive operations marked the beginnings of a radical rethinking of Soviet national security strategy. It also reopened the issue of the relationship between the Soviet Union and its WTO allies; in particular, the Soviets needed to reformulate the political underpinnings of the relationship. They needed to maintain a reasonable level of defensive reliability of the non-Soviet Warsaw Pact forces under condition of a protracted defensive stalemate fought not in the West but more likely on the very territory of their clients. The Soviets envisioned that the defensive phase of such a war would not last longer than twenty days, after which the Warsaw Pact would be able to resort to its traditional offensive strategy.

The Kremlin's decision to redefine the Soviet Union's military strategy implied a change in the political relationship between Moscow and the non-Soviet Warsaw Pact members. The fact that this change was coming after a decade of détente in the 1970s, which had opened up Eastern Europe to Western influence to an unprecedented degree, was the primary danger inherent in the undertaking. The protracted economic crisis in Eastern Europe in the 1980s caused by the legacy of economic mismanagement further complicated the task. The communist regimes of the WTO member countries were being asked to make their ties to Moscow more viable at the time when communism was exhausted after four decades of failed policies. Military reform came as Poland was struggling hopelessly with the debt crisis and the chronic economic crisis since the 1981 introduction of martial law. Czechoslovakia's growth and productivity rates were plummeting amid continued political repression, while Hungary's 1968 "new economic mechanism" reform program was failing to deliver a steady increase in the living standards of the population.

NOTES

1. Roy E. H. Mellor, *Eastern Europe: A Geography of the Comecon Countries* (New York: Columbia University Press, 1975), pp. 4–5.

2. Joseph Rothschild, *East Central Europe between the Two World Wars* (Seattle and London: University of Washington Press, 1974), p. 8.

3. C. A. Macartney and A. W. Palmer, *Independent Eastern Europe: A History* (London: Macmillan and Co., 1962), p. 98.

4. Mellor, p. 70.

5. Ibid., p. 72.

6. Rothschild, p. 86.

7. Macartney/Palmer, p. 130.

8. Mellor, p. 66.

9. Robin Okey, *Eastern Europe 1740–1985: Feudalism to Communism* (Minneapolis: University of Minnesota Press, 1986), p. 160.

10. Rothschild, p. 156.

11. Macartney/Palmer, p. 140.

12. Henry L. Roberts, *Eastern Europe: Politics, Revolution, and Diplomacy* (New York: Alfred A. Knopf, 1970), p. 58.

13. Macartney/Palmer, p. 162.

14. Antony Polonsky, *The Little Dictators: The History of Eastern Europe since 1918* (London and Boston, Mass.: Routledge & Kegan Paul, 1975), pp. 44–45.

15. Ibid., p. 49.

16. Roberts, p. 61.

17. Ibid., p. 63.

18. Rothschild, p. 10.

19. Eduard Benes, *Five Years of Czechoslovak Foreign Policy* (Prague: Orbis Publishing, 1924), pp. 12–19, in Alfred J. Bannan and Achilles Edelenyi, eds., *Documentary History of Eastern Europe* (New York: Twayne Publishers, 1970), p. 285.

20. Roberts, p. 64.

21. Polonsky, p. 52.

22. Ibid., p. 59.

23. Z. Anthony Kruszewski, "Nationalism and Politics: Poland," in George Klein and Milan J. Reban, eds., *The Politics of Ethnicity in Eastern Europe* (New York: Columbia University Press, 1981), p. 148.

24. Okey, p. 191.

25. Kruszewski, p. 177.

26. Peter Bender, *East Europe in Search of Security* (London: Chatto and Windus, 1972), p. 52.

27. Milan J. Reban, "Czechoslovakia: The New Federation," in George Klein and Milan J. Reban, eds., *The Politics of Ethnicity in Eastern Europe* (New York: Columbia University Press, 1981), p. 216.

28. Okey, p. 191.

29. Garrison E. Walters, *The Other Europe: Eastern Europe to 1945* (Syracuse, N.Y.: Syracuse University Press, 1988), p. 283.

30. Bender, p. 83.

31. Ibid., p. 83.

32. Ivan Volgyes has suggested that the defeat in World War II ended "once and for all" Hungary's irredentist claims. This appears to be questionable in light of the policy on Magyar minorities in Slovakia and Romania pursued by Budapest after 1989. Ivan Volgyes, "Legitimacy and Modernization: Nationality and Nationalism in Hungary and Transylvania," in George Klein and Milan J. Reban, eds., *The Politics of Ethnicity in Eastern Europe* (New York: Columbia University Press, 1981), pp. 134–135.

33. Volgyes, p. 139.

34. Bender, p. 100.

35. Okey, p. 191.

36. A. Ross Johnson, "Soviet Military Policy in Eastern Europe," in Sarah Meiklejohn Terry, ed., *Soviet Policy in Eastern Europe* (New Haven, Conn., and London: Yale University Press, 1984), p. 258.

37. See Michael MccGwire, *Perestroika and Soviet National Security* (Washington, D.C.: The Brookings Institution, 1991), p. 15.

38. Ross Johnson, p. 261.

39. Ibid., p. 262.

40. MccGwire, p. 23.

41. Ross Johnson, p. 263.

42. Teresa Rakowska-Harmstone, Christopher Jones, and Ivan Sylvain, *Warsaw Pact: The Question of Cohesion, Phase II*, vol. 2, *Poland, German Democratic Republic, and Romania* (Ottawa: ORAE Extra-Mural Paper No. 33, November 1984), p. 71.

43. The reference to bilateral military assistance among WTO members, excluding the Soviet Union, was contained in the Czechoslovak Ministry of Defense's 1968 Action Program. See Condoleezza Rice, *The Soviet Union and the Czechoslovak Army, 1948–1983: Uncertain Alliance* (Princeton, N.J.: Princeton University Press, 1984), p. 133.

44. Jeffrey Simon, *Warsaw Pact Forces: Problems of Command and Control* (Boulder, Colo.: Westview Press, 1985), pp. 62–67.

45. David Halloway, *The Soviet Union and the Arms Race* (New Haven, Conn.: Yale University Press, 1987), p. 88.

46. Michael MccGwire, *Military Objectives in Soviet Foreign Policy* (Washington, D.C.: The Brookings Institution, 1987), pp. 42–45.

47. *World Military Expenditures and Arms Transfers, 1987* (Washington, D.C.: U.S. Arms Control and Disarmament Agency, 1988), p. 30.

48. *The Military Balance, 1988–1989* (London: International Institute for Strategic Studies, 1988), p. 46.

49. MccGwire, *Perestroika*, p. 37.

2

THE COLLAPSE OF THE
WARSAW PACT

"NEW THINKING" ON SOVIET SECURITY

The redefinition of Soviet national security policy in the second half of the 1980s involved both a radical change in Soviet–West European relations and a transformation of the organizational structure of the Warsaw Pact. The envisioned change in Soviet military strategy harkened to Marshal Nikolay V. Ogarkov's insistence at the beginning of the decade that, in light of the existing nuclear stalemate between the two superpowers, the Soviet armed forces would have to adapt to the rapidly changing conventional weapons technology and shift their training to combined-arms operations (air power, air defense, field force firepower) concentrated in theaters of military operations.[1] The renewed importance of the conventional battlefield made it imperative for the Warsaw Pact to restructure its armies, both Soviet and satellite, to increase the reliability of the non-Soviet WTO forces, and to reequip the Combined Forces with technologically advanced conventional weapons systems. This need was made more urgent by the growing economic pressure on the Soviet defense establishment generated by the perceived necessity to match the American defense buildup of President Ronald Reagan's first term in office, including the critical challenge of the Strategic Defense Initiative program.

The Soviets were not ready, however, to give up on their traditional goal of weakening NATO's transatlantic connection, which had been the primary objective of both Khrushchev's and Brezhnev's defense policies. Instead of attempting to undercut the U.S. strategic guarantee to Europe, as Khrushchev and Brezhnev would have done, Gorbachev apparently decided in 1985 to degrade the value of the U.S. nuclear guarantee by lowering the overall threat of war on the Continent. In practical terms, this approach required Moscow to forgo a portion of its own nuclear forces in the region, as well as to reduce the level of the Warsaw Pact conventional forces.[2] The signing of the Intermediate Range Nuclear Forces treaty, in 1987 in Moscow, which removed from Europe the Soviet SS-20s in return for the elimination of the American Pershing 2 and cruise missiles, was a logical consequence of Gorbachev's redefinition of Soviet security in Europe.

After 1987 Moscow's decisions on military strategy became tied directly to the premise, propounded by Gorbachev on the counsel of Foreign Minister Eduard Shevardnadze, that Soviet national security had to be linked to a pan-European security arrangement based on the principle of mutuality. The period of Shevardnadze's ascendancy in the Soviet foreign policy–making establishment as Gorbachev's most trusted adviser, until his resignation on December 20, 1990, constitutes the time frame during which Moscow's "new thinking" on national security was implemented. The policy contributed to the 1989 anticommunist revolutions in Eastern Europe, led to the disintegration of the Warsaw Treaty Organization in 1991, and ultimately led to the collapse of the USSR itself. At the core of the Gorbachev-Shevardnadze redefinition of Soviet national security objectives lay the premise that the Soviet Union could provide for its security, and ultimately prevent war, primarily by political means. In his December 1988 address to the United Nations General Assembly, Gorbachev announced that this approach would constitute an official Soviet policy. Gorbachev also promised a 14.2 percent reduction in Soviet defense spending and a half-million cut in Soviet military personnel, including a 240,000 reduction in Soviet troops deployed in Europe.

The preparatory stage of the WTO reform began in April 1985 with dramatic changes in the top-level Soviet military personnel. The renewed European emphasis in Moscow's strategic redefinition, which translated into the Gorbachev-Shevardnadze vision of a new pan-European security paradigm, was implemented by a group of senior military personnel brought into the process by Gorbachev in 1985–1986. These army officers included General Pyotr G. Lushev, former commander-in-chief of Soviet forces in East Germany and the man who in 1988 replaced Marshal Viktor Kulikov as the commander-in-chief of the Warsaw Pact; Chief of the General Staff Mikhail A. Moiseyev, formerly an officer with Soviet forces in East Germany; General Yevgeniy F. Ivanovskiy, appointed commander-in-chief of the Ground Forces in 1985, who had been a training expert and commander-in-chief of the Group of Soviet Forces in Germany (GSFG) between 1972 and 1980; and the Main Political Administration (MPA) chief General Aleksy D. Lizichev, who had served between 1982 and 1985 as the MPA chief of the Group of Soviet Forces in Germany.[3] Finally, in May 1987 Gorbachev appointed General Dmitriy T. Yazov, who had extensive experience with the Central Group of Forces in Czechoslovakia, as the Soviet Union's defense minister. These senior officers were Gorbachev's choices to replace the top military echelon of the Brezhnev era. By early 1987 Gorbachev could claim control over the Soviet military; however, the army's enthusiasm for his reforms would wane shortly thereafter as the top brass blamed Gorbachev for undermining the Warsaw Pact and for weakening the Soviet Union itself. In January 1991 confusion over the aborted crackdown against the independence movement in Lithuania and Latvia, combined with the perceived setback to the Soviet Union's interests in the Middle East after the allied victory over Iraq in the Gulf War, brought to the fore the army's deep resentment over the government's national security policy.[4]

The decision to restructure the Warsaw Pact was first publicly hinted at during the June 1986 Budapest conference of the Warsaw Treaty Political Consultative Committee, which issued a general appeal to NATO for a radical reduction in conventional forces and weapons.[5] On January 11, 1986, at the close of the two-day Budapest meeting, the Pact called for the two alliances to reduce ground troops and tactical air forces on both sides of the European divide by 25 percent, or a half-million soldiers, within a decade.[6] The first step was to entail the demobilization of 150,000 soldiers over the next two years. A phased reduction of troops and armaments would continue into the early 1990s. The announcement, referred to by Warsaw Pact spokesmen as the "Second Budapest Appeal" in reference to the 1969 appeal which had preceded the Helsinki accords, was an amplification of the promise made by Gorbachev in April 1986 during a visit to East Germany that the Pact would soon unveil a plan for radical conventional arms cuts.

The Second Budapest Appeal was a breakthrough in Soviet thinking about strategy and arms control in Europe in that it allowed for on-site inspections and for the first time outlined a timetable for the WTO troop reductions. As such, it effectively eclipsed the deadlocked Mutual and Balanced Force Reduction (MBFR) talks in Vienna. The Second Budapest Appeal also symbolized the Soviet Union's "new thinking" on national security. At the heart of Gorbachev's redefinition of Soviet security in Europe was the reaffirmation of the principle that general world war—that is, war between the two social systems—was unacceptable and that it could be averted by political means par excellence.[7]

DEFENSE SPENDING CUTS AND WTO FORCE RESTRUCTURING

The Soviet plan to reduce defense spending and to restructure the Warsaw Pact's defensive posture was formally announced during the 1987 Berlin meeting of the Pact's Political Consultative Committee. While the appearances of unity were kept up, it was clear that the East European satellite regimes viewed the change with a mixture of anticipation and apprehension. In the core Northern Tier of the Warsaw Pact the least enthusiastic supporters of the plan were the East German and the Czechoslovak communist regimes, while the Polish government expressed a low-key approval. Hungary, which in the coalition's military planning was placed outside the Northern Tier, on the other hand made no effort to conceal its enthusiastic support for the changes.[8]

The Hungarian army began the process of restructuring in the spring of 1987, when it underwent a reorganization that replaced its five army divisions with three army corps, where each corps contained three to five brigades depending on the conditions and terrain of its possible deployment. The new Hungarian formations were configured to fight primarily a conventional war.[9] In the wake of Moscow's approval of the change, in late 1988 and 1989, the Hungarians engaged in an unusually frank public debate over their defense and disarmament plans. The discussion led to a reduction in military spending and a limited purge of the senior officer corps; in the process some fifty army generals and colonels were forced into an early retirement. Furthermore, although the defense spending cuts for 1989 originally set by the Hungarian government at 10 percent increased to 17 percent, even this figure was rejected by the country's parliament as inadequate.[10] In the end, the Hungarian defense budget was fixed at 40 billion forints ($2.2 billion). Simultaneously, the length of military service for Hungarian conscripts was reduced from eighteen months to twelve months, and the government promised to introduce a law providing for alternatives to military service for conscientious objectors.[11] In addition, General Ferenc Karpati, Hungary's defense minister at the time, called for a full disclosure of data on Warsaw Pact forces and defense spending levels prior to the upcoming conventional arms control talks scheduled to take place in Vienna in early 1989. Karpati suggested that, because of Hungary's geopolitical position, the country should serve as a "testing ground" in the area of disarmament and verification.[12] Karpati's statement was soon followed by Budapest's official announcement that some Soviet forces deployed in Hungary would be withdrawn in the near future. Reportedly, the Soviets had agreed to a 25 percent reduction in their 62,000-strong force in Hungary over a two-year period.[13]

In January 1989, Hungary's example was followed by Poland, which announced a 4 percent cut in its defense budget. According to a statement released by Poland's defense minister, General Florian Siwicki, the reduction had been approved in November 1988. The Polish army had already been cut by 15,000 personnel, and additional reductions were to be forthcoming shortly. The 4 percent cut in the defense budget, announced by Siwicki, amounted to 954 billion zlotys ($1.8 billion).[14] In an interview published in the Polish communist party daily *Trybuna Ludu*, Siwicki outlined the direction of reform within the Polish armed forces and indicated that the cuts were a prelude to substantial changes in Poland's defense doctrine in keeping with the changes in the defense doctrine of the Warsaw Pact as a whole.

As in the past, the new Polish defense doctrine placed the Polish army within the "coalition defense system."[15] The restructuring completed in 1988 included the reconstitution of two Category III mechanized divisions, as well as changes within several air force and artillery units. Poland's Sixth and Seventh Airborne Divisions were downgraded to the level of brigades, and a number of old tanks and artillery pieces were withdrawn from service. According to Siwicki, changes within the structure of the Polish army planned for 1989–1990 would include in addition:

—merging and streamlining of the army's central administration, with the possibility of merging branches of the armed forces;

—merging the military academies and officer schools with similar programs;

—reducing the number of units while increasing combat readiness and modernizing equipment;

—increasing the number of units *w stanie skadrowanym*, that is, with reduced readiness levels in peacetime (for example, reduction from Categories I and II to Category III);

—transforming regional defense units, engineering-construction units, rail and road units into civil defense units (thus placing them outside the armed forces);

—reducing the number of exercises for reservists and the extent of those exercises.[16]

Speaking on Polish television on February 26, 1989, Siwicki detailed the planned force reductions in Poland, scheduled for implementation over a two-year period. According to the plan, the size of the army was to be reduced by about 40,000 men; 850 tanks, 900 artillery pieces and mortars, 700 armored vehicles, and 80 combat aircraft would also be withdrawn. The plan called for the complete dissolution of the Second and Fifteenth Armored Divisions and a substantial manpower reduction of the Tenth and Sixteenth Tank Divisions.[17]

A year later in a January 4, 1990, interview for Polish television's Channel 1, Siwicki announced that the restructuring plan scheduled for 1989 had been partially implemented. In 1989 the Polish army was reduced by 33,000 soldiers and officers; 68 units were disbanded and 147 were restructured; 400 tanks were pulled out of service, as were 700 artillery pieces and mortars, 600 armed personnel carriers, and about 80 aircraft. In addition, about 30 military installations were turned over by the army to the government for civilian use. Future plans for the restructuring of the armed forces included combining the air force and the air defense forces (*wojska obrony powietrznej kraju*). All so-called political officers were to be replaced by "education officers" drawn from a new Education Officers Corps (*Korpus Oficerow Wychowawczych*). The plan also stipulated that, in 1990, 57 additional military units would be disbanded and about 70 units would be restructured. Cuts in equipment were to include the elimination of 450 tanks, 200 artillery pieces and mortars, and about 100 armored personnel carriers. After the anticipated 10,000 reduction of personnel by the end of 1990, the Polish army would number about 300,000, which would constitute approximately 0.8 percent of Poland's total population.

In October 1990 the Polish government reduced the required army service for draftees from two years to eighteen months; in addition, in the fall of 1990 two new military academies were opened: the National Defense Academy (*Akademia Obrony Narodowej*) and the Higher Army Engineering Officer School (*Wyzsza Szkola Oficerska Inzynierii Wojskowej*). The 1990 military budget was reduced by 5 percent relative to the 1989 appropriation.[18]

For economic as well as political reasons, the Polish army appeared determined to bring about important changes within its structure. Since August 1989 Poland had its first noncommunist government, led by Tadeusz Mazowiecki of the Solidarity Trade Union. In addition to the country's bankrupt economy, the new government had to deal with a considerable decline in the army's prestige caused by its role in the suppression of Solidarity in 1981. Throughout the 1980s, the Polish army faced growing problems in recruitment, especially to its officer schools. Because of the pressure from conscientious objectors, the former communist government had been forced to offer an alternative to military service; the law on alternatives to military service for Poland's youth had been passed in 1988, before the Mazowiecki government took office.[19] Similar laws were also introduced in East Germany and Hungary.

In contrast to Hungary and Poland, Czechoslovakia's hard-line communist regime was visibly more reluctant to undertake the restructuring of its defense establishment. As a result, the Czechoslovak army was less forthcoming than the Poles and Hungarians with the details of the reform program. Nevertheless, Prague had to adjust to the new situation, and in 1989 Czechoslovakia announced that it would follow Soviet directives. In an interview for the West German television network AES, rebroadcast in Prague on January 2, 1989, Czechoslovakia's Communist Party secretary general, Milos Jakes, stated that his country would "seek ways of reducing its military potential."[20] However reluctantly, by mid-1989 the Czechoslovak military was in the process of implementing military reforms to accommodate the Warsaw Pact's new defense doctrine.

The reductions in 1989 amounted to the cut of 12,000 men from military units and 20,000 from military support personnel. In addition, a number of armored regiments and air force units were slated for reduction. In sum, the organizational changes touched approximately 30,000 Czechoslovak military personnel.[21] Changes planned by the Ministry of Defense for 1989–1990 would affect some 200 Czechoslovak army units. The early reform plan was adopted during the summer 1989 session of the National Defense Council (*Rada obrany statu*), which redefined the country's defense policy to conform to the changes in the Warsaw Pact's military doctrine.[22]

WTO WAR PLANNING AFTER FORCE REDUCTIONS

The 1987–1989 restructuring of the Warsaw Pact was part of a dramatic change in the Soviet Union's contingency planning for a future war in Europe. In the new plan, the European territory from the Atlantic to the Urals was divided into three concentric zones: (1) the first zone was to include West Germany, Belgium, the Netherlands, Luxembourg, and Denmark in the West, and East Germany, Czechoslovakia, Poland, and Hungary in the East; (2) the second zone was to include Great Britain, France, six divisions in the United States to be used as reinforcements in Europe, and the border military districts in the USSR, that is, the Byelorussian and the Carpathian districts; and (3) the third zone was to include all remaining NATO countries in Europe and Turkey in the West, and Romania, Bulgaria, and the remaining eight military districts in the European part of the Soviet Union in the East.[23] The Soviets also envisioned that a portion of the U.S. territory, the U.S. Marine Groups of the Atlantic and the Mediterranean, and U.S. carriers and strike aviation would be included in the third zone.

The Warsaw Pact and NATO were to renounce the use of tactical weapons within the 150-kilometer border zone between West and East Germany and were to withdraw the highly maneuverable military equipment from the 100-kilometer direct contact zone between the two blocs; this would be augmented by up to 40 percent reductions of forces to bring both sides to an equal level. In effect, the Warsaw Pact would be eliminating 31 divisions, 11,200 tanks, and 5,500 artillery pieces and multiple rocket launch systems; NATO would be reducing 16 divisions, 4,700 tanks, and 2,000 artillery pieces and multiple rocket launch systems.[24]

According to Soviet Deputy Defense Minister Army General Mikhail Sorokin, in addition to the reduction in the number of tanks, the changeover from the traditional coalition warfare strategy to the "defensive" defense concept would include a 12 percent overall troop reduction that would amount to 240,000 troops in the west, 200,000 troops in the east, and 60,000 troops in the south. Six tank divisions would be disbanded in East Germany, Czechoslovakia, and Hungary by 1991.[25] In March 1989, Soviet Defense Minister General Dmitriy T. Yazov revealed that the first Soviet units to be pulled out of East Central Europe were the Thirteenth Tank Division at Veszprem in Hungary and two tank divisions from East Germany: the Thirty-second Guards Tank Division from Jueterborg and the Twenty-fifth Tank Division from Vogelsang.[26]

The complete schedule for Soviet force withdrawal from East Central Europe announced in early 1989 was as follows:

East Germany/Group of Soviet Forces in Germany:
   1989: Twenty-fifth Tank Division, Thirty-second Guards Tank Division, two independent training tank regiments, eight independent battalions.
   1990: Twelfth Guards Tank Division, Seventh Guards Tank Division, Air Assault Brigade, an independent training tank regiment, three training regiments, and several independent battalions.
Czechoslovakia/Soviet Central Group of Forces:
   1989: two independent battalions.

1990: Thirty-first Tank Division, an independent training tank regiment, an air assault battalion, and a fighter regiment; all forces to leave by June 1991.

Hungary/Soviet Southern Group of Forces:

1989: Thirteenth Tank Division, an independent training tank regiment, an air assault battalion, a fighter regiment; the remaining troops would be moved back to the rear in accordance with the new "defensive doctrine"; all forces to leave by June 1991.

Poland/Soviet Northern Group of Forces:

1989: a tank regiment, an anti-air regiment, and an independent helicopter regiment;[27] all forces to leave by 1994, pending the ongoing Polish-Soviet negotiations.

A NEW WTO MILITARY DOCTRINE

The new Warsaw Pact military doctrine, referred to for the first time publicly by General Dmitriy T. Yazov in the July 27, 1987, issue of *Pravda*, was formally adopted by the WTO member-states during the May 28–29, 1987, conference in Berlin. The doctrine was touted as "purely defensive," as it stipulated that military force could be used only when the socialist alliance was attacked. It reaffirmed the traditional Soviet "no first use" policy on nuclear weapons and asserted that the WTO had no territorial ambitions either in Europe or elsewhere. It also articulated the principle of "sufficiency" as the foundation of the Pact's security policy—that is, that no state was entitled to a greater level of security than other countries and also that no state could be expected to accept less. Yazov reaffirmed Gorbachev's position that "notions that wars can achieve political aims are outdated"; hence war lost its usefulness as a rational instrument of policy.[28]

While the statement was a startling repudiation by the Warsaw Treaty Organization of Lenin's definition of war, its impact on the West was diminished by considerable confusion as to the actual meaning of the term *defense* and its implications for Soviet military planning. In the Soviet definition, "defensive defense" appeared not so much to apply to actual war fighting but to express instead the Gorbachev/Shevardnadze line that war was preventable primarily by political means. In effect, it meant that deterring or deflecting an attack was now the key objective of the Warsaw Pact's military planners. In case of war, however, the WTO forces would retain the capability to resort to offensive operations. Most important, in the initial reformulation of the Pact's military strategy, NATO remained the enemy and war would be waged by the Soviet bloc as a whole, with each East European member-state contributing its prescribed military contingent. The "defensive defense" idea assumed that a reduction in the level of threat through diplomatic means did not preclude a return to offensive operations in case of war. As late as 1989 the Soviet General Staff maintained that American imperialism was as threatening as ever, and it therefore required constant vigilance on the part of the Warsaw Treaty Organization. In an interview for *Krasnaya Zvezda* in February 1989, Soviet Chief of the General Staff General Mikhail A. Moiseyev dismissed the idea of a lasting reconciliation with the United States and Western Europe as a "pacifist notion."[29]

The stated political goal of the Pact's doctrine was to prevent war through political means. It was defined as purely defensive in that the WTO member-states would "never, under any circumstances, start hostilities against any country or an alliance of countries, unless they become the target of an armed attack themselves."[30] It also asserted that the size, equipment, and structure of the WTO armed forces would not exceed the limits necessary for defense against aggression. The stated Soviet goal of the proposed reductions in conventional forces in Europe was to ensure that neither NATO nor the Warsaw Pact would have the ability to launch offensive operations against each other. In a major departure from the past, the Soviets made concessions on the question of arms control treaty verification to include a combination of satellite surveillance, international supervision, exchange of military information, and, most important, holding on-site inspections. Finally, they declared that the perpetuation of the two military blocs in Europe was contrary to the spirit of "new thinking" and called for the simultaneous dissolution of both NATO and the Warsaw Pact.[31]

By 1990 the Soviets became quite outspoken on the subject of military reform, including statements by high-ranking senior officers. According to Major General V. L. Manilov, chief of the Directorate of Information of the USSR Ministry of Defense, "beginning in 1987 a new modern military doctrine has been in the process of implementation."[32] The reform was drafted by a special commission including members of the USSR Supreme Soviet, departments of the CPSU Central Committee, the Council of Ministers, the Ministry of Defense, and "other institutions"—presumably the KGB. The proposed changes were to run through the year 2000.[33] The primary goal of the reform was to modernize the WTO armed forces and to increase the efficiency of Soviet military personnel. The successful achievement of the former depended on the improvements in the Soviet economy; the successful achievement of the latter rested on changes in the Soviet educational system. Already in January 1987 the "Reform of General Education and Vocational Training" laws were introduced. Their aim was to improve the quality of education in Soviet secondary and vocational schools; in particular, to boost Russian language training for non-Russians. The reform, first discussed in 1983 during Yuriy Andropov's brief tenure as CPSU general secretary, was developed by a special educational committee. Gorbachev, who had served on the committee, was a strong supporter of the new law. The law on education was also backed by the military, which saw it as a step toward increasing the size of the career NCO (noncommissioned officer) corps in the Soviet army.[34]

At no point did the Soviet General Staff contemplate a unilateral dissolution of the Warsaw Pact or a loss of control over satellite armies in Eastern Europe. The Soviet view that the WTO would remain in place as a sine qua non of Soviet strategy in Europe was reaffirmed as late as January 1990, after the anticommunist revolutions of the previous year had already made the preservation of the external empire doubtful. The Pact's commander-in-chief, General Pyotr G. Lushev, writing for the authoritative Soviet military journal *Voyennaya Mysl'*, argued at the time that the "key political criterion that links the [WTO] member-states is the principle of socialist internationalism," especially as "NATO continues to block the WTO efforts to reduce military tension in Europe."[35]

The Soviets did recognize, however, that some changes had to be made. The "renewed alliance," whose reaffirmation the Soviet military had sought since the beginning of the 1987 reform, meant that "ideological intelligibility" rather than the complete conformity of the Brezhnev period was now an acceptable formula for Moscow's relations with its satellites. However, the notion of "collectivism" as applied by the Soviet General Staff to the USSR's security meant first and foremost the fulfillment of intra-allied commitments within the Warsaw Treaty Organization. "National defense" meant the "defense of socialism," that is, the maintenance of the Soviet imperial position in the East. Hence, after 1987, "collective security" in the context of the Warsaw Pact for the Soviet military translated into the collective defense of socialism, which "under present conditions is expressed in the concept of all-encompassing, mutual, equal, and indivisible security."[36]

It is important to note that when the key concepts of "reasonable sufficiency" and the "defensive defense" approach were being discussed by the Soviet military, "sufficiency" was understood to encompass the potential of the entire Warsaw Pact. Lushev defined the Soviet military's understanding of "reasonable sufficiency" as follows:

By sufficiency in defense one understands the minimal level and nature of military potential of the *coalition members* of the military alliance which is commensurate to the external threat and at the same time guarantees the security and effective defense of *all allied states* [author's emphasis].[37]

The Soviet military understood "sufficiency" and "defensive defense" in coalition terms par excellence. Therefore, to the Soviet General Staff the transformation of the WTO into a renewed political alliance meant in effect the strengthening of alliance cohesion.

GERMAN REUNIFICATION AND WTO MILITARY PLANNING

Paradoxically, the Soviet military's view on the future of the Warsaw Pact did not change until late 1990, even though it had become ever more apparent that German reunification would constitute an irreparable breach in the WTO's security perimeter. In fact, senior Soviet officers argued that the reunification of Germany made it imperative for the Warsaw Pact to endure, as it would provide a necessary counterweight to the new Germany. Acknowledging that the WTO was being restructured, General Pyotr G. Lushev insisted as late as May 1990 that "the area of mutual obligations has not changed. These are defined by the Pact, whose goals are to provide for strong security of all member-states of the coalition."[38] Lushev was not willing to give up more control over the satellites than absolutely necessary. According to Lushev, changes in the structure of the "renewed WTO" could entail only a new agreement on the "location of the headquarters of the Pact's Combined Armed Forces, changes in the command structure, and the principle of personnel rotation"[39]—a concession to the Polish demand that the top-level military position in the WTO be staffed with East European officers. Still, the Soviet military adhered to the key position that NATO continued to pose a threat to Soviet security. This position was reiterated to West German Chancellor Helmut Kohl during his historic meeting with Gorbachev in Zheleznovodsk in July 1990. The Germans were told that the price of reunification was the clear understanding of the "unacceptability of extending NATO's military structures into the territory of the GDR."[40]

At no point in their negotiations with either the West or the WTO member-states did the Soviet General Staff concede that the Pact had lost its military role or validity. In an interview for *Krasnaya Zvezda* in commemoration of the thirty-fifth anniversary of the WTO, Lushev vigorously denied that the impending withdrawal of Soviet forces from

Czechoslovakia and Hungary constituted an end of the alliance. Lushev's reasoning ran as follows:

1. The governments of all member-states announced that they would fulfill their obligations as allies within the Pact;

2. They reaffirmed the position that both NATO and the WTO could only be dissolved simultaneously and only when a collective European security system was in place;

3. Most important, Soviet withdrawal from Hungary and Czechoslovakia was taking place "on the basis of bilateral rather than collective all-Pact agreements, and hence it did not affect relations within the alliance"; thus, it was not synonymous with the "liquidation of the Combined [WTO] Armed Forces."[41]

Lushev admitted that some changes would have to be made. The Soviets were willing to reduce the intensity of large-scale joint military maneuvers and replace them with lower-level training on the tactical level. The Warsaw Treaty Organization would also become more of a political structure than it had been in the past, but "politicization" as contemplated by the Soviet military did not include greater participation by the East Europeans in the decision-making process. In terms of its impact on the military structures of the Warsaw Pact, the "politicization of the alliance" would mean "the strengthening of cooperation on the General Staff level and an increase in the exchange of experiences on military matters."[42] All changes, therefore, had to be weighed against the Soviet General Staff's position that the WTO should continue into the foreseeable future. In Lushev's words:

As specified by the Warsaw Treaty the forces earmarked by each country to constitute their contingents of the Combined Armed Forces remain in peacetime under their national command and train according to their plans. In case of aggression, they should be ready to operate within the structure of the coalition forces.

Naturally, I cannot completely exclude the possibility of this or that country leaving the Warsaw Treaty Organization. In Hungary, for instance, the question of leaving the WTO has been raised by one of the factions of the newly elected national assembly. I have believed and still believe that every nation by itself determines its fate. However, from my point of view, the time for dissolving the WTO has not yet come. Today, the Warsaw Pact provides its member-states with guarantees of stability.[43]

In short, Lushev's insistence on the preservation of the Warsaw Pact reflected the Soviet General Staff's assessment of the European balance of power. The Soviet position articulated prior to the crucial June 1990 meeting of the WTO Political Consultative Committee in Moscow, which called for replacing the two-bloc security system in Europe with a collective security arrangement, was that NATO had not ceased to be a threat to the Soviet Union. In May, Lushev attacked the proponents of dissolving the WTO and argued that "NATO remains to us what it has always been—an adversary military bloc with a concrete military doctrine [directed at us] and with first strike nuclear capability."[44]

In the end, however, Gorbachev overruled the army's objections. The June 1990 meeting brought about a political redefinition of Soviet security objectives. By then, the army apparently no longer agreed with the Gorbachev/Shevardnadze formula for East-West cooperation and regarded it as a radical setback to Moscow's strategic interests in Europe.[45]

REBELLION WITHIN THE PACT

In the spring of 1990 the Soviet General Staff made one last push to salvage what it could from the disintegrating Warsaw Treaty Organization. The military's position was a restatement of Lushev's outline of the Pact's future, presented in May 1990:

In the near future the Pact will continue to undergird the allied relations of the East European countries, while taking into account new approaches to solving the problems of cooperation within the WTO. For the time being, the military organization of the Pact will also retain its role. Without a doubt, it is too early to speak now about the inevitable demise of the alliance.[46]

The June 8, 1990, meeting of the WTO Political Consultative Committee was the last-ditch effort by Moscow to reconcile its vision of the Pact's future role with that of its increasingly unruly former satellites. Challenged by the Hungarians and the Czechoslovaks, Gorbachev virtually pleaded for the conference participants to accept the Soviet position that it was premature to discuss the Pact's dissolution. The final communiqué was based largely on a draft submitted by Czechoslovakia, after its president Vaclav Havel contended that the Soviet version contained nothing new.[47]

The final document of the Moscow Warsaw Pact summit called for a transition from the current bloc security system to a pan-European structure at the earliest possible date. It declared that such a system was made possible by the present state of East-West relations; it referred to these developments as "irreversible" and called for the creation of "a new all-European security system, for one Europe of peace and cooperation."[48] In a move bound to anger the Soviet military, the declaration asserted that the "image of the enemy" was no longer applicable to East-West relations and that the "confrontational elements" in the military doctrines of NATO and the WTO "did not reflect the spirit of the times."

From the point of view of the Soviet General Staff, the most radical and dangerous portion of the Moscow document spoke to the need to redefine the structure of the Warsaw Pact in a way that would assist its members in an expeditious transition to collective security. The heads of state assembled in Moscow agreed to establish "a special temporary government-level commission of plenipotentiaries to report to the Political Consultative Committee by the end of October of 1990 on the ways to restructure the Pact."[49] These recommendations were to be reviewed before the end of November 1990, presumably during another summit-level meeting to determine the ultimate fate of the WTO. Finally, the WTO Moscow summit participants reaffirmed their commitment to the Helsinki process, declared their support for German reunification in the context of collective security in Europe, called for a speedy conclusion of the Conventional Arms Control negotiations in Vienna, and reaffirmed their support for human rights.[50]

The military had their worst fears confirmed a week after the Moscow summit of the WTO Political Consultative Committee. On June 14 and June 15, 1990, East German Minister of Defense and Disarmament Rainer Eppelmann hosted in East Berlin a meeting of the WTO defense ministers. After the session, the Soviet delegation insisted on seeing things its way, that is, that "the meeting stressed that the member-states of the Warsaw Pact will in their defense policies be guided by the [Warsaw Pact's] defensive military doctrine."[51] As far as the Soviet military was concerned, the East Berlin talks on the transformation of the Warsaw Pact were to be limited to the 1987 redefinition of the defense doctrine, and hence they did not signal the dissolution of the bloc. The Warsaw Pact's commander-in-chief, General Pyotr G. Lushev, flatly stated after the Berlin meeting that the dissolution of the WTO was out of the question.[52]

The Soviet military's position in Berlin failed to impress the East Central Europeans. Afterward, Poland, Czechoslovakia, and Hungary continued to work for the complete dissolution of the Warsaw Treaty Organization. They argued that their views were consistent with the WTO's stated commitment to pan-European collective security. The three also assured Moscow that they were not trying to push the Soviet Union out of Europe or to exclude it from the future European security system.

THE SOVIET TROOP WITHDRAWAL

Military withdrawal from Eastern Europe was a logical extension of Gorbachev's German policy. In any event, the Soviet Union's decision to pull its troops out from Czechoslovakia and Hungary in 1991 undermined the WTO 1987 military reform program. The Czechoslovak case provides a good illustration of this point. Since the Soviet military had insisted early on that the WTO was to remain in place until some unspecified future date when both NATO and the Warsaw Pact would be dissolved simultaneously, Gorbachev's ruling on the troop withdrawal from Czechoslovakia and Hungary forced the Soviet General Staff to reevaluate its European defense plans. In fact, the withdrawal of Soviet forces from Czechoslovakia compromised the Soviet Union's ability to defend effectively its position in Eastern Europe.

A permanent Soviet presence in Czechoslovakia had been established in 1968, following the WTO invasion to quash the Prague Spring. The Soviet Central Group of Forces in Czechoslovakia consisted of two tank divisions, three motorized rifle divisions, and one air division of over one hundred combat aircraft.[53] Following Czechoslovak-Soviet negotiations in 1990, the 75,000 Soviet contingent in Czechoslovakia was targeted to leave the country's territory completely by the end of June 1991. Its withdrawal weakened the Soviet military position in East Germany, as it made the Soviet Northern Group of Forces stationed in the GDR vulnerable to an attack by NATO forces against its southern flank. Even if Czechoslovakia had remained in the Warsaw Pact, the fitness and/or willingness of its army to hold the southern flank against a Western attack would always be questionable. The Czechoslovaks would be confronted with NATO's Central Army Group of German and American forces operating out of Bavaria—arguably NATO's strongest force in Europe. At the same time, control over Bohemia remained essential to Soviet plans to defend their position in Eastern Europe, as Czechoslovakia constituted a "corridor running from Germany straight into the Soviet Union."[54]

The Soviet withdrawal from Czechoslovakia was, therefore, synonymous with Gorbachev's decision to pull out of East Germany by 1994 and to fold the entire WTO forward deployment position in Eastern Europe. Had the Soviets decided to retain their troops in Germany after their withdrawal from Czechoslovakia, their strategic position would have deteriorated considerably, as their units in Germany would have to plan to engage the enemy from two directions at once. Under these conditions, the Soviet Northern Group of Forces could become encircled and cut off from the rear. Therefore, considering the impact of the Soviet troop withdrawal from Czechoslovakia, the Kremlin's decision to withdraw from Hungary was only a logical consequence of the USSR's new strategic situation in Europe.

In light of the Soviet military's position on the future of the Warsaw Pact—that is, its unswerving insistence through June 1990 that the organization be preserved—one can only begin to appreciate the amount of confusion caused by Gorbachev's decision to disengage from East Central Europe altogether. Indicative of the Soviet Union's declining sense of security after it had committed itself to leave Germany, Czechoslovakia, and Hungary was the increasingly bellicose attitude taken by senior Soviet officers in response to the calls for withdrawal from Poland. The Soviet military vented its anger during the negotiations with the Poles over the timetable for the withdrawal of two Soviet divisions from Legnica in southwestern Poland. In January 1991 the commander of Soviet forces in Poland, General Vyacheslav Dubynin, issued what amounted to an ultimatum to Warsaw. Dubynin stated that his troops would leave Poland only according to their own schedule and under conditions set by Moscow. Dubynin also charged that Poland was vilifying the Soviet soldiers as "occupiers and international criminals" and that the withdrawal of Soviet troops from Poland would not take place before 1994, when the Soviets would complete the withdrawal from Germany. At that time the Soviet troops would return home "with heads held high, with banners unfurled."[55] Warsaw reacted to Dubynin's outburst by launching a formal protest and restating their demand that the Soviets coming out of Germany be allowed to transit Poland only along the strictly defined routes, bypassing the capital, and with their weapons stored away from the troops.[56]

In 1991 the issue of the Soviet military withdrawal from Poland came to symbolize the rapid deterioration of Moscow's relationship with its former allies. The tense negotiations in January and February were in sharp contrast to the situation of only a year ago, when the Soviets had officially expressed their readiness to withdraw from Poland, even though they called for 1995–1996 as the final withdrawal date.[57] The negotiations over the mechanics of the Soviet withdrawal from Poland were further complicated by arguments over rent payments and property claims to the buildings erected on Soviet installations in that country. According to official Polish army data, in addition to the 1,157 storage buildings and 2,440 army barracks which the Soviets had rented from the Poles, the Soviet army constructed about 2,700 buildings with its own resources.[58] Now the Soviets demanded compensation for their investment.

There were other signs of the progressive hardening of the Kremlin's official position on troop withdrawal from Poland. The Soviets communicated their official position to Poland's President Lech Walesa on February 13, 1991, informing him that they did not intend to leave Poland before 1994, regardless of the Polish demand for the pullout by the end of 1991.[59] As the Soviets completed their scheduled withdrawal from Czechoslovakia and Hungary in June 1991, Polish-Soviet negotiations on the issue remained deadlocked, with Moscow arguing that a continued Soviet presence in Poland was needed to provide logistical support to the Soviet military units withdrawing from Germany.

THE COLLAPSE OF THE WTO MILITARY ORGANIZATION

The German-Soviet negotiations leading to the July 17, 1990, Zheleznovodsk agreements, which had cleared the path for German reunification, accelerated the process of the disintegration of the Warsaw Pact's military structures. Clearly, from the Soviet military's point of view, Zheleznovodsk was a strategic setback, as it exchanged Soviet military bases in East Germany for the German-Soviet agreement on the "unacceptability of extending NATO's military structures into the territory of the GDR."[60] Most important, the Federal Republic of Germany would remain a member of NATO. As the Soviet government tried to stall on setting the date for the decisive follow-up meeting to the June 1990 WTO Moscow summit, Poland, Czechoslovakia, and Hungary moved increasingly on their own to disentangle themselves from the Pact.

After the Soviet military crackdown in Lithuania and Latvia, the three former Soviet satellites moved jointly to pressure Moscow to dissolve the WTO's military organization at the earliest possible date. The Poles forcefully asserted their sovereignty on matters of national defense by refusing the Soviets the right to send their military convoys from Germany through Poland without first complying with Polish laws. On February 6, 1991, Poland's defense minister, Rear Admiral Piotr Kolodziejczyk, announced that his country's military alliance with the Soviet Union was over and that Poland was now "isolated and neutral."[61] Czechoslovakia's prime minister, Marian Calfa, echoed Kolodziejczyk's sentiment when he declared on the same day that Czechoslovakia was considering "some cooperation with NATO following its decision to leave the Warsaw Pact by June of 1991."[62] In a move that would dramatically underline the scope of East Central Europe's independence from Moscow, Czechoslovakia's president, Vaclav Havel, announced that in March 1991 he would visit Brussels to discuss the matter of Czechoslovakia's association with the North Atlantic Council.

The joint position of Poland, Czechoslovakia, and Hungary forced Gorbachev to agree to hold the promised meeting to discuss the dissolution of the military structures of the Warsaw Pact. In a message by Gorbachev to the East Europeans, confirmed on February 12, 1991, the Soviets proposed that the military structures of the Warsaw Pact be disbanded by April 1, 1991. Gorbachev also suggested that a preliminary meeting of the Pact's foreign and defense ministers be held in Budapest in late February 1991.[63]

On April 1, 1991, the Warsaw Treaty Organization military structures were officially disbanded, including the Committee of Defense Ministers, the Joint Armed Forces Command, the Military Council, the Staff and the Technical Committee, the Joint Command's Military Technology Council, and the Joint System of Anti-Aircraft Defense. According to Czechoslovak Deputy Foreign Minister Zdenek Matejka, who was also the general secretary of the Warsaw Pact's Political Consultative Committee at the time, the Soviets forbade the publication of the protocol formally dismantling the WTO military structures on the grounds that it was "a military document of a secret character and such documents were not published anywhere in the world."[64] The remaining political structures of the Warsaw Pact were abolished on July 1, 1991, marking the formal end of the organization's thirty-five years of existence. The Soviets were now faced with the reality of having to rely exclusively on their own resources for national defense.

A NEW STRATEGY FOR THE SOVIET ARMY

While resisting the dissolution of the Warsaw Pact, the Soviet military was nevertheless for some time preparing for such a contingency. In late 1990, the Soviet General Staff made public a reform program that would take the Soviet army into the next century. An outline of the timetable for Soviet military reform was given in November 1990 by Soviet Armed Forces Chief of Staff General Mikhail A. Moiseyev. In an interview published in *Krasnaya Zvezda* on November 18, 1990,[65] Moiseyev presented the following stage-by-stage program:

1. The first stage of military reform would run from 1987 through 1994; it would include reductions in nuclear and conventional forces, depending on the outcome of the Geneva and Vienna negotiations; it would include the withdrawal of Soviet forces from Czechoslovakia and Hungary by 1991, Mongolia by 1992, and Germany by 1994; internal reform would lead to the ex-

clusion of road construction units from the armed forces of the USSR Civil Defense; military construction units of other ministries would be disbanded; the entire mobilization plan would be reworked and reformulated, and it would be partially implemented; a new set of laws defining the military's place in the state would be adopted; the units withdrawn from Eastern Europe and Germany would be redeployed within the territory of the USSR; finally, new social welfare programs for military personnel, their families, and retirees from the army would be drafted and their implementation would begin.

2. The second stage of military reform would be limited to one year, 1994–1995; during that period the key reductions in personnel would be completed, as would the strategic redeployment of Soviet forces within the state's boundaries; at that time the central administration and command structure of the Soviet armed forces would be reorganized, and the internal hierarchy of the military districts would be streamlined; all military research and development (R&D) facilities would be reorganized; the implementation of the new mobilization system would be completed; and a new program to ensure that the army had ample access to sought-after technical specialists would be adopted.

3. The third stage of military reform would run between 1996 and 2000; it would include the completion of a 50 percent reduction in Soviet strategic offensive weapons, as well as the finalization of the modernization and reequipment of the army and the navy; the Ministry of Defense would continue to develop and perfect a new system of qualitative indicators for the army and the navy; the key command and supply structures of the services would complete their restructuring; and the social welfare programs for the military would be fully implemented.[66]

The stated goal of Soviet military reform was to create a less costly, yet highly effective, military force. In his *Krasnaya Zvezda* interview in November 1990, Moiseyev estimated that, pending the successful conclusion of the Strategic Arms Reduction Talks (START) Treaty with the United States, the Soviet Strategic Rocket Forces would undergo a 30 percent cut. In the year 2000 the Soviet Ground Forces would be reduced by 10 to 12 percent, while they would retain the ability to expand rapidly through a more efficient national mobilization system, should the Soviet Union's security position deteriorate in the future. The overall number of Soviet armies, corps, and divisions would be reduced, while they would undergo a thorough internal reorganization.

The Air Defense Forces (*Voyska Protivovozdushnoy Oborony*; PVO) would be cut by 18 to 20 percent, but they would retain their present high-readiness levels, with qualitative improvements in equipment, including new missile batteries, fighter aircraft, and a sophisticated radar detection system to compensate for the cuts in personnel. As a result, Moiseyev estimated, the total cost of the Air Defense Forces would fall. Next, the Air Force would shrink to a "reasonable sufficiency" level, which in practical terms would translate into a reduction in the number of equipment types, the shortening of the reequipment cycle, and a 6 to 8 percent cut in personnel. Again, the loss in personnel would be offset by enhanced pilot training and the restructuring of the aircraft deployment in the European part of the Soviet Union.

Moiseyev was less forthcoming on the details of the proposed modernization within the Soviet navy, saying only that qualitative improvements would be introduced and that the navy would be maintained at the level of "reasonable sufficiency." An interesting innovation tried in the Soviet navy, which should increase its overall professionalism, was the 1991 experimental program of staffing the positions that require high levels of technical skills on a contract basis. Moiseyev announced that, after a trial period, the contract system of recruiting professional naval personnel might be extended throughout the Soviet armed forces at the third stage of military reform.

Overall, the Soviet armed forces would be reduced to 3.0–3.2 million people, while the top level military personnel would be cut by 15 to 20 percent. This would include the retirement of 1,300 generals, as well as an overall reduction of the officer corps by 220,000 and the warrant officer corps by 250,000 by the year 2000. According to Moiseyev, in 1993 the Soviets would introduce a volunteer service program for warrant officers to be fully in place by 1996. In an attempt to increase the reenlistment rate of military professionals, in 1991 officers, warrant officers, and NCOs were given pay raises ranging from 90 to 150 rubles per month, while their sorties went up by 50 rubles. The Soviet Ministry of Defense also made public a plan to increase the conscripts' pay by up to 30 to 55 rubles per month.[67] Finally, it accepted the principle of alternatives to military service for conscientious objectors, which would last 3 years for draftees and 1.5 years for university graduates.

"NEW COOPERATION MODEL" AFTER THE WTO

The reform of the Warsaw Treaty Organization, as envisioned by General Moiseyev and his General Staff officers, was halted in midstream because of Gorbachev and Shevardnadze's decision to accept German reunification. This policy change dramatically undercut the Soviet Union's strategic position in Europe. The senior Soviet military reacted angrily to the policy change. In December 1990 Marshal Sergey F. Akhromeyev delivered a handwritten ultimatum to Gorbachev, signed by twenty top military commanders, blaming Gorbachev and Shevardnadze for undermining the Warsaw Pact. The note warned that the army would not tolerate the loss of strategically important border republics of the Soviet Union.[68] The ultimatum forced Shevardnadze's resignation and his dramatic warning of an impending coup. It also pushed Gorbachev in the direction of more hard-line policies on the Baltic states' independence. It was, however, too late to avert the disintegration of the WTO. The subsequent fragmentation of WTO military structures was the result of a concerted effort by former Soviet satellites, in particular Poland, Czechoslovakia, and Hungary, which had jointly pushed for the removal of the Joint High Command and the dismantling of the Joint Air Defense System. As was first mooted during the February 1991 Berlin meeting, the military structure of the WTO was finally dissolved on April 1, 1991, following a meeting in Budapest of the six WTO member-countries. The Pact's commander-in-chief, Army General Pyotr G. Lushev, was relieved of his duties and retired from his job as first deputy defense minister by President Gorbachev's decree of April 26, 1991.[69]

Gorbachev's decision to heed the calls for the complete dissolution of the Warsaw Pact's military organization by April 1, 1991,[70] spelled out the end of the organization's thirty-five years of existence. It also created a radically new security situation for the Soviet Union, whereby Moscow had to rely on diplomacy as the key to its security policy on a scale unprecedented in the past. As the withdrawal of the remaining Soviet troops from Czechoslovakia and Hungary neared completion, Soviet diplomats moved vigorously to sign new bilateral treaties with the former satellites in an effort to compensate for the loss of direct control in the region. More than ever before, in 1991 the question of Moscow's relations with its western neighbors acquired a "direct impact on [the Soviet Union's] security position."[71]

After the April 1, 1991, dissolution of the WTO military organization, the Soviets repeated their call for the simultaneous dissolution of NATO; however, they recognized all too well that this was wishful thinking. The

Soviet General Staff was now grasping at straws. As late as March 1991, the official Soviet position on the future of the Warsaw Treaty itself had been that the organization should be maintained, while relations between member-states should undergo deep changes "within the framework of the Warsaw Treaty, as it moves to acquire a political-consultative form."[72] This overall security policy objective became irrelevant in the second half of 1991, when Moscow was forced to recognize the growing differentiation among its former satellites, as it moved to negotiate bilateral treaties with each of them.

Gorbachev's shift to diplomacy as a principal means for providing for Soviet national security in East Central Europe further deepened the rift between the Kremlin and the Soviet General Staff. Senior Soviet army officers, embittered by the collapse of the Warsaw Pact and the resultant havoc in Soviet defense strategy, showed themselves in 1991 ever more eager to speak up on what they saw as the sorry state of the country's future security. In a telling indication of the army's mood, Colonel General Igor Rodionov, writing for the authoritative military journal *Voyennaya Mysl'*, charged that the belief in "war prevention through political means was meaningless if it was not backed by substantial military power."[73] These sentiments were echoed by Soviet Chief of the General Staff Army General Mikhail A. Moiseyev, who warned in a May 6, 1991, interview for TASS that the dissolution of the Warsaw Pact had made the implementation of the "Soviet model of security" problematic, as the Soviet Union was now facing NATO alone.[74]

The collapse of the former Soviet security position in Eastern Europe, of which the disintegration of the Warsaw Pact reform program was the most vivid symbol, forced upon the Soviet Union a thorough reevaluation of its relations with its former satellites. In January 1991, the Secretariat of the CPSU Central Committee held a special session devoted entirely to the region's place in the USSR's foreign and security policies. In the process, the Soviet party leadership recognized that, in light of revolutionary changes in Eastern Europe, the foreign policies of the former satellites "were undergoing an ever-faster reorientation."[75]

The disintegration of the Warsaw Pact and the impending complete withdrawal of Soviet troops from Europe forced Moscow for the first time since 1945 to plan for the defense of the Soviet Union's western borders. Furthermore, the collapse of communism in Eastern Europe had become an important destabilizing factor in the Soviet Union itself, as it encouraged the opposition in the USSR to push for the dismantling of the communist state. Since the Kremlin could not undo the damage to its strategic position in Europe caused by loss of the buffer zone in the west, it would now insist on political concessions from its former satellites to guarantee vital Soviet security interests, as these were being defined by Moscow. A new relationship between the Soviet Union and its former clients in East Central Europe would have to be based on "a new geopolitical reality and a pragmatic balance of interests."[76]

On March 13, 1991, *Pravda* published an in-depth overview of Moscow's policy vis-à-vis its former satellites. According to the article, the principal objective of Soviet foreign policy in bilateral negotiations with Poland, Czechoslovakia, and Hungary was to ensure that the new democracies remained friendly to the Soviet Union and, most important, that they refrained from any action that might contribute to internal instability in the USSR. In this perspective, Poland's declared support for Baltic independence and Czechoslovakia's decision to strengthen relations with Lithuania were regarded by the Soviets as acts detrimental to their vital national security interests. Moscow's minimum condition in the 1991 round of negotiations on new bilateral treaties between the Soviet Union and the three East Central European countries was that their territory "must remain free of foreign bases and foreign military forces."[77]

The Kremlin insisted that the Triangle refrain from joining any future security arrangements in Europe without its consent. This revealed the conviction on Moscow's part that, if given a chance, Poland, Czechoslovakia, and Hungary would opt for NATO membership as well as other possible European structures. The United States' position that NATO should constitute the skeleton of the future security framework in Europe and the May 28, 1991, NATO decision to create a rapid deployment force were viewed in Moscow as indications that NATO might indeed move in the future to become the key security organization in Europe, thus leaving the Soviet Union on the outside.

In 1991 a large section of senior Soviet military officers appeared particularly embittered over the loss of Soviet position in East Central Europe. On May 14, 1991, *Krasnaya Zvezda* charged that the disintegration of the WTO not only brought about the destruction of a "bastion to which [the Soviet Union had] become accustomed as durable and insuperable to any aggressor,"[78] but in fact led to the creation of hostile neighbors on the Soviet Union's periphery. Poland, Czechoslovakia, and Hungary were singled out by Major General M. Monin in *Krasnaya Zvezda* as the three most hostile of the former satellites. Pointing to Poland's "Armed Forces '90" concept of defense along two lines,[79] in the East and in the West, as well as the troop redeployment by Poland, Hungary, and Czechoslovakia along their eastern borders, Monin observed that the real objective of the Triangle was an immediate rapprochement with NATO. According to Monin, these actions could only be viewed as directed at the weakening of the security of the Soviet state. In effect, because of the hostile policies of Moscow's former allies in East Central Europe, the Soviet Union's strategic position had deteriorated, and "henceforth the correlation of forces in the world [would] be determined by the balance between the USSR and NATO, and not between the Warsaw Pact and NATO." Monin further complained that the Soviet army in Europe without its WTO allies was now "qualitatively inferior to NATO in terms of conventional weapons."[80]

In the second half of 1991 the view that the Soviet Union had suffered a setback by agreeing to withdraw its troops from Europe was increasingly shared by Soviet parliamentarians and government officials. Leonid Sharin, chairman of the Supreme Soviet Commission for Defense and State Security, in an interview for TASS on May 17, 1991, noted that many in the Soviet parliament were "not overly optimistic about the military-strategic situation in which the Soviet Union found itself as a result of current changes in Europe."[81] Sharin also charged that the balance of power in Europe had been dangerously upset, with one of the blocs ceasing to exist, while NATO continued its operations unhindered. In light of the growing conviction among Supreme Soviet deputies that the USSR's withdrawal from the region had serious negative consequences, the Soviet military found it easier to insist that the loss of the vital strategic region should be compensated for with security guarantees written into the new bilateral treaties with the former satellites. As *Krasnaya Zvezda* pointed out, the bilateral treaty signed by the Soviet Union and Romania in 1991, which included a special security clause demanded by the Soviets, was exactly the kind of agreement the country's security required.

In addition to charging that the former Warsaw Pact allies had changed sides after 1989, the Soviet Union expressed a particular hostility toward regional cooperation in East Central Europe. In an attack on the emerging Triangle of Poland, Czechoslovakia, and Hungary, *Pravda* described these tripartite consultations as attempts to create "new *cordon sanitaires*" or "little ententes"[82] directed against the USSR. For its part, *Pravda* was unambiguous about what kind of regionalism it would find acceptable, offering as a model the Soviet Union's relationship with Finland. In 1991 the goal of Soviet security policy in the region was to replace the defunct Warsaw Pact structures with "a model of bilateral relations of the Soviet-Finnish type."[83] In addition to the "Finnish-type" security arrangement, the Soviets asked for the establishment of a new trading association in the region, based on a "planned centralized trade mechanism," to take the place of the defunct Council for Mutual Economic Assistance

(COMECON) and to revive the Soviet Union's moribund trade with its former satellites. Finally, Moscow called for the strengthening of cultural exchanges and the building of good relations between the CPSU and left-wing parties in East Central Europe.

In sum, the general policy outline for the "New Cooperation Model," introduced by Moscow after the April 1, 1991, collapse of the Warsaw Pact included (1) a security component in the form of a security clause in future bilateral treaties; (2) an economic component in the form of a trade association to replace the COMECON; and (3) a cultural component built around "people-to-people" diplomacy, such as the creation of sister cities, various cultural exchanges, and so on, which in the Soviet view would "help to build good neighborly and mutually beneficial relations between [the USSR] and its neighbors."[84]

The successful negotiation of the Soviet-Romanian treaty was viewed in Moscow as a hopeful sign that the damage to the USSR's strategic position in Europe, suffered in 1989–1991, could be partially undone by diplomacy. Valeriy Musatov, the deputy director of the CPSU Central Committee's International Department, described the relations with East European nations as "bottoming out." He pointed to "new invigorating contacts and the Soviet-Romanian treaty"[85] as evidence of an important change for the better. The Soviet position at the beginning of the summer of 1991 reasserted that the territories of Moscow's former satellites "should never be a source of real or potential threat to the USSR's security and that, whatever the developments, the countries in the region should remain free from foreign bases and armies." Diplomatic pressure from the Kremlin would continue, as it was "necessary to take measures to keep ex-Soviet allies from joining [hostile] military blocs and groupings."[86] According to *Pravda*, the "New Cooperation Model" had to be implemented regardless of the reluctance on the part of Poland, Czechoslovakia, and Hungary to accept the Soviet Union's definition of its security needs in the region. As far as the communist government in Moscow was concerned, East Central Europe's sovereignty was far from assured.

The failed Soviet coup attempt of August 19–22, 1991, and the subsequent breakdown of the Soviet state threw Moscow's entire East European policy in disarray. The "new cooperation" formula collapsed together with the disintegration of the Stalinist formula for the Soviet Union. The September 6, 1991, decision by the new Soviet Council of State, headed by Gorbachev, to recognize the independence of the Baltic republics followed by the dissolution of the Soviet Union itself in December 1991 laid the foundations for a new round of bilateral negotiations between the reconstituted Soviet successor states and the Triangle. At the same time, however, while the climate for the bilateral talks vastly improved because of the aborted coup's failure, the immediate domestic economic and political challenges facing the Soviet successor states as they braced themselves for the harsh winter ahead took precedence over regional foreign policy and security issues.

NOTES

1. For an extensive discussion of Marshal Ogarkov's reorganization plans, see John Erickson, "The Soviet Union and the Warsaw Pact: Military and Security Affairs," in George Schopflin, ed., *The Soviet Union and Eastern Europe* (New York and Oxford: Facts on File Publications and Muller, Blond, and White, 1986), pp. 218–230.

2. This interpretation of Gorbachev's redefinition of the WTO position on nuclear weapons has been suggested by Christopher Jones. See Christopher D. Jones, "The Military Alliance," in Richard F. Staar, ed., *United States–East European Relations in the 1990s* (New York: Crane Russak, 1989), p. 63.

3. "Changes in the Soviet Military High Command," *Jane's Defence Weekly*, October 25, 1986, pp. 956–961, and Robert Hutchinson, "Gorbachev Tightens Grip on Soviet High Command," *Jane's Defence Weekly*, June 13, 1987, pp. 1192–1199. At the close of the twenty-eighth CPSU Congress in July 1990, the surprise announcement was made that Lizichev had been replaced by Colonel General Nikolai Shlyaga. Shlyaga appears to be committed to the preservation of the party's presence in the army. See Stephen Foye, "Soviet Army's New Political Chief on Reform of Military-Political Organs," *Report on the USSR*, vol. 2, no. 31 (Munich: RFE/RL, August 3, 1990), p. 14.

4. David Remnick, "The Hard-Liners' Bad Boy Challenges Gorbachev," *Washington Post,* February 8, 1991.

5. This was confirmed in an interview with General Tadeusz Cepak of the Polish General Staff, who at the time was intimately involved in the conventional arms control process. Interview with the author, Polish Ministry of Defense, Warsaw, January 8, 1991. In 1987 the proposals to reduce conventional weapons were augmented by a general propaganda-oriented Warsaw Pact proposal for nuclear and chemical weapons free zones in Central Europe and in the Balkans.

6. Michael T. Kaufman, "Soviet Proposes Major Troop Reductions in Europe," *New York Times,* June 12, 1986.

7. For a discussion of the evolution of Soviet strategic thought, see Michael Mcc-Gwire, *Perestroika and Soviet National Security* (Washington, D.C.: The Brookings Institution, 1991), pp. 306–309.

8. "Eastern Europe Responds to Gorbachev Cut-Backs," *Jane's Defence Weekly*, January 7, 1989, p. 22.

9. Christopher Donnelly, "Future Trends in Soviet Military-Technical Policy," in Susan L. Clark, ed., *Gorbachev's Agenda: Changes in Soviet Domestic and Foreign Policy* (Boulder, Colo., San Francisco, and London: Westview Press, 1989), p. 209.

10. David Fouguet, "Hungary in Defense Plan Debates," *Jane's Defence Weekly*, January 7, 1989, p. 6.

11. "First Soviet Troops to Leave Hungary Soon," *Jane's Defence Weekly*, January 21, 1989, p. 82.

12. Fouguet, "Hungary in Defense Plan Debates."

13. "First Soviet Troops to Leave Hungary Soon," p. 82.

14. "Poles Plan 4% Spending Cut," *Jane's Defence Weekly*, January 4, 1989, p. 43.

15. "Przemiany w Wojsku Polskim: Rozmowa z czlonkiem Biura Politycznego KC PZPR, Ministrem Obrony Narodowej, gen. armii Florianem Siwickim," *Trybuna Ludu*, January 4, 1989.

16. Ibid.

17. "Polish Minister Details Forces Cuts," *Jane's Defence Weekly*, March 18, 1989, p. 473.

18. "Zasadniczo przebudowujemy armie akcentujac jej obronny charakter," *Zolnierz Wolnosci*, January 5–7, 1990.

19. "Problems Facing Polish Army," *Jane's Defence Weekly*, February 11, 1989, p. 232.

20. *RFE/RL Situation Report: Czechoslovakia*, December–January 1989.

21. "Zmeny v armade," *Rude Pravo*, July 12, 1989.

22. "Vojenske stavebni kapacity," *Rude Pravo*, August 5, 1989.

23. "Soviet View of Future War after Arms Cuts," *Jane's Defence Weekly*, January 28, 1989, p. 141.

24. Ibid.

25. "Arms Cut Details Revealed," *Jane's Defence Weekly*, February 18, 1989, p. 279.

26. "Tank Unit Withdrawals Revealed," *Jane's Defence Weekly*, March 18, 1989, p. 472.

27. Ibid.

28. Christopher Bellamy, "What the New Warsaw Pact Military Doctrine Means for the West," *Jane's Defence Weekly*, December 5, 1987, p. 1310.

29. General Mikhail A. Moiseyev, "S positsiy oboronitel'noy doktriny," *Krasnaya Zvezda*, February 10, 1989.

30. "Pact Military Doctrine," *FBIS-SOV-87-104*, June 1, 1987, p. BB19.

31. Ibid., p. BB21.

32. "Voyennaya reforma: opyt, problemy, perspektivy—'krugloy stol,' " *Voyennaya Mysl'*, April 1990, p. 31.

33. General V. L. Manilov and Lieutenant General S. Ya Karpov, chief of the Directorate of the Soviet General Staff, quoted in "Voyennaya reforma: opyt, problemy, perspektivy—'krugloy stol,' " *Voyennaya Mysl'*, April 1990, p. 35.

34. "Education Reform to Boost Military Efficiency," *Jane's Defence Weekly*, January 31, 1987, pp. 149–150.

35. General Pyotr G. Lushev, "Edinstvo oboronnykh usiliy stran Varshavskogo Dogovora—faktor nadezhnoy zashchity sotsializma," *Voyennaya Mysl'*, January 1990, p. 4.

36. Ibid., p. 3.

37. Ibid., p. 7.

38. General Pyotr G. Lushev, "Varshavskiy Dogovor: istoriya i sovremennost'," *Voyennaya Mysl'*, May 1990, p. 22.

39. Ibid., p. 26.

40. "Rabochiy vizit G. Kola," *Krasnaya Zvezda*, July 17, 1990.

41. General Pyotr G. Lushev, "Varshavskomu dogovoru—35 let," *Krasnaya Zvezda*, May 13, 1990.

42. Ibid.

43. Ibid.

44. Ibid.

45. Remnick, "The Hard-Liners' Bad Boy Challenges Gorbachev."

46. Lushev, "Varshavskomu dogovoru—35 let."

47. *RFE/RL Daily Report*, June 9, 1990.

48. "Deklaratsya gosudarstv-uchastnikov Varshavskogo Dogovora," *Krasnaya Zvezda*, June 8, 1990.

49. Ibid.

50. Ibid.

51. "Kommyunike zasedaniya komiteta ministrov oborony gosudarstv-uchastnikov Varshavskogo Dogovora," *Krasnaya Zvezda*, June 16, 1990.

52. Douglas L. Clarke, "Warsaw Pact: The Transformation Begins," *Report on Eastern Europe*, vol. 1, no. 25 (Munich: RFE/RL, June 22, 1990), p. 36.

53. Douglas L. Clarke, "The Military Implications of a Soviet Troop Withdrawal from Czechoslovakia," *Report on Eastern Europe*, vol. 1, no. 5 (Munich: RFE/RL, February 2, 1990), pp. 48–51.

54. Ibid., p. 50.

55. *RFE/RL Daily Report*, January 17, 1991.

56. Interview by the author with Jacek Szymanderski, member of the Sejm Military Commission, Warsaw, January 7, 1991.

57. "ZSRR gotow do rozmow na temat wycofania swoich wojsk z terytorium Polski," *Zolnierz Wolnosci*, February 12, 1990.

58. "Scisle Jawne," Polish Television, Channel 1, January 6, 1991.

59. Mary Battiata, "Soviets Rebuff Poles on Troop Pullout," *Washington Post*, February 13, 1991.

60. "Rabochiy vizit G. Kola."

61. "Poland Neutral," *Financial Times*, February 7, 1991.

62. "Czechoslovakia Considering Links with NATO after Leaving Pact," *Financial Times*, February 7, 1991.

63. *RFE/RL Daily Report*, February 13, 1991.

64. "Foreign Ministry Official on Warsaw Pact Session," *FBIS-EEU-91-040*, February 28, 1991, p. 10.

65. General Mikhail A. Moiseyev, "Voyennaya reforma: deystvitel'nost' i perspektivy," *Krasnaya Zvezda*, November 18, 1990.

66. Ibid.

67. Ibid.

68. Zhores Medvedev, "Before the Coup: The Plot inside the Kremlin," *Washington Post*, September 1, 1991.

69. *RFE/RL Daily Report*, April 29, 1991.

70. *RFE/RL Daily Report*, February 13, 1991.

71. "Vostochnaya Evropa: Chto gryadet za peremenami" (interview with Deputy Foreign Minister Yuliy A. Kvitsinskiy), *Pravda*, March 18, 1991.

72. Ibid.

73. *RFE/RL Daily Report*, April 30, 1991.

74. *RFE/RL Daily Report*, May 7, 1991.

75. Valeriy Musatov, "Vostochnaya Evropa: Tayfun peremen," *Pravda*, March 13, 1991.

76. Ibid.

77. Ibid.

78. "Pact's Future Pondered on 36th Anniversary," *FBIS-SOV-91-097*, May 20, 1991, p. 2.

79. See chapter 3.

80. "Pact's Future Pondered on 36th Anniversary," p. 3.

81. "Deputy Cited on Troop Withdrawal from Germany," *FBIS-SOV-91-097*, May 20, 1991, p. 22.

82. Musatov, "Vostochnaya Evropa: Tayfun peremen."

83. Ibid.

84. Ibid.

85. "CPSU's Musatov on Relations with East Europe," *FBIS-SOV-91-096*, May 17, 1991, p. 34.

86. Ibid.

3

POLAND BETWEEN TWO GREAT POWERS

DILEMMAS OF POLISH GEOGRAPHY

The dissolution of the military organization of the Warsaw Pact on April 1, 1991, formally concluded the process of alliance disintegration, which had been under way since 1989. It meant a recognition by the USSR of the new security situation in East Central Europe. In 1991 the WTO no longer existed, while NATO refused to extend its guarantees to the former Soviet satellites. The region was now in a security vacuum. This radically new situation accelerated the search for pan-European solutions, forcing the postcommunist democracies to examine their ability to sustain their newly found independence. As the largest and historically the most vulnerable among the Triangle, Poland has sought to define its security in a way that would resolve its traditional geopolitical dilemma.

In terms of national security, arguably the greatest challenge facing Poland as it entered the 1990s was to find an acceptable compromise between the nation's aspirations for independence and sovereignty, and the realities of power distribution in the region. Despite all the uncertainty about the future, it was clear in 1991 that Moscow could reassert control over Poland only if it resorted to an all-out military invasion. Considering the protracted internal crisis and the ongoing domestic turmoil following the demise of the Soviet Union in December 1991, this was a highly hypothetical scenario. Poland's ability to shed its former communist regime owed at least as much to the incessant pressure from Solidarity opposition for pluralism and democratic reform as it did to the implosion of Moscow's imperial controls.

For over two hundred years Poland's basic security dilemma has been the country's place on the map between two powerful states: Germany and Russia. The two have remained and will remain great regional powers whose potential Poland could never hope to match. Since the collapse of communism, the key challenge to Polish security policy has been to replace the historical legacy of hostility between Poland and its neighbors with good neighborly relations. Still, in 1991 history was always close on the minds of Polish politicians. In the past, Poland vanished from the map four times because Germany and Russia had decided to divide up its territory between themselves. Poland's instinctive fears about future relations with its powerful neighbors were encapsulated by Andrzej Micewski, a leading adviser to Lech Walesa during his 1990 presidential election campaign, who argued that it was imperative for Poland's security to make Polish-German relations and Polish-Russian relations better than the overall German-Russian relationship.[1]

Micewski's fears were a reaction to the past. In 1990 Poland took great comfort in Germany's continued commitment to NATO and the European Community. Germany's Western orientation meant that one element of the Polish security equation was undergoing a dramatic change. This presented a historic opportunity for Poland to redefine its place in Europe through a new relationship with Germany. Even if in the final analysis Poland could not affect the extent of future German-Russian cooperation, Warsaw knew that it had a chance to build a working partnership with the democratic and economically powerful German state. Since 1990 Poland's national security policy has been based on the axiom that both in domestic and foreign policy Germany will remain fundamentally a Western European power. Germany's continued membership in NATO has assured the Poles that, in contrast to the interwar situation, even if Germany were eventually to refocus on its historical interests in the East, the extent of its entanglement in the West would limit the impact of German-Russian cooperation on Poland's security position. Any putative pressure on Poland from Germany in the future would therefore become a pan-European security issue.

This new view of Germany's role in Europe determined Warsaw's reformulation of its German policy in 1990. Polish Foreign Minister Krzysztof Skubiszewski, its principal architect, saw his country's relations with Germany as part of Poland's overall effort to join the community of Western European nations. The short-term Polish security policy objectives vis-à-vis Germany included (1) obtaining an explicit German recognition of Poland's western border on the Oder-Neisse rivers and (2) negotiating a new bilateral treaty on cooperation that would redirect

Polish-German relations away from the historical legacy of hostility and mistrust.

In contrast to Warsaw's 1990 formula for dealing with Germany, future relations with the Soviet Union presented a much more confused picture. Formulating an Eastern policy was a challenge to Polish diplomacy first and foremost because of the very uncertainty about the outcome of the Soviet domestic crisis. Furthermore, traditional Polish hostility toward Russia was strengthened by the forty-five years of Soviet domination, which has led to justified Polish suspicions and mistrust about Moscow's intentions in the region. In 1990–1991, Warsaw's Eastern policy was marked on several occasions by uncertainty and an often contradictory duality of purpose. On the one hand, the Polish government welcomed the disintegration of the Soviet state as it both vindicated the principle of self-determination and lowered the threat posed to Poland's security by a diminished future Russia. On the other hand, it feared that the internal fragmentation of the Soviet Union, which might easily explode into chaos and civil war, would threaten directly Poland's eastern border and could generate a range of irredentist claims against the country's territory. The clarity and predictability of the Polish policy toward Germany in 1990–1991 contrasted sharply with the often erratic and inconsistent initiatives in Warsaw's dealings with Moscow.

A new and mutually acceptable Polish-Russian modus vivendi has been a critical condition for both Poland's independence and regional stability. A redefinition of the country's relations with the former Soviet Union's successor states has remained an essential task for Polish foreign policy for the foreseeable future. In practical terms, this process started in 1990 when Poland and the Soviet Union broached for the first time the subject of a new treaty on cooperation and good neighborly relations between the two countries. However, follow-up talks between Warsaw and Moscow soon became bogged down over issues ranging from the Soviet troop withdrawal timetable to a Moscow-dictated security clause. Although Polish Foreign Minister Skubiszewski had proposed the signing of a new treaty with the Soviet Union already during his October 1990 meeting with Soviet Foreign Minister Eduard Shevardnadze,[2] the negotiations made little progress in the first half of 1991.

Although the question of Poland's relations with Germany and the Soviet Union has been a foremost concern of the Polish government, since 1990 Poland has also worked to develop a future pan-European security system embodied in the Conference on Security and Cooperation in Europe (CSCE). During his January 1990 official visit to Strasbourg to address the Parliamentary Assembly of the Council of Europe to petition for Poland's membership, Prime Minister Tadeusz Mazowiecki spoke of the urgent need to bring postcommunist Eastern Europe into an all-European security system.[3] Mazowiecki called for the creation of a Council of European Cooperation (*Rada Wspolpracy Europejskiej*) to serve as a bridge between the East and the West. Throughout 1990 and 1991, Warsaw remained an active supporter of the CSCE process, on par with the other members of the Triangle.

At the same time, however, the Poles entertained few illusions about the CSCE's ability to meet their security needs in the near future. Privately, Polish government officials seemed to consider direct bilateral negotiations, tripartite regional cooperation, and especially cooperation with the existing Western security organizations, such as NATO, as the best short-term solution to the dilemma of Poland's relations with reunified Germany and the disintegrating Soviet Union.[4]

POLISH-GERMAN RELATIONS

In contrast to the pressure from the East, in the years to come the German threat to Poland will remain a highly hypothetical possibility. Here the best guarantees to Poland are Germany's political and cultural orientation toward the West and Germany's foreign policy anchored in NATO or its successor alliance. The Polish Deputy Minister of Defense Janusz Onyszkiewicz expressed a broad-based consensus within the Polish government when he argued on the record that the "German threat to Poland has been overstated," and should it arise it would come from the former GDR rather than the Federal Republic.[5] Potential for future conflict between Poland and Germany will be progressively eliminated as the Polish-German border becomes porous, leading to increased contacts of the two populations and greater trade. Despite friction between the Germans and Polish traders in Berlin, which often reinforces cultural stereotypes, the potential gains from the visa-free travel agreement signed by Poland and Germany is by far worth the risk. Polish-German relations appear easier to improve today than only a decade ago, as the current generation of Poles have no memories of the wartime experience, while the German government has publicly repudiated territorial ambitions in the East.

The new Polish-German bilateral treaty on good neighborly relations, initialed in May 1991 and signed during Polish Prime Minister Jan Krzysztof Bielecki's visit to Bonn on June 17, 1991,[6] has significantly contributed to improved Polish-German relations. The border treaty, signed in November 1990, confirmed the existing Polish-German frontier on the Oder-Neisse rivers. In Article 2 of the treaty, both sides pledged to respect each other's sovereignty and territorial integrity.[7] The "friendship and cooperation treaty" of 1991 for the first time since 1945 recognized formally the existence of the German minority in Poland, estimated at about 200,000 people. The Polish concession on the German minority issue was welcomed by Bonn as a radical departure from the past. According to an official German statement, the new treaty "will fundamentally alter the previously strained relations between the two countries."[8] Stressing this historic opportunity to change the geopolitical equation in the region, Bonn also expressed its commitment to build the same relationship with Poland as it has with France, another of its historical enemies.

The thirty-eight-article draft treaty, negotiated by German Foreign Minister Hans-Dietrich Genscher and Polish Foreign Minister Krzysztof Skubiszewski, not only reverses Poland's post-1945 position of denying the existence of the German minority but commits Warsaw to grant full equality to the Polish Germans, including equal educational, religious, and cultural rights. From now on, the Polish Germans, rather than the Polish government officials, will determine their ethnicity, and they will have the right to use their German last names. The same rights will be extended to Poles living in Germany. In turn, Germany has committed itself to support fully Polish associate membership in the European Community, with the stipulation that this will constitute a first step toward full membership. In addition, Poland and Germany have pledged to work jointly to build "cooperative structures" for Europe, including the CSCE process.

The negotiations leading to the signing of the treaty were not without problems. In 1991 the Polish-German friendship and cooperation treaty came under strong criticism from the Federation of Expellees in Germany, which blamed Foreign Minister Genscher for allegedly ignoring its demands on the rights of ethnic Germans expelled from Poland after World War II. In addition, some members of the Christian Social Union (CSU) of Chancellor Helmut Kohl's center-right coalition accused the government of excluding them from negotiations with the Poles and threatened to hold up the signing subject to additional talks with Warsaw. In particular, the Bavarian CSU demanded that the treaty include the right to education in German for the German minority in Poland and for bilingual street signs in areas where ethnic Germans live. Bonn resisted these pressures and chose to proceed with the signing of the treaty despite the objections.[9]

After the border and the friendship treaties have been ratified, Poland and Germany will be launched in earnest on the road to genuine national reconciliation. From a purely economic point of view, good relations with Germany will be essential to the success of Poland's reform program, to its economic recovery, and ultimately to its goal of becoming a member of the new Europe. Most important, the two agreements will go a long way to reduce mutual suspicion and to calm Polish fears about German revanchism. Recognizing the historic opportunity to break the past cycle of mutual hostility, in an interview for *Sztandar Mlodych* in April 1991, Polish Foreign Minister Krzysztof Skubiszewski referred to the two treaties as a "breakthrough in Polish-German relations."[10] For the first time since 1945 Poland and Germany are positioned to overcome the legacy of antagonism and suspicion. A transformation of Polish-German relations similar to that in French-German relations after World War II, if it indeed takes place, will constitute a radical improvement in Poland's security position and in the overall stability of East Central Europe.

SKUBISZEWSKI'S TWO-TRACK EASTERN POLICY

As much as Poland's future relations with Germany hold considerable promise, the picture of its relations with the former Soviet Union remains bleak. Poland needs to improve its relationship with the Soviet successor states in order to lower tension and to concentrate on domestic reforms. This is clearly a daunting task, as the instability in the former Soviet Union and the disintegration of the postwar European order have left Poland uncertain about its place in the emerging European security framework. Prospects for good future relations with Russia are further hampered by the fact that the Poles blame Moscow not only for the forty-five years of communism, with its attendant repression and economic ruin, but in a more fundamental sense for having been cut off from Western Europe. These legitimate grievances, injury to the Polish national pride notwithstanding, and the Polish government's goal of rejoining the West have resulted in an implicit rejection of the Warsaw-Moscow axis.

Since 1990, Polish Eastern policy has followed a dual-track pattern: on the one hand, Warsaw has continued to deal directly with Moscow; on the other hand, it has tried to build ties to the emerging national movements in the Soviet border republics. Polish Foreign Minister Krzysztof Skubiszewski has promoted this policy design in an effort to hedge against the uncertain outcome of the Soviet domestic crisis. In its official policy vis-à-vis the USSR, Poland has pursued the course of noninterference in the ongoing conflict between the Kremlin and the breakaway republics. At the same time, the government and Polish society have expressed repeatedly their sympathy for the struggling national independence movements in the disintegrating Soviet Union.

Skubiszewski's two-track Eastern policy attempts to ensure that, if the former Soviet state erupts into civil war, the chilling impact of this turn of events on Polish domestic politics would be minimized. Protracted civil war behind Poland's eastern frontier is a disturbing prospect in light of the country's fragile new systemic foundations. If democratic reforms in the former USSR fail while Russia reconstitutes the postcommunist Soviet Union around Moscow's central authority, Poland will most likely face a powerful authoritarian regime poised on its borders. Such an outcome would constitute a permanent potential threat to Poland, which the country would never be able to address based on its own human and material resources. Hence, if Russia shifts toward an authoritarian option at home, Poland's foreign policy will instinctively move in the direction of NATO and existing European institutions. In the meantime, Poland has explored collective and regional security arrangements that would ensure that pressure and potential military conflict on Poland's eastern border could not be relegated to the ranks of local confrontations, but rather would inevitably become a pan-European problem. Considering the weakness of the CSCE institutions, however, it is an open question whether pan-Europeanism as it exists today can provide an answer to Poland's national security dilemma.

In the immediate future Poland will face a much greater threat from the postcommunist Soviet successor states than from Germany. The remaining unpredictability of the future direction of change in the former USSR, and hence the unpredictability of residual Soviet military power, will continue to remain a grave security concern for Poland. In practical terms, this potential threat to Poland is not likely to diminish as long as the Soviet army remains the only imperial institution that has retained the old structure and the old cadres, especially below the very top of its bureaucracy. Therefore, Poland's security position in the East will be greatly affected by the successful reduction in the size of the Soviet army and the purge of its senior military echelon, promised in the aftermath of the failed August putsch by Russian President Boris Yeltsin. For now, the prospect of an accidental crisis becoming a military confrontation between Warsaw and Moscow will be compounded by the continued presence of Soviet troops on Polish territory, as well as the fact that at least until 1994 Poland will be the transit route for Soviet troops leaving Germany. Finally, there is always the danger that, should civil war erupt along the western periphery of the former USSR, it may spill over into Poland. It is in Poland's vital national security interest to ensure that the breakup of the Soviet empire and the reconstitution of the Russian state take place peacefully. The gradual and nonviolent dissolution of the USSR will (1) limit the danger of a Soviet civil war engulfing Poland and (2) will carry with it an immediate improvement in Poland's overall security position, as a diminished Russia will pose a lesser threat to its neighbors in both absolute and relative terms.

In 1990 Poland's political and military leaders based their long-term national security policy toward the East on the premise that the centralized structure of the Soviet Union could not be maintained very much longer. The election of Lech Walesa as Poland's president helped to crystallize the governing elite's view on the country's place in Europe. By early 1991 the Polish military was increasingly convinced that the internal problems within the Soviet Union simply could not be resolved within a Moscow-controlled structure—the position subsequently vindicated by the collapse of the Soviet Union. The key question is the future shape of the Soviet successor states. If democratic reforms fail and the postcommunist Russia remains an authoritarian power, Poland will have little choice but to push for direct Western security guarantees. Furthermore, the Poles believe that, even if the former Soviet Union transforms itself successfully into the new Commonwealth of Independent States, it will remain for some time to come outside Europe's periphery. In the view of a number of senior Polish military, if the reformed or renewed Soviet Union endures, "at the beginning of the 21st century two large confederations will emerge: the European and the Soviet, which only subsequently could be united in a 'common European home.' "[11] If the postcommunist Soviet successor states become paralyzed by internal turmoil, the Poles see no alternative for the postcommunist Eastern Europe but "to rush to join the West and to separate itself from the East."[12]

INSTABILITY IN NON-RUSSIAN REPUBLICS AND KALININGRAD

Regional instability in the East may pose a security threat to Poland in this decade, but it is unlikely to endanger the country's territorial integrity. The eastern frontier issue is the only one likely to present future potential problems for Poland, depending on the outcome of the Soviet nationalities crisis. This is a qualitatively new situation, because from 1945 through 1987 Poland's eastern border had been officially viewed as the so-called border of peace, which simply meant that the Kremlin's power precluded territorial grievances on either side of the border from surfacing. Today, considering Moscow's formal recognition of the Baltic states' independence and in light of the newly acquired independence of the Ukraine and Byelorussia, Poland can have the border question reopened by (1)

Lithuania, (2) the Ukraine (which has territorial claims not only against Poland but also against Russia), (3) Byelorussia, and (4) the Kaliningrad region. The urgency of the border problem may be eclipsed by an even more disturbing prospect of systemic instability within the border states or the question of the extent of their political independence and sovereignty vis-à-vis Russia.

One of the principal failures of Skubiszewski's two-track Eastern policy has been the inability to improve relations with individual Soviet republics bordering on Poland. Today, in light of the Soviet Union's disintegration, Poland has acquired three new neighbors, Lithuania, Belarus (Byelorrussia), and the Ukraine, while the legal status of the Kaliningrad district remains unclear. Although the new Soviet successor states do not by themselves constitute a security threat to Poland, mutual grievances and tension along the country's eastern border can become a perpetual source of crisis and instability. Little in Polish Eastern policy in 1990–1991 inspired confidence that Warsaw would be able to build good neighborly relations with its potential future neighbors.

In 1990 and 1991, relations between Poland and Lithuania were strained, despite the fact that the Polish government was outspoken in its support of Lithuanian independence. Lithuanian political and cultural leaders expressed concern over being dominated by Poland once independence was achieved. These are understandable considerations because Lithuania is a much smaller country than Poland, one whose national culture has developed largely in opposition to Polish influence. Territorial concerns also figure prominently in the uncertainty surrounding future Polish-Lithuanian relations. At the core of the potential territorial dispute between Poland and Lithuania lies the future status of the city of Wilno/Vilnius, which before World War II belonged to Poland. While so far Poland has not made any irredentist claims on Vilnius, the Lithuanians are well aware of the strong sentiments among the older generation of Poles who still regard the city as Polish. In the future, Polish-Lithuanian relations will also be complicated by the presence of a large Polish minority in Lithuania, estimated in 1990 to number about 800,000.[13] In 1990–1991 Polish official policy, as outlined by Foreign Minister Krzysztof Skubiszewski, was to support to some degree the aspirations of Lithuania's independence movement without, however, challenging Moscow directly on the issue. As Skubiszewski remarked in 1991, Lithuania's road to independence "will depend on negotiations between Vilnius and Moscow."[14] In 1990–1991, Polish parliamentarians as well as government officials met several times with their Lithuanian counterparts, but these contacts yielded little of substance, save for a general joint declaration on the foundation of future friendly relations between Poland and Lithuania. In light of Lithuania's regained independence, recognized by Moscow on September 6, 1991, Poland faces the challenge of developing a bilateral relationship with its new neighbor that will transcend the legacy of past suspicions.

Belarus (Byelorussia) is another Soviet successor state that by virtue of its size, location, population, and resources will play an important role in the region. Prospects for Byelorussia's good relations with Poland are less than encouraging. The republic's largely peasant population appears hostile to Poland because of a history of past domination by the Polish gentry. The leaders of the Byelorussian independence movement look at Poland with suspicion as a potential danger to Byelorussian self-determination on par with the Russian threat. In the perception of many among the Byelorussian nationalist intelligentsia, the 1921 Treaty of Riga, which had formally ended the 1919–1920 war between the Soviet Union and Poland, amounted to a partition of Byelorussia between the two combatants. The anti-Polish sentiment in the republic surfaced with considerable force during the 1990 elections there. The feeling that one's cultural tradition is vulnerable to Polish influence is particularly true of Byelorussia, whose rather tenuous sense of national identity has been all but obliterated by the years of Russian domination. At the same time, Byelorussia appears to harbor territorial claims against Poland. During his October 1990 visit to Byelorussia, Polish Foreign Minister Krzysztof Skubiszewski was reminded of Byelorussia's alleged rights to the Bialystok region in eastern Poland.[15] Skubiszewski's response to these demands was to insist that the existing borders are nonnegotiable, and as such they form the foundation of international relations in Europe. Skubiszewski discounted the significance of such claims on Polish territory as not representing the mainstream of political opinion in Byelorussia;[16] nevertheless, Poland has to take them into consideration now that Byelorussia has achieved independence.

Potential problems in Polish-Lithuanian and Polish-Byelorussian relations pale in comparison with the history of antagonism bordering on mutual hatred that has marked the relationship between Poland and the republic of the Ukraine. Polish-Ukrainian relations have been strained by past Polish domination and the Ukrainian struggle against it, often punctuated by appalling atrocities on both sides. As late as 1947, the Polish army played a key role in the destruction of the Ukrainian national independence movement. The so-called Vistula operation, launched by the Poles in 1947 in cooperation with the Soviets, annihilated the Ukrainian Resistance Army, while in the process uprooting and forcibly resettling entire Ukrainian villages. More recently, the Poles were for their part embittered by the 1990 decision of Lvov's democratically elected city council to make this formerly Polish city temporarily off-limits to the Poles. Since 1990 Warsaw has looked with concern at repeated expressions of irredentist sentiments on the part of the Ukrainian *Rukh* independence movement, fearing that, even if at present these claims could not be more than a minor annoyance, they might become in the future a source of constant friction after the 1991 Ukrainian declaration of statehood.

Relations between Poles and Ukrainians living in Poland is another side of the Polish-Ukrainian question. Tension between the Poles and their Ukrainian minority has surfaced with a renewed force after the collapse of communism in Poland. By 1991 the Ukrainians living in Poland became considerably more assertive in their demands for compensation for past repression and for the full recognition of their minority rights. In March 1991, the Head Council of the Union of the Ukrainians in Poland demanded that the Sejm (the lower house of the Polish parliament) follow the example of the Senate and condemn the repression suffered by the Ukrainians under communist rule, including the notorious Vistula pacification operation of 1947 conducted by the Polish army against Ukrainian nationalist resistance. The council also demanded that all past government decrees confiscating Ukrainian property be repealed and that Warsaw provide a "moral and material compensation to those Ukrainians who had suffered discrimination [in the past], as well as assist those Ukrainians who may want to resettle on the formerly confiscated land."[17]

Poland's future relations with its eastern neighbors are also complicated by the presence of a large Polish minority on their territory. While a precise count is not yet available, according to a rough Polish estimate, there are about eight million ethnic Poles living in the former Soviet Union. It is only a matter of time before the Polish government's concern for the rights and well-being of those ethnic Poles becomes a source of friction between Warsaw and Moscow, or Warsaw and individual Soviet successor states. Polish diplomacy in the 1990s will have to face up to the complex and delicate task of building friendly working relations with the country's eastern neighbors under conditions of lingering suspicion, mistrust, and past grievances. In 1991 the Polish military expressed its concern that, if the western Soviet republics manage to break away from the USSR, Poland may be confronted with the prospect of persistent low-level instability along its eastern border.[18] In May 1991, during a symposium on Poland's national security organized by the Polish National Defense Academy, several officers repeatedly stressed that neighboring republics, once independent, may even try to divert attention from their internal problems by making territorial claims against Poland.[19]

The worst-case scenario for Poland's security in the East would be a complete disintegration of the Soviet Union followed by anarchy and civil war. The potential outflow of Soviet refugees, estimated to number in the millions, would without a doubt exceed Poland's ability to resettle them or to facilitate their transit to other countries for resettlement. The Sejm Commission on Foreign Policy estimated in 1991 that, even if the Soviet Union does not collapse into internal chaos, once the Soviets become free to travel it is reasonable to expect that about five million people from the former USSR will travel through Poland by the middle of the decade.[20] Again, good working relations between Warsaw and Moscow, and between Warsaw and the key non-Russian successor states, are imperative in order to handle effectively the modalities of such dramatic migrations of the population and to prevent them from becoming a source of conflict in the region.

Potentially, the most thorny territorial issue in Polish-Russian relations, with implications for Polish-German relations as well, may be the future status of the Kaliningrad district, a remnant of former East Prussia which was incorporated into the Russian republic after World War II. In light of the Baltic states' independence, the Kaliningrad district is a major Russian military base, sandwiched between Poland and Lithuania, and therefore it is cut off from Russia proper. In 1990 the fate of Kaliningrad became a point of intense discussion between Germany and Moscow in connection with the future of the German minority in the USSR.[21]

The root cause of the Kaliningrad problem is the anticipated increase in migration from Soviet Central Asia to Germany of two million so-called Volga Germans, who have lived in Soviet Central Asia since their expulsion from European Russia during World War II. Descendants of the eighteenth-century colonists of the Volga River basin, these people are entitled under current German law to automatic rights of citizenship. According to the German Interior Ministry, the number of Volga Germans returning to Germany increased from only 753 in 1986 to 147,950 in 1990.[22] The German government anticipated that, once exit visa requirements have been waived by the Soviets in 1993, an estimated one million, if not more, Volga Germans would emigrate to Germany. An alternative, preferred by both Bonn and Moscow, is to resettle the Volga Germans somewhere in the European part of Russia. Already in 1989, in a radio interview, German Chancellor Helmut Kohl expressed his support for the creation of a homeland for the ethnic Germans in the Soviet Union, stressing that they "want to retain their identity as ethnic Germans" and expressing hope that "an ethnic German territory or republic can again be set up there."[23]

In the aftermath of the July 1990 Zheleznovodsk Soviet-German summit, Moscow and Bonn reviewed the German proposal to make the Kaliningrad district an area of resettlement for the close to two million Volga Germans. Bonn apparently viewed such a solution as a way to defuse the pressure of yet another wave of immigrants coming to Germany at a time when the reunification process had already strained the government's ability to assist the East Germans migrating to the West. The German government had initially contemplated the idea of resettling the Volga Germans in the depopulated territories of the former German Democratic Republic, but it abandoned the scheme in favor of a solution that would keep the ethnic Germans on Soviet territory, while according them their own autonomous region. As an inducement to the Soviets, the proposal also envisioned giving the Kaliningrad district a special open economic zone status, in order to turn it into a hub of German-Soviet commerce.

The idea of transferring the Volga Germans to the Kaliningrad region was raised after the opposition of the Soviet military and local residents of the territories comprising the original prewar Volga German autonomous republic had prevented the implementation of the resolution, passed by the Supreme Soviet in November 1989, to restore the prewar ethnic German homeland in the Soviet Union. The Kaliningrad option apparently enjoyed some support from the Soviet government and from Germany's Deutsche Bank, which proposed turning Kaliningrad into a duty-free port.

The Polish government reacted to the news of Soviet-German talks on the Kaliningrad issue with visible concern. Polish Interior Minister Krzysztof Kozlowski disclosed to the press the contents of Soviet-German negotiations, stressing his government's opposition to any such deal on Kaliningrad.[24] Warsaw insisted that territorial issues in Europe ought not to be reopened at all. The Poles informed the Soviet Union that they would view the implementation of the scheme to resettle the Volga Germans in the Kaliningrad district as a direct threat to their country's security. They argued that the resettlement would recreate the Polish territorial dilemma of the interwar period, with a Polish "corridor" running in between Germany proper and an area that would gravitate toward Germany politically and economically. Most of all, the Poles feared that changes in the status of Kaliningrad could constitute a precedent that might lead to other territorial revisions. Bronislaw Geremek, chairman of the Sejm Commission on Foreign Policy, expressed the official Polish view that such a precedent would have a ripple effect not only on Poland but also on

Romania, Hungary, Czechoslovakia, and Lithuania. The Polish position has been that the Kaliningrad territory should remain a part of Russia, with the existing population pattern remaining unchanged.[25]

In mid-1990 the Polish government delivered a formal protest to Moscow, demanding that the resettlement scheme be dropped altogether and notifying the Soviets that it viewed the plan as detrimental to its vital national security interests. In reply, Foreign Minister Eduard Shevardnadze assured Warsaw that the proposal to resettle the Volga Germans in the Kaliningrad district had been shelved and that this position of the Soviet government had been communicated to the representatives of the Volga Germans at one of the sessions of the USSR Supreme Soviet.[26] In a meeting in the summer of 1990 with the leaders of the Volga Germans "Rebirth Society," Soviet Deputy Prime Minister Vladimir Gusev, the man in charge of Soviet policy on nationalities, offered the Volga Germans Moscow's official recognition of their special status as a people, but with no territory of their own.[27]

In 1991 German-Soviet discussions on the future of Kaliningrad shifted away from the Volga German question and concentrated on the economic aspect of the proposal, including the suggestion to grant Kaliningrad a duty-free status of an open port. Nothing has been decided yet, as the outcome of the talks depends on the final resolution to the postcommunist succession in the former Soviet Union. It is apparent, however, that the territorial question of the district's future will remain one of the potentially most difficult territorial issues in Europe.

RELATIONS WITH NATO AND REGIONAL COOPERATION

Since 1990 Poland has regarded collective security in Europe, tied to the NATO alliance framework, as the only viable guarantee of its own national security interests. Hence, Poland considers the preservation of NATO, including continued American troop deployment in Europe, to be the linchpin of European security today. The issue of Poland's close ties to NATO had been raised already during the presidency of General Wojciech Jaruzelski, the country's last communist leader. On June 1, 1990, an international affairs expert in Jaruzelski's chancellery caused a minor sensation by publishing an article in the daily newspaper *Zycie Warszawy*, in which he addressed the issue of NATO troop deployment on Polish territory.[28] Moscow's reaction was strong enough to warrant a formal disclaimer from Jaruzelski, who "rejected such views as counter to Poland's policy and goals."[29] At the time, as General Tadeusz Cepak of the

Polish Army Foreign Liaison Office put it, "NATO still suffered from an image problem in the East."[30]

The issue of Poland's ties to NATO resurfaced six months later, however, after the election of Solidarity's Lech Walesa as Poland's president. In 1991 the new Polish government of Jan Krzysztof Bielecki began in earnest to search for an acceptable model for Poland's association with NATO, as part of its commitment to establish links to a range of Western European organizations. Privately, Polish government officials have regarded NATO as the only real working security structure in Europe, which both can keep Germany firmly within Western Europe and can offset Russia's influence in East Central Europe.

While Warsaw realizes that Poland's membership in NATO as it is presently constituted would have been unacceptable to the communist regime and the hard-line military in the Soviet Union, the postcommunist government may be less opposed to the idea. Poland's goal nevertheless is to become as closely tied to NATO's structures as possible. Throughout the 1990–1991 negotiations with the Soviets on the future of the Warsaw Pact, Poland maintained that NATO and America's presence on the Continent contributed significantly to its stability and collective security. In private, Polish government officials expressed the view that Poland's membership in the Atlantic Alliance would be a preferred solution to its security dilemma.

At the same time, the Poles have recognized that their future membership in NATO remained questionable not only because it offended Moscow's sensibilities but also because of NATO's reluctance to open itself up to new members. Geopolitical barriers aside, some more mundane matters, such as differences in military training and weapons incompatibility, have also been raised as an obstacle to integrating the postcommunist democracies in NATO. Since 1990 NATO has been in transition, which is likely to continue for some time before its new military posture has been fully articulated and the organizational changes agreed upon. In the meantime, Warsaw has repeatedly expressed its open support for NATO's continued existence. The Polish government believes that, even if it may not be absolutely essential for Poland's security to be a member of NATO, it is crucial nonetheless that NATO remain an anchor for Western Europe.

In 1990–1991 Poland worked vigorously to establish closer ties to NATO. Those efforts resulted in a partial success. On May 23, 1991, Polish Defense Minister Rear Admiral Piotr Kolodziejczyk visited Brussels to discuss the format for Poland's future cooperation with the alliance. After his meeting with NATO's Secretary General Manfred Woerner, Kolodziejczyk announced that NATO agreed to expand military contacts with

Poland, including the exchange of information on military doctrine and technical issues, as well as exchanges of officers. In turn, Woerner assured the Poles that NATO "would not ignore Warsaw's security interests" as it drafted a new strategy and a force structure to respond to the new conditions in Europe.[31] Possibly, after NATO's strategy has been reformulated, the future European military rapid deployment task force, announced after the NATO defense ministers' meeting on May 28, 1991, will have a contingency plan to operate on Polish territory.

In the Polish government's view, following the demise of the Warsaw Pact and in light of the absence of formalized CSCE security structures, NATO has become by default the only viable linchpin of the all-European security framework. Hence, Poland's petition for associate membership is considered in Warsaw a logical response to the new situation. At the same time, the Poles do not expect that NATO in its present form can provide Poland with a security guarantee against the Soviet threat. It is quite unlikely that the governments and public opinion in the United States and Western Europe will entertain any time soon the prospect of extending the strategic nuclear umbrella to Poland, or any other East Central European country for that matter. In the short term, Polish security vis-à-vis the former Soviet Union will depend primarily on the climate of Poland's relations with its eastern neighbors. Still, Warsaw looks to NATO as the badly needed reassurance of last resort in case its relations with Russia or another Soviet successor state become unmanageable.[32]

In addition to its focus on NATO, Poland has also been a proponent of regional cooperation in East Central Europe. Resistance to continued pressure from the East is arguably the strongest tie binding Poland's security interests with those of Czechoslovakia and Hungary. Critics of Poland's regional concept of security often describe it as a futile parliamentarian vision intended by the Solidarity government to assert its "Europeanness" and its separation from Russia. A regional security framework in East Central Europe, promoted by Poland, is still an idea rather than a practical solution to the threat of regional instability. Poland's plans for a regional security framework that would encompass political, economic, and limited military cooperation among the three newly emerging democracies, proposed by Solidarity's Bronislaw Geremek in 1990, may ultimately be hampered by different economic needs, political traditions, and a pattern of relations with Germany and Russia. Geremek's concept of a Baltic suballiance, in which Poland could find its regional anchor, has tough sailing ahead, and it is likely to remain an idea rather than a formal treaty. In 1990–1991, however, regionalism did yield concrete results. Tripartite consultations among Poland, Czechoslovakia, and

Hungary on the future of the Warsaw Treaty Organization contributed significantly to the Pact's dissolution.

Another reason why Poland has encouraged regionalism is the need to present the West with a common agenda. Since the 1989 collapse of communist power, Poland, Czechoslovakia, and Hungary have competed to a degree against one another in the race to join the European Community. Hungary is scheduled to join the European Economic Community (EEC) as an associate member in 1992 and has targeted 1995 as the goal for full membership. Poland is in the process of negotiating for associate membership in the EEC, and these negotiations are expected to be concluded by the end of 1991. Czechoslovakia has been lagging behind the two in its bid for membership in the common market largely because of the slow process of economic reform at home. A common agenda for negotiating the region's return to Europe, as advocated by Geremek and supported by Czechoslovakian President Vaclav Havel, is important to coordinate and accelerate the integration process.

In the area of limited regional military cooperation in East Central Europe, prospects are good as well, if only because they are dictated by practical considerations, including the reliance on standardized Soviet weapons and over four decades of joint military training. It has been the Polish position that such regional cooperation need not be formalized into an alliance in order to be effective. For instance, Polish generals have maintained close ties with their Czechoslovak and Hungarian counterparts, and such contacts will continue to grow in the future. The Poles have expressed a strong interest in cooperating with the Czechoslovaks and the Hungarians in an effort to diversify their weapons supply sources; in particular, to negotiate en bloc with Western suppliers on the purchase price and on joint licensing agreements for their armaments industries.[33] Poland signed a limited military cooperation agreement with Czechoslovakia in February 1991 and with Hungary in March of the same year. Regional military cooperation in those areas, without a formal alliance commitment, does not hinder East Central Europe's integration in a larger European community. It will most likely remain limited to the Triangle states.

The Poles also look to regionalism as a source of tangible economic benefits. For example, the February 15, 1991, Polish, Czechoslovak, and Hungarian summit in Visegrad, Hungary, resulted in a treaty on economic and environmental cooperation.[34] In May 1991, Poland took another important step toward regional economic cooperation and integration by gaining admission to the Pentagonale group, which includes Italy, Austria, Hungary, Czechoslovakia, and Yugoslavia. Polish Foreign Minister Krzysztof Skubiszewski described the country's admission to Pentagonale on May 17, 1991, during the group's Bologna summit, as a foreign policy objective the country "has consistently sought since 1990."[35] Poland was formally admitted into the Pentagonale in July 1991, with the group extending its infrastructure projects to cover the northern region as well.

"ARMED FORCES '90" MILITARY REFORMS

The first stage of military reform in Poland followed the 1987 Warsaw Pact guidelines for the restructuring of the army, combined with personnel reductions. Since Defense Minister General Florian Siwicki, a communist appointee of General Wojciech Jaruzelski, resisted change at the top of the army's bureaucratic apparatus, the personnel cuts were largely confined to the middle and lower ranks. Siwicki rationalized the direction of the restructuring in fiscal terms, often resorting to arbitrary decisions to dissolve selected military units. Already in February 1990, Poland's parliamentarians charged that the "restructuring was hitting the junior professional cadres, while protecting . . . the bureaucratic apparatus and the senior personnel."[36] The Sejm Commission on National Defense (*Sejmowa Komisja Obrony Narodowej*) attacked Siwicki's plan for restructuring as poorly thought through, because it had failed to take into account the "role and place of the Polish army in the new Europe."[37] In effect, already in the winter of 1990 the reform was stalled, caught in between two competing conceptions of the future of the Polish army: (1) Siwicki's plan to ensure that, while changes take place within the Polish army, they follow the guidelines of the 1987 Warsaw Pact reforms and that the army continues to operate within the Warsaw Pact command structure, and (2) the vision of the Solidarity deputies to the Sejm who considered national control over the army the sine qua non of state sovereignty and Polish independence. Confusion was an all too predictable result of the disagreement.

At the beginning of 1990 the Sejm took the initiative to block Siwicki's plan to replace the defunct Main Political Administration (*Glowny Zarzad Polityczny*; GZP) with the Main Educational Administration (*Glowny Zarzad Wychowawczy*; GZW). In late February 1990, three Solidarity deputies on the Sejm Commission on National Defense—Jacek Szymanderski, Jan Rokita, and Bohdan Kopczynski—called in Rear Admiral Piotr Kolodziejczyk, Siwicki's choice for the chief of the GZW, to testify before the commission. During the hearings, Kopczynski demanded that all former political officers in the Polish army be fired, Rokita called for the immediate dissolution of the GZW as well as the army's Education

Officers Corps, while Szymanderski flatly stated that "the education of the soldiers should be left to their commanders."[38] The Sejm then proceeded to challenge the size and structure of the defense budget, demanding that Siwicki present a comprehensive plan of military reform before any monies were to be appropriated.[39]

Repeated attacks in the Sejm on Siwicki's reform contributed to the unprecedented decision by Poland's National Defense Committee (*Komitet Obrony Kraju*; KOK) to make public the country's new defense doctrine, adopted by the KOK on February 21, 1990.[40] The text, approved by Siwicki, described the Polish defense doctrine as based on the country's *raison d'état,* the term used by Polish communists to refer indirectly to the need for an alliance with the Soviet Union. The doctrine argued along the lines of the 1987 Warsaw Pact redefinition of security that the two-bloc system at the heart of Europe would take several years to "crystallize," and hence Poland would continue to live up to its alliance commitments. In case of war, the Polish contingent of the Warsaw Pact would operate within the Pact's command structure, although its immediate command would be Polish. Siwicki's doctrine also outlined a plan to integrate the air force and the air defense forces, thus mirror-imaging the proposed changes in the Soviet army.[41] Finally, it reaffirmed the right of the president to declare war when the Sejm was not in session, which reaffirmed Jaruzelski's prerogative written into Poland's 1983 Law on National Defense.

The publication of the military doctrine was Siwicki's last important act as the country's defense minister. By that time a wave of radical political changes was sweeping across Poland. Pressure from Solidarity parliamentarians led in March 1990 to the dissolution of the GZW as well as the Education Officers Corps; the post of deputy commander for education was also eliminated. The new Education Department of the Polish Army (*Departament Wychowania Wojska Polskiego*) marked a clear break with its ideologically oriented predecessors, its primary task being the preparation of texts and audio/video materials needed for professional military training.[42] In a belated attempt to pacify the junior cadres, Siwicki launched a campaign to "humanize relations in the army," hoping to win back the junior officers' and NCOs' loyalty by improving their welfare. These efforts earned Siwicki a three-month extension but could not save his job. In April 1990, under continuing pressure from Solidarity deputies, President Jaruzelski accepted the appointment of two civilian deputy ministers of defense; the posts went to Bronislaw Komorowski and Janusz Onyszkiewicz.[43] Two months later, in June 1990, General Florian Siwicki, Jaruzelski's long-time friend and confidant, was removed from office.

On account of the randomness of the cuts introduced by Siwicki, by the spring of 1990 the Polish army found itself in a severe crisis which had come very close to an all-out rebellion by middle-level and junior military officers. Emboldened by democratic changes in the country, delegations of these officers took their grievances to the parliament and, testifying before the Sejm Commission on National Defense, demanded that the arbitrary cuts be halted until a long-term plan for the restructuring of the army, reflecting the requirements of a new defense doctrine, was approved by the government.[44] Under such conditions of internal instability, the Polish army entered the second phase of the reform process, this time to reflect a new political system in the country, a new foreign policy, and, most important, a new military doctrine.

Since 1990 the blueprint for the restructuring of the army, called "Armed Forces '90," has shaped both the military doctrine and the organizational structure of the army.[45] The program is to be completed by the year 2000.[46] The highlights of "Armed Forces '90" were first outlined by the chief of the Polish General Staff, General Zdzislaw Stelmaszuk, in late November 1990. The plan calls for a redefinition of the function of defense minister to focus on personnel and budgetary matters and to address the broad questions of national defense strategy and objectives through direct supervision of the ministry's Institute of Strategic Studies (*Instytut Badan Strategicznych*). The armed forces will be led either by the general inspector of the armed forces (*Glowny Inspektor Sil Zbrojnych*; GISZ) or the chief of the General Staff, who will be appointed commander-in-chief of the army in time of war. The GISZ or the chief of the General Staff will supervise the General Staff, logistics, and military training.

According to "Armed Forces '90," the Polish armed forces will be organized into three services under GISZ/chief of the General Staff's command: (1) the ground forces (*wojska ladowe*), (2) the air force and the air defense forces (*wojska lotnicze i obrony powietrznej*), and (3) the navy (*marynarka wojenna*). The ground forces will be divided into four military districts/army groups, with each district including the commander-in-chief's reserve units as well as a rapid deployment force (*sily szybkiego reagowania*) subordinated to the district commander. The air force and air defense force will be radically restructured to provide for the air defense of Polish territory from all directions, including the eastern frontier. Poland's radar detection systems will be relocated to cover equally the entire territory of the country. The navy will undergo a general program of reequipment to reflect its new coastal defense role. The army's central bureaucracy, which by the close of 1990 constituted roughly 1.1 percent of the armed forces' total personnel, will be reduced to about 0.6 percent of the total. The logistics of the Polish army will be organized into two inspectorates: (1) quartermaster general (*Glowne Kwatermistrzostwo*) and (2) chief inspector of technology (*Glowny Inspektor Techniki*), while the army's supply system will be reworked to rely on the local civilian economy.[47]

The new model of the Polish army assumes that the economy can support between 230,000 and 250,000 active military personnel, which can be expanded in wartime to between 750,000 and 800,000. The overall political control over the army will belong to the president as the commander-in-chief; he will be assisted in this role by his National Security Council (NSC) (*Rada Bezpieczenstwa Narodowego*). The bimonthly meetings of the council will be chaired by the president and will provide him with a current assessment of the country's security situation. The National Security Council will include the GISZ/chief of the General Staff, as well as the ministers of defense, foreign affairs, internal affairs, finance, transportation, maritime economy, and industry. The president may also bring in representatives from the Sejm, the Senate, political parties, and the Catholic church.[48] In 1991 President Lech Walesa moved to strengthen the National Security Council. According to Lech Kaczynski, minister of state for national security affairs in the president's chancellery, Walesa's goal has been to transform the NSC from an advisory and review body into "a constitutional body [with] extensive powers to issue binding decisions regarding the whole state security sphere and to monitor and exercise supervision over it."[49] Under the NSC reform plan proposed by Walesa, the president will have the power not only to appoint the commander-in-chief of the armed forces in time of war but to use the army for purposes other than the defense of the country. In 1991 the proposal generated considerable opposition in the Sejm, with several deputies charging that Walesa was after dictatorial powers.

TOWARD A PROFESSIONAL ARMY AND CIVILIAN CONTROL

The military reform program has changed the organizational structure of the Ministry of Defense. The ministry has been reorganized into two branches, the civilian branch and the military branch. Presently, the civilian side includes the position of the undersecretary for education, the Information Bureau, the Institute for Social Research, the Field Church (*kuria*), the defense minister's staff (*Urzad Ministra Spraw Wojskowych*), the Sejm Liaison Office, the Personnel Office, the Finance Office, the Institute of Strategic Studies, the Legal Affairs Office, and the Military Police Directorate (*zandarmeria*). In April 1991 the General Staff was reorganized into three branches: (1) the inspectorate for training (*inspektorat szkolenia*), (2) General Staff department for strategic planning (*szefostwo sztabu planowania strategicznego*), and (3) technical department of the armed forces (*pion techniczny wojska*).[50] The plan envisions the creation of regional defense brigades and special "reserves of the commander-in-chief" (*odwod naczelnego dowodcy sil zbrojnych RP*), rapid deployment forces (*sily szybkiego reagowania*), and a mountain brigade to operate in southern Poland.[51]

At present the army is attempting to shed its former image as a pillar of the old communist establishment. The most obvious changes in the current round of reform have been the reduction in the size of the armed forces and its increased professionalization. The Polish army will have shrunk from the present level of over 300,000 to approximately 230,000 officers and soldiers by the end of 1991.[52] In addition, the entire top-level echelon of the Ministry of Defense has already been purged of Jaruzelski's appointees. All military district commanders have been replaced, as have the generals heading the individual services of the Polish armed forces. In the process, thirty-nine generals and admirals were forced into an early retirement in 1990. In January 1991 Poland had eighty-eight general officers, which was close to the prewar size of the senior officer corps; the average age of Polish generals was fifty-four.[53]

The Polish army entered 1991 as a force still largely based on draftees, with only 38 percent being professional officers, NCOs, and warrant officers. The goal of the reform is to raise this percentage to reach a ratio of 50 percent professional to 50 percent draftees by the year 2000. This ratio of professional to nonprofessional military would put Poland on par with the German, French, and Dutch armies.[54] The ratio can be achieved, because the overall size of the Polish army has been contracting faster than the size of its professional cadres. At the end of 1989, professionals numbered 112,000, or 32 percent of the army, which numbered close to 330,000. A year later, as of January 1, 1991, the army numbered 94,000 professionals, which approached 35 percent of the total. More important, in 1990 the officer corps became much less "top-heavy"; at the end of 1989, Poland had 138 generals, while at the end of 1990 the number stood at 88. In January 1991, the middle-level cadres of the Polish army were as follows: 4,000 colonels, approximately 9,000 lieutenant colonels, and about 8,000 majors in the army of 304,000.[55] In order to accelerate the professionalization of the army, on January 29, 1991, Polish President Lech Walesa instructed his defense minister to devise a plan to shorten compulsory military service to twelve months, to be offset by the hiring of specialists on a contract basis to ensure the army's operational viability.[56] An all-volunteer professional Polish army is, however, a long-term goal, rather than a realistic short-term prospect. The current reform is trying first to redress the imbalance between the draftees as officers before exploring the feasibility of creating a professional army.

In addition to administrative changes, the Polish army has moved to reclaim its national character and symbols. The Poles are in the process of returning to the prewar uniform, including the traditional four-square cap (*czapka rogatywka*); the honor guard and the military police have already been issued the new national uniform. In addition, the institution of army chaplain, which the Polish army has retained since the end of World War II despite considerable Soviet pressure to abolish it, is being strengthened to ensure that soldiers are not hindered in their religious practices. On January 31, 1991, the Polish army got its first postwar military diocese, set up by the government in cooperation with the Vatican. Leszek Slawoj Glodz of the Warsaw Garrison church was appointed the first postwar field bishop of the Polish armed forces.[57]

By 1991 Polish military training had been purged of all remaining vestiges of communist ideology; it now emphasizes the army's patriotic tradition and its role in Poland's struggle for national independence. The return to national symbols and the emphasis on the national character of the armed forces were instrumental in bringing about a change in the manner in which the military was viewed by Polish society. By 1991 the army managed to remove the stigma of General Wojciech Jaruzelski's martial law. A public opinion poll, released by the Center for Public Opinion Research (*Centrum Badania Opinii Spolecznej*) in April 1991, for the first time in Polish postwar history placed the army at the top as the most trusted national institution, ahead even of the Catholic church.[58]

Once the military reform has been fully implemented, the Ministry of Defense will become largely a civilian organization. Within the ministry, the strictly military functions will be separated from political functions, so as to isolate the military from domestic politics and, presumably, to ensure against the army's interference in the country's domestic affairs. The position of the minister of defense will become a civilian cabinet appointment. He will control the overall strategy, the budgetary process, personnel appointments, and the administration.[59]

As a part of the move toward civilian control over the army, including parliamentary oversight, already in 1990 the government of Tadeusz Mazowiecki appointed Janusz Onyszkiewicz, a former spokesman for the Solidarity trade union, as deputy defense minister. In addition, the twenty-one-member Sejm Commission on National Defense was revamped and staffed with some Solidarity deputies from the Citizens Parliamentary Caucus (*Obywatelski Klub Poselski*; OKP). The commission is authorized to call before it any army officer or civilian employee to testify under oath, including the minister of defense. In 1990 there appeared to be some confusion about how to deal with sensitive material, as none of the members of the commission had been formally cleared for access to classified information. Since the commission deals with general questions of national defense policy, rather than military hardware per se, this has not become a major obstacle to its work.

The issue of the precise relationship between civilian and military structures within Poland's national defense establishment has remained a focus of national debate. In order to address the problem, in 1991 the government set up an interdepartmental Commission on Organizational Reform of National Defense, chaired by Minister Krzysztof Zabinski. According to Zabinski, the principal goal of the commission was to "facilitate the transformation of the Ministry of Defense into a civilian state agency."[60] Other issues raised by the commission in March and April 1991 concerned civil defense, the division of authority on national defense within the government, and the reform of the army and of the defense industry. The commission recommended that the minister of defense become a civilian political appointee. He will be assisted in his work by a deputy defense minister for social and educational affairs, a deputy defense minister for defense policy and planning, and a deputy defense minister for armaments and military infrastructure. The commission also recommended that the army itself be headed by the general inspector of the armed forces who would also function as the chief of the General Staff. If the recommendations are accepted, these two functions will be combined.

The present restructuring of the Polish army also addresses the role of the army in Polish society. The goal is to break completely the organic tie between the army and state power, which had developed during the forty-five years of communism in Poland and became especially pronounced in the 1980s following the introduction of martial law. In order to eliminate past practices, the army has been depoliticized. In 1989 the Sejm voted to forbid the professional military to belong to any trade union, political party, or organization; the draftees are also required to suspend their political affiliation and activities for the duration of their military service. Depoliticization of the army, the early retirement of some senior officers, and the reintroduction of prewar uniforms are the most visible elements of change within the Polish army. The National Defense Committee, traditionally the nation's highest agency concerned with national security in the communist period, has been slated for elimination; it will be replaced by the president's National Security Council.

NEW MILITARY DOCTRINE

For the first time in over four decades, questions about the utility of military force are at the center of Poland's national security concerns. This has been reflected in the new Polish military doctrine, to be adopted by the end of 1991. The draft proposal of the new doctrine has repudiated the previous document, published in February 1990 by former Minister of Defense General Florian Siwicki.[61] The current doctrine describes Poland's national security policy and the role of its army as follows:

—Poland is committed to the principle of a European collective security system; the task of the Polish army is purely defensive; it is to defend the country's territory against any and all possible threats;

—the Polish army can be used only in accordance with decisions by the country's constitutional bodies, which retain complete sovereignty over the armed forces;

—the army can be deployed outside Poland's borders only in accordance with international agreements, such as United Nations peacekeeping missions;

—Poland's political and military leadership recognizes that the country alone cannot defend itself against an all-out attack; since under the most favorable conditions Poland can put in the field an army of only 800,000 men, the only kind of military conflict that the Polish army can plan to fight in the future is a limited border war; although not openly articulated, it is implicitly understood by both Polish politicians and the military that in this decade the threat of local wars can arise along the country's eastern border with the former USSR;[62]

—in light of Poland's geopolitical position in Europe between Germany and the former Soviet Union, the country is determined to ensure that its territory not be used for aggression in any direction; the government believes that this principle of national security policy will have a stabilizing impact on the security of Europe as a whole, and therefore it will contribute to Poland's own security;

—the army's objective in case of war is to engage the potential aggressor long enough to raise the political price of aggression and to make the conflict a threat to European security as a whole; armed resistance after the defeat of the Polish army in the field under conditions of total conflict is excluded, as its price in human life and material destruction would be unacceptably high;

—Poland's national security is inextricably tied to collective security in Europe; in this sense, the Polish army is to acquire a purely deterrent value, that is, it must be capable of exacting a high price from an aggressor; the potential aggressor must be aware that Poland's political ties to the West and the professionalism of its small army will make it impossible for the war to remain limited and local for any length of time;

—in line with the "Armed Forces '90" reform program, Poland has restructured its military districts, including the creation of an additional district in the east; the army's operational and tactical command structure is now built around (1) the Pomeranian District in the northwest, (2) the Silesian District in the southwest, (3) the Malopolski/Krakow District in the southeast, and (4) the Kujawski-Mazurski District in the northeast between the Vistula River and the Bug River; the last two districts have been created from the former Warsaw Military District;[63] the redeployment of army units within Poland's borders constitutes a pivotal element of the new military doctrine; in the past, Poland's deployment was approximately 40 percent in the west, 35 percent in the center, and 25 percent in the east;[64]

—in case of war, the two districts facing the aggressor will become immediately engaged, while the other two will remain in reserve and will constitute a rear echelon of the Polish armed forces;[65]

—the redeployment of troops to the east (the Malopolski and Kujawski Districts) reflects the stated foreign policy goal of equidistance between the east and the west; the army is to be equally prepared to defend Poland from all directions;[66]

—increased troop mobility (rapid deployment capabilities) and reduction in armored divisions are essential for the army to meet the requirements of the new military doctrine;

—in order to provide for the defense of all of the country's borders, the army will establish several new units, including mountain infantry; training arrangements for the professional cadres of a mountain infantry brigade are being negotiated with the Italians;

—cooperation in the area of training with Western armies, including Great Britain, France, Germany, and the United States, as well as the armies of Czechoslovakia and Hungary, is the country's stated goal; Poland has approached the Western governments with a direct request to admit Polish officers into their military academies for training;

—future diversification of equipment will decrease the Polish army's dependence on Russia as a sole-source supplier; in particular, Poland is interested in purchasing military hardware from the United States and other Western countries jointly with Hungary and Czechoslovakia in order to lower the unit cost; cooperation between the Polish and the Czechoslovak defense industries will continue, including the coproduction of self-propelled guns designed by Czechoslovakia.

EQUIPMENT MODERNIZATION

A fundamental problem facing the Polish army today is that its training and equipment are inappropriate to the new defensive strategy and the new defensive doctrine. Prior to the collapse of communist power in Poland, the Polish army was trained to fight an offensive war against the West as part of the Warsaw Pact coalition strategy. Hence, the Polish army's organization and supply system was geared toward mobile offensive operation, while its equipment emphasized heavy armor and artillery. Under the now defunct Warsaw Pact coalition warfare strategy, Poland had been assigned to move rapidly against the northern segment of NATO's central front and occupy Denmark and portions of German territory. However unrealistic this war scenario for the Polish army might have been, the fact remains that the officers and soldiers were trained according to tactical plans built around the Soviet offensive military doctrine. Change in Poland's defense doctrine demands the reworking of the equipment requirements to emphasize antitank weapons, helicopters, and interceptor aircraft, as well as a change in the entire logistical and supply structure left by decades of Warsaw Pact coalition warfare planning.

Under the new geopolitical conditions, the question of partial self-sufficiency in weapons production has become an important issue for Poland's defense planners. The government hopes that through budgetary reform it can affect directly the weapons procurement process and funding, contributing in the future to the development of potential defense contractors, as Polish heavy industry completes the privatization cycle.

At present, Polish industry is unable to supply the armed forces with modern jet engines and state-of-the-art electronic equipment. The strength of the country's defense industry lies in airframe design, small weapons design, and ammunition manufacturing. Poland also produces under license the Soviet T-72 tank, a 122 mm howitzer, and an armored personnel carrier, the MTLB.[67] The Polish air force is largely obsolete, despite the purchase in the late 1980s of ten MiG-29 aircraft from the Soviet Union. While the defense industry has developed some very promising original designs, such as the Lublin landing ship, it badly needs to have access to Western technology in order to modernize and become less dependent on Soviet supplies.

On June 13, 1991, in order to address the problem of the sorry state of the Polish defense industry, a special interdepartmental Commission on Organizational Reform of National Defense, chaired by Minister Krzysztof Zabinski, recommended to the prime minister that a thorough reform of the industry take place as soon as possible. The commission recommended the creation of a state defense industry corporation which would operate under separate laws, including a ban on trade union activity. This state-owned company, referred to in the Zabinski report as State Defense Industries (*Panstwowe Zaklady Zbrojeniowe*), would operate between eight and ten military plants.[68] In addition, the Polish army would be authorized to award contracts for supplies and equipment directly to the private sector.

In 1991 Poland decided to increase its self-sufficiency in military technology. Current plans call for an increase in domestic R&D and in the production of aircraft, communications equipment, armor, ships, electronic equipment, and ammunition. The accepted short-term delivery schedule will provide the armed forces with a new Polish-designed armored personnel carrier, a new all-terrain small vehicle, a new Polish trainer aircraft, and a newly designed ground support aircraft.[69] The modernization plan calls for the eventual termination of equipment purchases from Russia, especially since Moscow has refused to sell Poland its most up-to-date weapons systems. The goal of the modernization program is to ensure that in the future state-of-the-art military equipment constitutes between 33 and 40 percent of the hardware used by the Polish army; in 1991, modern equipment constituted between 27 and 30 percent of the total.[70]

As part of the modernization program, the Polish General Staff and the Ministry of Defense have expressed a strong interest in purchasing Western weapons systems.[71] The army is eager to break the sole-source pattern in Poland's weapons acquisition, to select the best state-of-the-art hardware, and in the process to make the Polish army's equipment more compatible with that of NATO forces. For example, the Poles have expressed interest in acquiring the F-16 and the F-18 aircraft from the United States, but such purchases are not likely to be finalized any time soon. Cost is not the only obstacle to the Polish plan to purchase Western weapons. Even more important, Poland lacks qualified military personnel capable of practically evaluating competing designs under simulated battlefield conditions. Hence, the future acquisition of Western military hardware is contingent upon the Polish army's ability to send its procurement officers for training in the West. Finally, financial constraints and procurement problems aside, Poland will not be ready to make weapons purchases in the West until its army has been fully restructured and the requisite personnel changes completed. Considering the present structure of the Polish army, as well as the four decades of close integration in the Warsaw Pact, it is fair to say that for now Poland will remain dependent on Russia for weapons and spare parts. As a shortcut to military modernization, in 1991 Warsaw asked Bonn to transfer to Poland without compensation some of the Soviet-made weapons of the former East German army, but the Germans refused the request.

PROSPECTS FOR THE FUTURE

The basic geopolitical reality for Poland is that the country cannot match the military power potential of its western or eastern neighbors. In theory, this will always constitute a potential threat to Poland and, under the hypothetical scenario of an all-out aggression, would spell the end of Polish independence. Hence, the Polish government's security policy in the 1990s will continue to emphasize the political aspects of security, as the country searches for a workable all-European security formula that will ameliorate the reality of its difficult geopolitical position. Poland will also look for ways to bring itself closer to NATO. Warsaw believes that prospects for finding a workable security solution are encouraging and that the current internal problems experienced by the Soviet successor states give Poland the necessary time to develop a security policy under conditions devoid of an immediate threat. As Polish Defense Minister Rear Admiral Piotr Kolodziejczyk argued in May 1991, an outright military threat to Poland could come about only under extreme conditions, such as the return to the Cold War or the rise of irredentist claims in Europe.[72]

The most probable danger Poland may face in the 1990s is a regional crisis caused by instability in the East, which, if intensified, could lead to a limited military conflict. Considering the length of the Polish eastern border, Poland must be ready to respond to such an eventuality in order to prevent a civil war in the western part of the former USSR from spilling into its territory. Hence, for the rest of the decade, Polish army plans will focus primarily on low-intensity and limited war.

So far, Poland appears capable of handling a limited military confrontation. In the words of Defense Minister Kolodziejczyk, "[I]t so far has maintained defensive sufficiency, which means that a fight on any of its borders would be extremely costly for the aggressor."[73] More important, the country has backed military preparedness with intense diplomatic efforts in Western Europe to ensure that Poland will not face a future aggressor alone. In effect, the key to its security in the 1990s lies in Poland's successful integration with the European Community, rather than in the unattainable self-sufficiency of its armed forces.

NOTES

1. Polish Television, Channel 1, January 7, 1991.
2. "Rozmowy Skubiszewski-Szewardnadze," *Polska Zbrojna*, October 12–14, 1990.
3. "Nadszedl czas, aby Europa przeszla do tworzenia konkretow wspolpracy," *Zolnierz Wolnosci*, January 31, 1990.
4. Conversations with the author, Warsaw, January 1991.
5. "Jeden dzien z Januszem Onyszkiewiczem," *Zolnierz Rzeczypospolitej*, June 1–3, 1990.
6. *RFE/RL Daily Report*, June 18, 1991.
7. "Polska i RFN podpisaly traktat o potwierdzeniu istniejacej miedzy nimi granicy," *Polska Zbrojna*, November 15, 1990.
8. "Warsaw and Bonn Agree to Goodwill Treaty," *Financial Times*, May 3, 1991.
9. "Bonn Says Polish Pact to Go Ahead," *Financial Times*, May 29, 1991.
10. "Wielkie Zmiany," *Sztandar Mlodych*, April 19–21, 1991.
11. Colonel Stanislaw Koziej, "Problem strategii wojskowej: polityczno-militarna przyszlosc Europy," *Polska Zbrojna*, December 11, 1990.
12. Ibid.
13. "Wielkie Zmiany."
14. Ibid.
15. According to Polish Deputy Defense Minister Janusz Onyszkiewicz, the question of the future of Bialystok was raised in private discussions between Foreign Minister Krzysztof Skubiszewski and his Byelorussian hosts, but it was kept off the official agenda. Interview with Deputy Defense Minister Janusz Onyszkiewicz, Warsaw, January 8, 1991.
16. "Wielkie Zmiany."
17. "Zadania Ukraincow," *Rzeczpospolita*, March 22, 1991.
18. Interview with Brigadier General Tadeusz Cepak of the Polish Army Foreign Liaison Office, Ministry of Defense, Warsaw, January 7, 1991.
19. *RFE/RL Daily Report*, May 16, 1991.
20. Interview with Bronislaw Geremek, chair of the Sejm Commission on Foreign Policy, Warsaw, January 3, 1991.

21. "Sie taten morgen kommen wolle," *Der Spiegel*, January 7, 1991, pp. 124–127.

22. "2 Million Volga Germans Pose Settlement Issue for Bonn, Moscow," *Washington Post*, February 4, 1991.

23. Ibid.

24. *National Review*, December 1990.

25. This is the argument advanced by Bogumil Rychlowski of the Polish Institute of International Affairs. See Bogumil Rychlowski, *Niestabilnosc Europy Wschodniej i Problemy Bezpieczenstwa Miedzynarodowego* (Warsaw: PISM, 1991).

26. Professor Bronislaw Geremek, Chairman of the Sejm Commission on Foreign Policy. Interview with the author, Warsaw, January 3, 1991.

27. "2 Million Volga Germans Pose Settlement Issue for Bonn, Moscow."

28. Waldemar Piotrowski, "Wojska NATO w Polsce," *Zycie Warszawy*, June 1, 1990.

29. *Zolnierz Rzeczypospolitej*, June 6, 1990.

30. Interview with the author, Ministry of Defense, Warsaw, January 7, 1991.

31. *RFE/RL Daily Report*, May 24, 1991.

32. Interview with Deputy Jacek Szymanderski of the Sejm Commission on National Defense, Warsaw, January 5, 1991.

33. Interview with Polish Deputy Defense Minister Janusz Onyszkiewicz, Warsaw, January 8, 1991.

34. *Commercial Appeal*, February 15, 1991.

35. "Skubiszewski on Entry into 'Pentagonal Group,' " *FBIS-EEU-91-097*, May 20, 1991, p. 28.

36. "Sprawa armii jest sprawa niezwyklej wagi (rozmowa z Jackiem Szymanderskim, wiceprzewodniczacym Sejmowej Komisji Obrony Narodowej)," *Zolnierz Wolnosci*, February 13, 1990.

37. Ibid.

38. "Wychowawczy to znaczy jaki," *Zolnierz Wolnosci*, February 19, 1990.

39. "Czy za 'te pieniadze' mozna miec lepsza armie," *Zolnierz Wolnosci*, February 26, 1990.

40. "Doktryna Obronna Rzeczypospolitej Polskiej," *Zolnierz Wolnosci*, February 26, 1990.

41. See the discussion of Soviet reform, as outlined by Soviet Chief of the General Staff General M. Moiseyev, in chapter 2.

42. "Powstanie nowa sluzba wychowawcza WP," *Zolnierz Wolnosci*, March 16–18, 1990.

43. "Nowi wiceministrowie obrony narodowej," *Zolnierz Rzeczypospolitej*, April 4, 1990.

44. Interview with Deputy Jan Rokita of the Sejm Commission on National Defense, Warsaw, January 5, 1991.

45. Rear Admiral Piotr Kolodziejczyk, "Model lat 90-tych," *Polska Zbrojna*, November 16–18, 1990.

46. Interview with Polish Deputy Defense Minister Janusz Onyszkiewicz, Warsaw, January 8, 1991.

47. General Zdzislaw Stelmaszuk, "Jakie zmiany w WP," *Polska Zbrojna*, November 16–18, 1990.

48. General Zdzislaw Stelmaszuk, "Nowy model armii," *Polska Zbrojna*, November 22, 1990.

49. "Kaczynski Walks out of Defense Meeting," *FBIS-EEU-91-100*, May 23, 1991, p. 15.

50. "Kontrowersje w sprawie KON," *Zycie Warszawy*, April 23, 1991.

51. Stelmaszuk, "Nowy model armii."

52. Polish Defense Minister Admiral Piotr Kolodziejczyk in an interview for *Express Wieczorny*, January 3, 1991.

53. Defense Minister Admiral Piotr Kolodziejczyk in *Gazeta Wyborcza*, January 10, 1991.

54. Ibid.

55. Interview with Brigadier General Tadeusz Cepak of the Polish Army Foreign Liaison Office, Ministry of Defense, Warsaw, January 7, 1991.

56. *RFE/RL Daily Report*, January 30, 1991.

57. *RFE/RL Daily Report*, February 1, 1991.

58. "Sondaze Centrum Badania Opinii Spolecznej," *Rzeczpospolita*, April 15, 1991.

59. Ibid.

60. "Struktury cywilne i wojskowe: prace nad nowym ksztaltem systemu obronnosci panstwa," *Zycie Warszawy*, April 16, 1991.

61. *Zolnierz Wolnosci*, February 26, 1990.

62. Interview with Deputy Jacek Szymanderski of the Sejm Commission on National Defense, Warsaw, January 5, 1991.

63. *Polish Army: Facts and Figures* (Warsaw: Ministry of Defense, 1990).

64. General Franciszek Puchala, "Zmiana dyslokacji jednostek WP: to wynika z naszej racji stanu," *Polska Zbrojna*, December 12, 1990.

65. Interview with Polish Deputy Defense Minister Janusz Onyszkiewicz, Warsaw, January 8, 1991.

66. Defense Minister Admiral Piotr Kolodziejczyk in *Gazeta Wyborcza*, January 10, 1991.

67. "Polski przemysl zbrojeniowy: czolgiem do Europy," *Gazeta Bankowa*, April 14–20, 1991.

68. "Struktury cywilne i wojskowe: prace nad nowym ksztaltem systemu obronnosci panstwa."

69. "Czym sie bronic? Nasza armia znalazla sie praktycznie w slepej uliczce," *Wokanda*, May 12, 1991.

70. Ibid.

71. Interview with General Tadeusz Cepak and Deputy Defense Minister Janusz Onyszkiewicz, Warsaw, January 6 and 7, 1991.

72. "Temat: Nowa Polska w Europie. Z ministrem obrony narodowej wice-admiralem Piotrem Kolodziejczykiem rozmawia Jerzy Papuga," *Konfrontacje*, May 1991.

73. Ibid.

4

CZECHOSLOVAKIA IN SEARCH OF CONFEDERATED EUROPE

COLLECTIVE SECURITY AND SOVIET PRESSURE

In 1990 and 1991 Czechoslovakia became a leading proponent of European federalism and regional cooperation as a solution to the Continent's future security needs. With respect to East Central Europe, Prague's foreign policy was based on the premise that collective security can be a viable option in the region only if the concerted efforts of all governments generate a "common feeling of confidence . . . and the perception of shared security or insecurity."[1] In effect, the future security of the Triangle would rest on shared co-responsibility for each country's peace and independence. In the words of Czechoslovak Foreign Minister Jiri Dienstbier, "Czechoslovakia and Hungary cannot feel secure if Poland does not, and vice versa."[2] Czechoslovakia's vision of future pan-European security assumes a voluntary partial loss of state sovereignty by all European nations and the eventual shared co-responsibility for the security of Europe as a whole.

The Czechoslovak government has been much more emphatic than Poland and Hungary in its focus on the Conference on Security and Cooperation in Europe as the solution to the regional security dilemma. It has argued that, in order for the general CSCE framework to work, it will have to be supplanted by strong all-European institutions empowered to deal with specific regional crises. The Czechoslovak notion of pan-European security presupposes that the web of international relations in Europe would eventually become complex enough so as to prevent any individual country, no matter how powerful, from breaking out of the common agreements without critically endangering its own survival.

Czechoslovakia's special emphasis on collective security and regional co-responsibility reflects its strong sense of vulnerability, as it begins to grapple with the mechanics of domestic reform. Moreover, Czechoslovakia's constitution, which is based on the principle of federalism, as well as the country's historical experience, makes a supra-national security option an attractive solution. In contrast to Poland and Hungary, Czechoslovakia is a two-nation federation which must find a working formula for the preservation of the state. In light of its own experience, Czechoslovakia sees the axiom of mediated compromise inherent in the principle of collective security as the best solution to Europe's historical legacy of competing nationalisms.

In 1990–1991, in contrast to Poland's paramount preoccupation with the residual Soviet military threat, Czechoslovakia appeared more concerned about internal instability at home. Forty-five years of communist rule in Czechoslovakia have given political and economic reform a particular security connotation. Unlike Poland or Hungary, Czechoslovakia has no postwar experience with the market, having missed de-Stalinization in the 1950s and having been governed from 1968 until 1989 by one of the most hard-line communist regimes in the former Soviet bloc. Therefore, in 1991 Czechoslovakia faced the prospect of the inevitable social dislocations associated with market reforms with little experience in dealing with them, while the federation's new democratic institutions were challenged by internal nationalist discord.

Prague's preoccupation with the danger of domestic instability has had a particular Soviet dimension to it. While sharing with Poland and Hungary the concern over the outcome of the domestic crisis in the former USSR, Czechoslovakia has a concrete reason to worry about the state of its relations with the Soviet successor states. Today Czechoslovakia is almost completely dependent on Russia for its energy needs. It gets close to 90 percent of its oil and natural gas supplies from Russia,[3] which makes the country highly vulnerable to Moscow's political pressure. In 1991 Prague moved to reduce this dependency by negotiating for purchases of oil from the Middle East, in particular Iran, and of natural gas from Algeria and Norway. It has also launched a large-scale construction project to tap into the European pipeline in Germany. Still, for at least the next two years, Czechoslovakia will remain potentially vulnerable to Moscow's economic blackmail. If the new Russian state chooses to exercise its economic leverage, it may seriously hurt the country's prospects for successful economic reform, for Czechoslovakia lacks sufficient hard currency reserves to replace the lost oil supplies through market purchases.

SLOVAK SEPARATISM

The inevitable disruptions generated by economic change could fuel popular discontent in Czechoslovakia and strengthen the hand of Slovak separatists. In 1991 there were signs that Slovak nationalists could use the difficult domestic situation to their advantage. Shortly before his forced resignation as Slovakia's prime minister, Vladimir Meciar claimed that during his visit to Moscow he had secured future Soviet defense orders for Slovakia's factories as a viable alternative to Slovakia's continued economic ties with Bohemia and Moravia. In order to appreciate the appeal of Meciar's rhetoric to Slovak public opinion, one has to keep in mind that the country's 111 weapons manufacturing plants are located in Slovakia. As reported by Czechoslovak Foreign Minister Jiri Dienstbier, on May 2, 1991, the country faced the possible loss of 70,000 to 80,000 jobs in the defense industry, with the bulk of it occurring in Slovakia. Although in 1991 Prague managed to sign several weapons export deals, overall Czechoslovakia's weapons sales declined from 1988 through 1990 by $7 billion, falling from $8 billion in 1988 to only $1 billion in 1990.[4] The rising unemployment in the Slovak defense industry has become a powerful divisive issue between Prague and Bratislava.

Domestic instability generated by the inevitable economic and social dislocations caused by the present reform appears to be a greater potential threat to Czechoslovakia's security than it is in Poland and Hungary. In 1991 the Czechoslovak government was seriously concerned that, if the Slovak economy collapsed, the democratic process in the country might suffer a serious setback. In order to communicate to the West the urgency of the problem, Prague asked the CSCE to focus on the economic aspects of regional security, arguing that Western economic assistance was essential to the stability of East Central Europe. In June 1991, supported by Poland and Hungary, Czechoslovakia presented a position paper on the economic aspects of regional security to the CSCE meeting of foreign ministers in Berlin.[5]

Because of the danger of Slovak separatism, Czechoslovakia's future European Economic Community (EEC) membership also has an important domestic policy dimension. In contrast to Poland and Hungary, Czechoslovak officials believe that the country may not be ready to join the EEC for another fifteen years. In 1991 the Czechoslovak government estimated that Poland and Hungary were about three years ahead of Czechoslovakia in terms of economic reform. Still, the country hoped to achieve associate EEC membership by the end of 1992 or in 1993.[6] Prague has considered associate membership in the

EEC an important symbolic development, as it would constitute a strong signal of Western Europe's commitment to assist Czechoslovakia in reforming its economy. Associate EEC membership would therefore contribute to greater domestic stability in Czechoslovakia.

The Czechoslovak government has been most concerned about the impact of current secessionist pressures in Slovakia on the country's future as a federal state. Although in 1991 the Moravian republic also demanded the restoration of its autonomy, which had been abolished by the communists, it was the leading Slovak nationalist politicians who have applied strong pressure for fully independent statehood. The actual power of Slovak separatism will depend on the degree of economic hardship encountered by Czechoslovakia in the years to come. In 1990 the challenge of Slovak separatism appeared to be a long-term rather than an immediate threat, as public opinion polls conducted in Slovakia in December 1990 indicated that 70 percent of the Slovaks preferred to remain within the Czechoslovak federation.[7] It is far from certain, however, that the federation will hold when Slovakia finds itself in a deep economic recession.

Even if in the final analysis the majority of Slovaks will probably opt for the preservation of the federal republic, the separatist movement in Slovakia is bound to constitute a problem in the years to come. In 1991 the demand by Slovak Prime Minister Jan Carnogursky that "in 1992 Slovakia join the new Europe under its own banner" generated enough concern in Prague to prompt the Czech parliament to consider a contingency plan for Bohemia and Moravia, if the federation were to split up after all. On May 22, 1991, following the floor debate of a contingency plan for the breakup of the republic, submitted by Czech Prime Minister Petr Pithart, Czech parliament chairman Dagmar Buresova admitted that "despite efforts made by all to preserve the federation we must also be prepared for failure."[8]

Prague hopes that the pressures of Slovak separatism will be alleviated by the new constitution, which will grant Slovakia extensive autonomy rights. The negotiations between the Czech National Council and the Slovak National Council on the Czech and Slovak Federal Republic's (CSFR) constitutional and legal arrangement, which began in 1991, cover the procedural provisions for secession as well. According to the 1991 constitutional proposal, for a republic to secede from the federation, it will have to hold a popular referendum on the issue. Next, even if the majority of the republic's population votes to secede, the republic will still have to secure the Federal Assembly's consent to dissolve the union.[9] The federal government expects that these procedural constraints, strongly criticized by the secessionist Slovak National Party, will prevent the breakup of the state even if economic conditions in Slovakia worsen dramatically. Moreover, the complex legal and constitutional procedures that would have to be followed after Slovakia's formal bid for independence would take several years to complete. This by itself would give the federal government the chance to integrate further the Czech and Slovak markets and, hopefully, defuse separatist pressures.

Inflammatory nationalist rhetoric aside, in May 1991 there were also the first signs that the Slovak government might temper its demands for independence. Slovak Premier Jan Carnogursky in an interview on May 17, 1991, observed that the new treaty on relations between the Czech and Slovak republics "should contain fundamental principles of *Czechoslovakia's* constitutional setup. This means fundamental principles of relations between the Czech and Slovak republics in a *common state* [author's emphasis]."[10] The apparent change in Carnogursky's position on independence—that is, his implicit recognition that Czechoslovakia should remain as a federal state—has opened up the possibility for negotiation on far-reaching autonomy for Slovakia within the framework of a new federal constitution. Carnogursky's relative moderation has become in effect a critique of former Slovak Prime Minister Vladimir Meciar's demands for immediate independence and statehood. In a May 15, 1991, interview for *Narodna Obroda*, Carnogursky criticized Meciar unequivocally for leading Slovakia in the direction of "political and strategic defeat and isolation."[11] When asked about the future sovereignty of Slovakia, Carnogursky reaffirmed his commitment to "the realization of the national idea" but argued that, since the current trend favored Slovakia's independence, his primary task was "not to accelerate this trend, [but] rather the opposite [*sic*]" because "acceleration might turn into a free fall."[12] Carnogursky asserted that the road to independence led through the constitutional process, while attempts at immediate sovereignty would only isolate Slovakia internationally and possibly lead to civil war, as it did in Yugoslavia.

The Czechoslovak federal government and its Ministry of Defense have recognized that in the immediate future secessionist pressures in Slovakia are bound to increase, as the heavy defense plants located in that republic bear the brunt of the planned reductions in weapons manufacturing. The government hopes that in this respect the army will constitute a stabilizing factor by bringing together the Czech and the Slovak servicemen and educating them on the benefits of continued federation. Over the years, supporters of Slovak independence have complained repeatedly of underrepresentation on the level of the Ministry of Defense. An article entitled "Federal Army: Few Slovaks at the Ministry of Defense," published in

Narodna Obroda on May 14, 1991, charged that "the much-discussed problem of personnel representation in the high-ranking positions remains unresolved."[13] The article blamed the underrepresentation of Slovaks at the command level on a policy of discrimination dating back to the creation of the federal state in 1918. Reportedly, the number of Slovaks at individual departments of the federal Ministry of Defense ranged in 1991 from 5 to 23 percent, well below the overall 34.7 percent of professional soldiers of Slovak nationality in the federal army as a whole.[14] In 1991 the federal government moved quickly to remedy the situation. In order to defuse tension between the Czech and Slovak servicemen, the Ministry of Defense has instituted a form of "affirmative action" for the officer corps, whereby if the commanding officer of an army unit is a Czech, his first deputy commander must be a Slovak, and vice versa.[15]

NATIONAL SECURITY POLICY

The key issue of Czechoslovakia's security was taken up shortly after the 1989 "Velvet Revolution" by First Deputy Chief of the Czechoslovak General Staff Lieutenant General Josef Vincenc in an interview for Radio Free Europe in July 1990.[16] At the time, Czechoslovakia's position was that the preservation of the political institutions of the Warsaw Pact as a vehicle for negotiations with NATO remained in the country's interest, as the sudden dissolution of the WTO would isolate Russia and might cause additional tensions in the region. Still, even as early as 1989, the Czechoslovaks maintained that the Pact would cease to exist once a pan-European collective security system had been put in place. According to Vincenc, the new collective security system would be modeled after the Council of Europe, providing for the representation of all European countries as well as the Soviet Union and the United States. In the interview, Vincenc also echoed Foreign Minister Jiri Dienstbier's position that serious tensions in postcommunist Eastern Europe could develop due to growing economic problems and ethnic pressures. At the same time, Vincenc rejected out of hand the idea of neutrality as a viable option for Czechoslovakia and spoke critically about Hungary's push for an immediate withdrawal from the Warsaw Pact.

By 1991 Czechoslovakia's thinking about national security evolved away from the old bloc structures and refocused on the principles of collectivism and pan-Europeanism. At the same time, the federal Ministry of Foreign Affairs assumed the leadership of policy formulation, with Foreign Minister Jiri Dienstbier becoming the driving influence behind the policy change. In mid-1991 Prague was able to articulate an elaborate vision of the future European security system as well as Czechoslovakia's place in it.

The stated security policy objective of the Czech and Slovak Federal Republic in the 1990s is to develop a cooperative pan-European security system within the broad context of the CSCE process. In the words of Jiri Dienstbier, the ultimate goal is to "transfer security on the Continent from a bloc basis to an all-European one."[17] The long-term future goal is to create a "confederated Europe, a Europe of regions" tied together by shared economic and security interests. Czechoslovakia has pursued this admittedly broad goal through a three-pronged security policy design, including (1) bilateral treaties; (2) cooperation with NATO, the Western European Union (WEU), the Council of Europe, and the European Economic Community; and (3) the Conference on Security and Cooperation in Europe.[18]

BILATERALISM

Among the new bilateral treaties, the most important for Czechoslovakia's security are the agreements with the Soviet Union's successor states and Germany. Prague's position has been that the new treaties must reaffirm the equality and full partnership as the foundation of good neighborly relations between the parties. As in the Polish case, Czechoslovak-German negotiations proceeded apace, notwithstanding the disagreements over the Sudetic Germans' claims to compensation for property confiscated by Czechoslovakia in 1945. In early 1991, however, bilateral treaty talks between Czechoslovakia and the Soviet Union became bogged down over Moscow's insistence on special concessions in the area of national security.

The bilateral negotiations process revealed a deep strain in the Soviet-Czechoslovak relationship after 1989. In the course of negotiations with the Soviet Union, Czechoslovakia insisted on a clause in the new agreement outlining a mechanism of political consultations to settle disputes and manage potential crises in Soviet-Czechoslovak bilateral relations. In addition, Czechoslovakia insisted that, as a general principle, all new bilateral treaties signed by the states in the region include an express commitment of the parties to the creation of a cooperative pan-European security system.[19] As in the Polish case, the principal issue that has stalled the 1990–1991 Soviet-Czechoslovak negotiations of the new ten-year good relations treaty was the Soviet insistence on a clause that would prohibit Czechoslovakia from joining any future security alliance if Moscow deemed it hostile to its security interests. The clause, which was in line with Moscow's "New Cooperation Formula" for relations with its former satellites, has been privately described by Czechoslovak diplomats as a "Finlandization agreement." As of the summer of 1991 the Soviet security clause had been accepted by only one former Soviet satellite, Romania, which on March 22, 1991, signed a new bilateral treaty with the Soviet Union.

In the spring of 1991 Prague rejected the special Soviet security clause on the grounds that it would compromise Czechoslovakia's sovereignty. The Czechoslovaks refused to accept the Soviet draft of the new bilateral agreement, and the talks became deadlocked. The Czechoslovak side contended that a new bilateral treaty with the USSR, if it contained the "Finlandization security clause," would run counter to the country's most vital national security interests, that is, the goal of joining a new all-European security system. The Soviet version of the draft treaty was viewed in Prague with considerable concern as a throwback to the thinking on national security typical of the Cold War era, as well as an attempt by the Soviets to exercise veto power over Czechoslovakia's foreign policy. In April 1991, Czechoslovak President Vaclav Havel formally repudiated the Soviet treaty proposal, calling it simply "unacceptable."[20] Four months later, in August 1991, the collapse of communist power in the Soviet Union and the subsequent breakup of the USSR have reopened the issue and made future relations between Prague and Moscow dependent on the final settlement among Soviet successor states.

By contrast, the 1991 bilateral treaty negotiations with Germany, Italy, and France proceeded smoothly. In addition, Czechoslovakia strengthened its relations with Poland and Hungary by negotiating bilateral friendship and cooperation agreements within the Triangle. Prague extended the regional tripartite cooperation to the military sphere as well. On January 20, 1991, Czechoslovakia reached a five-year technical military cooperation agreement with Hungary, and on February 27, 1991, a military cooperation agreement with Poland. Both accords commit Prague to an exchange of information and experiences with Budapest and Warsaw in the area of military planning and to the exchange of students at the three countries' military academies, with possible cooperation in weapons maintenance.[21] The three agreements were reached at the Ministry of Defense level and do not have the status of a full-fledged military treaty.

RELATIONS WITH THE WEST

Association and close cooperation with established Western organizations such as NATO, WEU, EEC, and the Council of Europe are the second direction of Czechoslovak security policy outlined in 1991, likely to continue well into the 1990s. Czechoslovakia became a full member of the Council of Europe on February 21, 1991; it was the second former Soviet satellite, after Hungary, to join the council.[22] Two months later, President Havel's highly symbolic visit to NATO headquarters in Brussels, in April 1991, explored the extent of Czechoslovakia's possible association with the North Atlantic Alliance, including political as well as military cooperation. In light of NATO's decidedly unenthusiastic response to this particular Czechoslovak initiative, Prague settled for the alliance's pledge of more limited cooperation, as well as associate membership for the Czechoslovak Federal Assembly in the European Parliament. Like Poland and Hungary, in 1991 Czechoslovakia submitted formal letters of intent asking for close association with the Western European Union, NATO, and the European Economic Community.[23]

President Havel's April 1991 visit to Brussels forced Prague to realize that, at least for the remainder of the decade, full membership in NATO is not likely to become an available national security option, pending the internal transformation of the North Atlantic Alliance. Like Poland, however, Czechoslovakia has been reassured by the fact that NATO will remain for the foreseeable future an essential factor in European security. As Czechoslovakia's foreign minister put it in his address to the federal parliament in April 1991, "NATO is important because it fulfills in Europe the irreplaceable function of a link with the U.S.A., safeguards against risks issuing from the unpredictability of European developments, and makes it possible to coordinate procedures in case of a threat by extra-European factors."[24] In this perspective, it is apparent that like the other two Triangle states, Czechoslovakia will attempt to move as closely to NATO as the North Atlantic Alliance will permit it. This common regional policy vis-à-vis NATO has been agreed upon by Poland, Czechoslovakia, and Hungary during the February 1991 summit of the tripartite group in Visegrad, Hungary.[25]

Czechoslovakia's cooperation with the West in the economic sphere enjoys much better short-term prospects than its membership in NATO. Associate membership in the European Economic Community is considered in Prague to be a realistic possibility, with full membership becoming available to Czechoslovakia together with Poland and Hungary possibly by the end of the decade. Czechoslovakia's eventual entry into the EEC has been strongly supported by the German government, which already in November 1990 went on the record with its strong backing for Czechoslovakia's membership both in the EEC and in the Council of Europe.[26] The immediate objective of Czechoslovakia's efforts to forge close ties to established Western institutions, however loose they might be at the moment, is to ensure the country's presence at the European fora where vital regional security issues are debated. Prague, like Warsaw and Budapest, wants to make certain that, in the event of a regional crisis, its representatives will be invited by the key Western institutions to present their views on the issue. In line with this policy, Czechoslovakia has been particularly vocal in its request for observer status in arms control negotiations and future regional and pan-European security conferences. Multifarious contacts with Western alliances and institutions are regarded by Prague as the necessary first steps toward Czechoslovakia's future membership in a new pan-European security framework. Finally, foreign policy initiatives, such as Havel's 1991 visit to Brussels, constitute a strong declaration of intent; they emphasize Prague's position that close contact with the West is fundamental to Czechoslovakia's security.

Prague has also worked to develop new ties to the Western military. In a July 19, 1990, interview for *Hospodarske Noviny*, General Josef Vincenc stated that Czechoslovakia would henceforth base its defense on collective security rather than bloc security principles.[27] Shortly thereafter, the Czechoslovak army signaled its interest in developing close military relations with NATO. As reported by *Narodna Obroda*, Czechoslovak First Deputy Defense Minister Major General Anton Slimak, during a visit to the United States in the summer of 1990, called for frequent consultations with the Western military, including an invitation to Chairman of the U.S. Joint Chiefs of Staff General Colin Powell and U.S. Secretary of Defense Richard Cheney to visit Czechoslovakia.[28] These two events were symbolic of a new thinking on military strategy under way in the Czechoslovak Ministry of Defense. The reevaluation of the country's new strategic position led in 1991 to the formulation of a new Czechoslovak military doctrine.

THE CSCE PROCESS

The third pillar of Czechoslovakia's national security policy for the 1990s consists of a strong commitment to the Conference on Security and Cooperation in Europe. In an address to the Royal Institute of International Affairs in London in April 1990, Czechoslovak Foreign Minister Dienstbier outlined a broad long-term proposal for the CSCE's evolution into a pan-European security system. The first step in this direction would be for the thirty-four CSCE members to sign a new treaty obliging them to give military assistance to any signatory under attack. The treaty would be implemented by a new bicameral "Commission on Security in Europe," which would include a political chamber and a subordinate military chamber. Next, Dienstbier envisioned the creation of an "Organization of European States" (OES) as the second stage in the development of the new security framework. The OES would incorporate and expand the existing Western institutions, such as the Council of Europe and the European Parliament. The third and final stage would consist of political integration of Europe in the form of a "United Confederated Europe."[29]

The Czechoslovaks consistently have displayed a much greater enthusiasm for the CSCE than have the Poles or the Hungarians. President Vaclav Havel as well as his foreign minister described the CSCE summit meeting in Paris, in November 1990, as a milestone on the road to the creation of the new security system in Europe. Havel referred to the meeting as "the beginning of a new historical era [in Europe], an end of the cold war period, and actually an end to World War II and its consequences."[30] In Havel's view, the Paris summit also symbolized the end of bipolarity and of the division of Europe into hostile blocs. He expressed his strong conviction that the future Helsinki summit in 1992 would lead to specific binding security agreements between member-countries in place of the recommendations issued by the CSCE conferences to date. For his part, Dienstbier viewed the decision to locate the CSCE Secretariat in Prague both as a major success of Czechoslovak diplomacy and a symbol of a new Europe.[31]

The Czechoslovak government's enthusiasm about the future of the CSCE process was sorely tested only two months later, when the aborted Soviet crackdown in the Baltic republics brought home the difference between the high expectations of future pan-European security cooperation and the remaining realities of Soviet power. Prague was clearly shaken by the CSCE's inability to condemn the human rights violations perpetrated by the Soviets in Lithuania and Latvia, or to act in unison to force a change in Soviet policy. President Havel described the military crackdown in the Baltics as "shocking" and called upon Gorbachev to resolve the problem through peaceful negotiations.[32] Since January 15, 1991, Havel and Dienstbier's vision of a future security system covering a new integrated Europe has been complemented by a search for more pragmatic short-term solutions. Immediately after the crisis, President Havel announced his intention to seek closer ties with NATO, including, if possible, associate membership for Czechoslovakia. Prague also became a much more vocal proponent of the complete dissolution of the Warsaw Pact, threatening if need be to initiate a unilateral withdrawal from the alliance.

Havel's decision to seek additional assurances from NATO did not mean, however, that the Czechoslovaks were giving up on the CSCE. In

April 1991, in his address to the parliament, Dienstbier reaffirmed Czechoslovakia's commitment to the creation of the OES as a "distant perspective" and called for the strengthening of the existing CSCE institutions, in particular the Council of Ministers of Foreign Affairs, to give the CSCE an increased ability to respond to crises. Dienstbier even suggested that the 1992 CSCE summit in Helsinki should initiate the development of a multinational armed force, to include contingents from all CSCE member-states.[33] The new, more somber appraisal by Prague of the CSCE's ability to resolve crises is in large measure the result of the CSCE's failure to prevent the Baltic crisis from escalating into an all-out violent confrontation in the winter of 1990–1991. Likewise, the eruption of violence in Slovenia and Croatia in the aftermath of the Yugoslav republics' 1991 declarations of independence, despite repeated appeals from CSCE foreign ministers meeting in Berlin for the preservation of a unified Yugoslav federation, further underscored the institutional weakness of the nascent pan-European security organization based on the CSCE.

Still, despite its shortcomings, the CSCE remains unquestionably important as a broad security policy framework for Czechoslovakia as well as the other two Triangle states, especially as it is at present the only all-European institution in which the Triangle can play a significant role. For East Central Europe the value of the CSCE process consists in the simple fact that the formula supplies the transatlantic connection to the United States, as well as keeps the Soviet Union's successor states engaged in the search for a commonly acceptable security arrangement. Short of an alliance with the United States, the CSCE provides a forum for Czechoslovakia's direct association with America and the other members of the North Atlantic Alliance.

Prague hopes that within the next five years the existing conflict management institutions of the CSCE, such as the Secretariat in Prague or the Crisis Prevention Center in Vienna, will become effective instruments for settling regional disputes. In addition, Czechoslovakia proposed to the 1991 CSCE Berlin meeting of foreign ministers the creation of a permanent policy-making body, to be located in Helsinki, with the goal of transforming the conference into a permanent platform for negotiating common European policy goals. Since the most acute problem facing the CSCE is the absence of effective enforcement procedures, Prague also proposed in Berlin a resolution on the need to create a so-called emergency mechanism, that is, a set of clearly defined procedures to be invoked in a crisis.[34] The Czechoslovak proposal on the emergency mechanism significantly increases the ability of small states to raise their security concerns within the CSCE structures, although for a decision on how to resolve the crisis to be binding, the consensus of the members will still be required.

MILITARY REFORM: VACEK'S LEGACY

The current restructuring of the Czechoslovak military and the articulation of a new military doctrine go back to the November 1989 demands by the Civic Forum that the army be placed under civilian control. At the time, Prime Minister Ladislav Adamec agreed to meet those demands halfway by replacing the unpopular Defense Minister General Milan Vaclavik with another officer and a former deputy defense minister, General Miroslav Vacek. When Marian Calfa became Czechoslovakia's prime minister in place of Adamec, he retained Vacek at his cabinet post.

Although a member of the Communist Party, Vacek moved quickly to gain credibility with the democratic forces. On December 6, 1989, the pledge of allegiance to the Communist Party was deleted from the Czechoslovak military oath as a direct consequence of the new legislation eliminating the leading role of the Communist Party from Czechoslovakia's constitution. The so-called Instructions for Ideological Work in the Armed Forces were invalidated, and the mandatory instruction in Marxism-Leninism at military high schools and colleges was abolished.[35] After December 6, 1989, Czechoslovak soldiers no longer required permission to travel abroad, while officers with security clearances could apply to their immediate superiors for a permit to go abroad, rather than having to go through the cumbersome bureaucracy of the Ministry of Defense.

The army became partially depoliticized. On December 15, 1989, Vacek announced that he had decided to cancel all Communist Party operations inside Czechoslovakia's armed forces. As of December 31, 1989, all party organizations were banned from the army, the Border Guards units, and the armed detachments of the Ministry of Internal Affairs. In the same month, Vacek moved to accommodate additional demands from the opposition, which had called for the elimination of all political instruction from the military, the replacement of political officers with priests, and a new law allowing for alternative service for conscientious objectors.[36] In contrast to the approach taken by the Poles, whereby all political activity in the armed forces was banned, the Czechoslovaks opted for a formula that allows military personnel to belong to nonpolitical organizations, such as the Military Forum or military trade unions, as long as they refrain from campaigning directly for political parties.

Prior to Vaclav Havel's election as Czechoslovakia's president, the Czechoslovak senior officer corps had already undergone a limited purge. In his capacity as the country's interim president, Prime Minister Marian Calfa appointed Major General Anton Slimak as the new chief of the General Staff, with a rank of deputy defense minister, and replaced Deputy Defense Minister Lieutenant General Emil Liska with Major General Rudolf Duchacek; Duchacek was subsequently dismissed by Havel in November 1990 as part of the restructuring of the Czechoslovak Ministry of Defense undertaken by the new Defense Minister Lubos Dobrovsky. Calfa also fired three heads of the Czechoslovak army's Main Political Administration, as well as the commander of the military-political college in Bratislava, Lieutenant General Jiri Reindl; all of the dismissed officers were also retired from active duty.[37]

In 1990 the Czechoslovak federal parliament passed a new law on military service. The new law reduced compulsory military service from twenty-four to eighteen months and gave conscientious objectors the option of performing twenty-seven months of nonmilitary duty. It disallowed membership in a political party for the duration of service and limited the government's ability to use the armed forces for internal security purposes. It also prohibited drafting women in peacetime, which the Law No. 92 of 1949 had permitted, while making provisions for volunteer military service by women. The new law also guaranteed freedom of religion to all military personnel, allowed priests to enter military installations, and permitted soldiers who were not on duty to attend Sunday mass, if they chose to do so. In addition, every draftee was guaranteed a month's leave during his eighteen months of service. The new law prohibited the employment of soldiers as free labor on civilian projects, unless lives or important national property were at risk; all decisions concerning the internal deployment of army troops became the prerogative of the president of the republic as the commander-in-chief of the Czechoslovak armed forces.[38] At the time, the federal parliament also voted to rename the "Czechoslovak People's Army" simply the "Czechoslovak Army," in order to emphasize its regained national character and its primary loyalty to the parliament and the federal government.[39] The parliament also asked the Ministry of Defense to submit a proposal for a new military doctrine.

MILITARY REFORM: DOBROVSKY'S TENURE

General Miroslav Vacek was dismissed from the post of defense minister on October 17, 1990. Vacek, who had been compromised by his extensive ties to the former communist regime, was briefly retained as an adviser at the Ministry of Defense and was subsequently retired in February 1991. In October 1990 Vacek was replaced by Lubos Dobrovsky, formerly a deputy foreign minister and the Foreign Ministry's spokesman. Dobrovsky's appointment marked the first time in Czechoslovakia's postwar history that its army was led by a civilian. A prominent former dissident who had been expelled from the Czechoslovak Communist Party after the Prague Spring of 1968, Dobrovsky was instrumental in organizing the Civic Forum and transforming it into the leader of the "Velvet Revolution" in November 1989. In addition to Dobrovsky, another civilian in the Ministry of Defense was Antonin Rasek, the deputy defense minister for culture and education. Rasek had been chosen for the position by Prime Minister Marian Calfa in December 1989.

Dobrovsky's appointment as Czechoslovakia's defense minister led to a further purge of the senior officer corps. Dobrovsky retained General Anton Slimak as the chief of the General Staff for a year and a half, until May 1991. On November 2, 1990, Havel decided that Dobrovsky would henceforth have two deputies: Lieutenant General Anton Slimak, who thus far had been Dobrovsky's first deputy, and Lieutenant General Imrich Andrejcak, who had been commander of the Eastern Military Zone. At the same time, Havel dismissed Lieutenant General Rudolf Duchacek, Lieutenant General Josef Vincenc, and Major General Ondrej Kubizniak from the posts of deputy defense ministers.[40]

Less than a month after his appointment as Czechoslovakia's defense minister, Dobrovsky went public with his plans for continued military reform. Testifying on November 5, 1990, before the Defense and Security Committees of the two houses of the Czechoslovak federal parliament, Dobrovsky outlined his program for creating a smaller semiprofessional army by the year 2005.[41] The outline included the gradual reduction of the army's numerical strength as well as the shortening of compulsory military service to one year from the current eighteen months. Dobrovsky set the target figure for the army at 140,000. He argued that since the mass departures of career soldiers in the preceding months had already reduced the size of the army to barely over 150,000, the target figure of 140,000 would not be difficult to attain. Dobrovsky announced the suspension of the vetting of the military for their past political record but spoke strongly in favor of continuing the purge of the old-style communists from the former military intelligence and counterintelligence service. He also announced a 10 percent reduction in the military budget for 1991, which would amount to a 15 to 16 percent reduction in defense spending after taking into account the projected inflation rate. In his testimony before the parliament, Dobrovsky came out strongly in favor of the continued professionalization of the army, projecting that the percentage of the professional military in Czechoslovakia's armed forces would go up in the near future from the current 35 percent level to 42 percent.

In the course of his testimony, Dobrovsky also disclosed the expected ceilings on Czechoslovakia's conventional weapons adopted in accordance with the November 3, 1990, Warsaw Pact agreement. The compromise allowed Czechoslovakia to have 1,435 tanks (against the original 3,832), 1,430 infantry vehicles (1,920), 620 armored personnel carriers (3,047), 1,150 artillery pieces (3,243), 40 rockets (81), 1,032 antitank weapons (1,127), 315 combat aircraft (430), and 75 helicopters (134).[42] The number of combat aircraft was further reduced in February 1991 by a decision of Czechoslovakia's Defense Council, which decreed that as of December 31, 1991, the Air Force would operate only 270 aircraft, with the balance of the planes allowed under the Treaty on Conventional Armed Forces in Europe (CFE) limitations kept in storage.[43]

Dobrovsky's testimony was followed by a November 7, 1990, official statement on the military reform program, delivered during a press briefing at the Ministry of Defense by Miroslav Purkrabek, an adviser to one of the deputy defense ministers. Purkrabek confirmed that the army would be reduced by 60,000 men in total, with the share of professionals in the army increasing to 43 percent by the year 1993. The ministry expected that by 1997 the share of professional soldiers and officers in the army would rise to 60 percent of the total. The decision on the ultimate size of the Czechoslovak army will be made in the context of the future international situation. Depending on circumstances, around the year 2000 the army will be 75 to 78 percent professional. Purkrabek emphasized that the transition to a professional army will be expensive but that the plan constituted the best option for Czechoslovakia in light of its small population as well as the growing complexity of modern equipment. Deputy Defense Minister for Education and Culture Antonin Rasek disclosed that a growing number of draftees in the Czechoslovak army were unable to operate some of the more sophisticated military hardware and that this trend would only deepen unless more professionals were brought into the armed forces.[44]

The 1990 military reform also restructured the Border Guards (*Pohranicni Straz*; PS), which prior to 1989 had been formally subordinated to the Ministry of Defense and used to guard Czechoslovakia's frontier with Germany and Austria, and the Border Units of Public Security (*Pohranicni Oddily*; PO), which had been subordinated to the Interior Ministry and used to guard the borders with former Warsaw Pact countries. Already in January 1990, President Havel submitted a law to the parliament that removed these troops from under the control of the interior and defense ministries and subordinated them directly to the president's authority. Havel also announced that by the end of 1992 Czechoslovakia would establish a professional border police of about 2,000 officers.

Czechoslovakia's defense spending has declined rapidly since 1989. Already in February 1990, then Defense Minister General Miroslav Vacek announced that Czechoslovakia planned to cut the 1990 military budget of sixty billion korunas by 10 percent. He also promised to make the military budget public before the end of the year. Vacek's press conference statements were followed by Premier Calfa's announcement, also made in February, telling the press that the government decided to increase the planned reduction in defense spending to about 12 percent for the fiscal year 1990; this was confirmed in March 1990 by Finance Minister Vaclav Klaus, who disclosed that the military budget would go down by 12.5 percent relative to the figures prepared by the former communist government. The second round of military budget cuts came shortly after Defense Minister Lubos Dobrovsky took office in November 1990. Dobrovsky revealed that the budget would again be reduced by another 10 percent in 1991.

SEMIPROFESSIONAL ARMY: MILITARY REFORM THROUGH 2005

The Czechoslovak army is the second largest in East Central Europe. The current plans for its modernization extend into the year 2005.[45] This long-term military reform program, adopted by the Ministry of Defense in late 1990, calls for a three-stage transformation to a smaller semiprofessional army. The initial phase of the reform is to be completed by 1993, the second phase by 1996–1997, and the final phase by the year 2005.[46] According to Defense Minister Lubos Dobrovsky, "the goal is to professionalize the army" and to bring about its "thorough democratization and humanization."[47]

The first phase of the reform is considered crucial to the success of the overall program. It calls for a 60,000 cut in the size of the Czechoslovak army between 1990 and 1993. In effect, by 1993 the army would have gone down from about 200,000 to 140,000, with the duration of service for draftees reduced from twenty-four to eighteen months and for university graduates from eighteen to twelve months.[48] The new military doctrine, adopted by the federal parliament in 1991, stipulates a 25 percent cut in the size of the army by the end of 1992.[49]

While the first phase of the reform concentrates on personnel, the second phase, running from 1993 through 1996–1997, will focus primarily on reductions in the overall number of weapons systems and the badly needed modernization of equipment. In April 1991, Czechoslovakia negotiated with the other members of the "Group of Six"—the former WTO—the ceilings on particular weapons systems to be permitted to Czechoslovakia within the overall Vienna and Paris CFE limits. By the end of 1993, Czechoslovakia expects to have the remaining differences concerning the numbers of individual weapons systems allocated its army resolved through further negotiations with its former Warsaw Pact allies.

The third and final phase of the reform program will focus primarily on transforming the army into a semiprofessional force. As stipulated in the new Czechoslovak military doctrine, the army will rely on draftees for no more than 60 percent of its personnel needs, with 40 percent being filled by professional soldiers and officers. Depending on a successful transformation of the country's economic system and Czechoslovakia's overall economic performance, the Ministry of Defense may ask the parliament to authorize the reversal of this ratio—that is, for a 60 percent professional army. The new system will also allow draftees to remain in the army as professionals, if they choose to, by signing a contract for a three- to five-year period of extended military service. As a result, by the year 2005 the Czechoslovak army will have entire units composed exclusively of professional soldiers, NCOs, and officers.[50]

Compared to Poland and Hungary, the Czechoslovak army is the closest of the three to achieving the goal of building a largely professional army. The reform program calls for the transition to a professional force to begin in 1995, with conscription to be substantially limited by the year 2000.

CIVILIAN CONTROL AND PARTIAL DEPOLITICIZATION

In addition to the reduction in personnel and equipment, the 1990–1991 military reform in Czechoslovakia also addressed the core question of civilian control over the military. Already in 1990 the Czechoslovak government decided to restructure the administration of the country's defense establishment. The so-called Commission of Defense, formerly an agency of the Communist Party of Czechoslovakia, was dissolved after the collapse of the old regime. Shortly thereafter, the reconstituted State Defense Council was charged with the preparation of a new military defense doctrine. On May 22, 1990, the government announced that the new doctrine would be defensive and would affirm that Czechoslovakia "harbors no aggressive intentions against any of its neighbors."[51]

The country's three defense councils, the Czech, Slovak, and State (federal), were reformed in February 1990. On February 9, 1990, President Vaclav Havel dismissed all members of the State Defense Council except for General Miroslav Vacek and appointed Prime Minister Marian Calfa as the council's chairman and Deputy Prime Minister Valter Komarek as the deputy chairman. Other key members of the State Defense Council appointed by Havel at the time included Foreign Minister Jiri Dienstbier, Czech Prime Minister Petr Pithart, and Interior Minister Richard Sacher.[52] Havel followed up three months later with a formal request to the federal parliament to make the federal prime minister automatically the chairman of the State Defense Council. As part of the organizational reform program, the chairman of the State Defense Council was given the authority to appoint the members and the chairmen of the Czech and Slovak defense councils. In April 1990, Prime Minister Calfa appointed the new Slovak Defense Council, chaired by Federal Deputy Prime Minister Milan Cic. In 1991 Czechoslovakia's three defense councils, the Czech Defense Council, the Slovak Defense Council, and the State Defense Council, were further reorganized to bring in additional government officials, including several ministers. The State Defense Council was instrumental in the drafting of the country's new military doctrine. Another round of reorganization of the defense councils is planned for 1993.

A further step toward greater civilian control over the military was taken in December 1990, when the Czechoslovak government reviewed the proposal to establish the Armed Forces General Inspectorate, a specialized body of the federal parliament charged with the overall supervision of the army. Under the proposal, the general inspector would answer both to the parliament and to the republic's president.[53]

As part of the campaign to depoliticize the armed forces, the Military Political Academy of Klement Gottwald in Bratislava was shut down in December 1989 and replaced with a Military Higher Pedagogical School.[54] In contrast to the Polish solution, which prohibits the military from belonging to any political organization, the Czechoslovak government has permitted political groups to operate in the armed forces. In 1991 there were seven such political organizations, the most important among them being the Military Forum, formed on December 5, 1989, as a counterpart to the Civic Forum; the Military Revival Association; the Association of Slovak Soldiers (registered in Slovakia on January 17, 1991); and the Free Legion, a right-wing organization of military and former military personnel formed in mid-1990. In October 1990, the Free Legion was temporarily suspended and its members transferred to the army reserves on the orders of Defense Minister Lubos Dobrovsky, but subsequently the Ministry of

Defense reinstated its members.[55] In early 1991 the Czechoslovak Army Career Soldiers Union, the largest of the seven organizations operating within the army with a membership of 17,000, filed for admission to "Euromil," the European Association of Military Unions.[56]

The process of purging the armed forces of communist influences has also included the removal from military manuals of all references to the Communist Party. Marxism-Leninism has been dropped altogether from the curriculum at Czechoslovak military schools. Instead, the Ministry of Defense introduced special seminars devoted to the discussion of domestic and international political events. As of January 2, 1990, all Communist Party cells in the Czechoslovak armed forces have been abolished. Also since January 1990, the form "comrade" has been replaced with "sir" as the proper form of address in the military, to follow the change in the name of the armed forces from the "Czechoslovak People's Army" to simply the "Czechoslovak Army."

In 1991 the administrative structure of the Czechoslovak Ministry of Defense was overhauled to increase the degree of civilian control over the army. The appointment of Lubos Dobrovsky, a civilian, as the country's defense minister marked a clear break with the past practice of giving the post to army officers. The Ministry of Defense has been reorganized into three departments: (1) the Economic Planning Department, (2) the Strategic Planning Department, and (3) the Social Affairs Department. It has been made completely independent of the army's General Staff and has become more like the other civilian agencies of the federal government. In addition, several changes have been introduced in the structure of the General Staff itself, the most important among them being the dual appointment of the chief of the General Staff as the commander-in-chief of the armed forces. As a result, the chief of the General Staff has gained control over the day-to-day operation of the Czechoslovak army, with the president of the republic retaining authority as the supreme military commander. In May 1991, General Karel Pezel was appointed the army's new chief of the General Staff in place of General Anton Slimak, who was retained in the Ministry of Defense as an adviser on strategic planning. Slimak's effective retirement was symbolic of the Ministry of Defense's commitment to remove senior officers politically tainted by their work for the former communist regime. As of mid-1991, over 50 percent of all senior Czechoslovak officers had been retired, bringing the number of active duty Czechoslovak officers with a rank of general to less than fifty.[57]

In addition to personnel changes, the government moved to improve the conditions of military service. In May 1991, Defense Minister Lubos Dobrovsky submitted to the Federal Assembly a package of military laws defining the service conditions for Czechoslovakia's soldiers and officers. One of the new laws sets a minimum ten-year service period for professional career military in place of the former traditional age limit for each rank. Another new law on military discipline expands the appeal process and reduces the maximum length of disciplinary imprisonment from twenty-one to fourteen days.[58]

NEW MILITARY DOCTRINE

The new military doctrine was formally adopted by the Czechoslovak Federal Assembly and made public in March 1991. The document reaffirms the principle of civilian control over the military, with the Federal Assembly being the supervisor over the entire military reform process. The new doctrine bases the country's defense on the principle of "reasonable defensive sufficiency." The army's primary task is to defend Czechoslovakia's national sovereignty and frontiers in accordance with "the spirit of the United Nations Charter and in the context of the emerging European security system."[59] The doctrine emphasizes that the army cannot operate outside the country's territory. Essential to the defense of Czechoslovakia's borders is a redeployment of forces within the country, so as to "provide for equal defense in every direction, with equal distribution of forces in both republics."[60]

The Czechoslovak army's principal goal is to provide for a balanced territorial defense in place of the former westward concentration against NATO. By the end of October 1991, one tank division and one mechanized division, or between 38 and 39 percent of all Czechoslovak troops, will be deployed along the country's eastern border. The redeployment will be completed by 1993 to coincide with the first stage of reform leading to a semiprofessional military. Following the relocation of its army bases to the east, Czechoslovakia will have troops stationed along its Soviet border for the first time since World War II.[61]

The redeployment of troops on Czechoslovakia's territory, mandated by the new military doctrine, is based on the general assumption that threat to the country's security can come from any direction. The change has led to a redrawing of the country's military districts. During its membership in the Warsaw Pact, Czechoslovakia had two military districts, the Western Military Zone and the Eastern Military Zone, with the bulk of the army and most of the air force stationed in the western part of the country; the eastern part of Czechoslovakia had virtually no defenses in place. In the late spring of 1991, the Czechoslovak army's General Staff moved to draft new defense plans, including the establishment of three military districts:

(1) the Bohemian Military District, with headquarters in Tabor; (2) the Moravian Military District, with headquarters in Olomouc; and (3) the Slovakian Military District, with headquarters in Trencin. The air force and air defense headquarters will remain in Prague.[62] The General Staff plans to complete the changeover to the new military districts by 1993. In the process, the old army headquarters in Pribram and Pisek will be closed down. In case of war, the three military districts will constitute a skeleton of three Czechoslovak army groups. If in the future the army continues to shrink in size, however, its organizational structure may change to the corps system similar to the one used by the Hungarian army.

In 1991 the Czechoslovak General Staff also drew up plans for the levels of troop deployment in each of the three new districts. In the past, Czechoslovakia's armed forces were organized in four armies, including three operational armies (two in the Western Military Zone and one in the Eastern Military Zone) and the staff structure of a reserve army. Under the new system, each of the three military districts will have one full-strength division and one low-readiness-level division; the overall command for all army units in the district will rest with the district's military commander. The three commanders will be directly subordinated to the chief of the General Staff, who will also be the commander-in-chief of the army. The air and air defense forces deployed throughout the three districts will be under the direct control of the chief of the General Staff.

The redeployment of forces began in 1991; the General Staff estimates that by the middle of 1992 about 38 percent of the federation's armed forces will be stationed in Slovakia. In addition, in line with the new military doctrine, the Czechoslovak armed forces abandoned all nuclear battlefield training and have focused primarily on training for a limited conventional war. The new military training program emphasizes defense operations par excellence, with the stipulation that the Czechoslovak army will not advance into another country, limiting its task to the expulsion of the invader from the home territory.

WEAPONS MODERNIZATION AND REGIONAL COOPERATION

In order to implement the new operational defense doctrine, Czechoslovakia needs a small, highly mobile modern army. In the immediate future, most of the Czechoslovak equipment will remain Soviet-made or Soviet-licensed. While the General Staff expects that eventually the army will be able to purchase Western equipment, for the rest of the decade the shrinking defense budget will make large-scale reequipment with Western weapons virtually impossible. Czechoslovakia's defense budget for 1991 was reduced by 9.4 percent relative to 1989; in absolute terms defense spending went down from thirty-four to thirty-one billion korunas.[63]

The country hopes to earn badly needed foreign exchange to modernize the army through the selective export of arms. In the past, weapons export was a major source of revenue for the government; as late as 1987 Czechoslovakia ranked fourth in the world as a weapons exporter, after the Soviet Union, the United States, and France.[64] While under the new conditions weapons exports will be much more selective than previously, Czechoslovakia will continue selling weapons abroad on a hard currency basis. On April 26, 1991, Czechoslovak Prime Minister Marian Calfa announced, upon his return from a three-day visit to Nigeria, that Prague will supply Lagos with twenty-seven two-seat L-39 Albatros military trainer aircraft. The contract with Nigeria includes the delivery of the aircraft, a repair shop, spare parts, and training, and it is to be paid for by Nigeria with the delivery of one million tons of oil to Czechoslovakia. Defense Minister Lubos Dobrovsky disclosed that, in addition to the L-39 sale, the Czechoslovaks have been negotiating to build an ammunition plant in Nigeria.[65]

It is likely that Czechoslovakia will continue to export weapons, especially considering the fact that in 1991 its defense industry employed close to 140,000 workers. In addition, the country has a large inventory of weapons, particularly armor and heavy trucks, which have not yet been delivered to the armed forces and which now have to be eliminated in compliance with the CFE ceilings. From the purely economic point of view, it would make more sense for the Czechoslovak government to sell these weapons abroad, instead of bearing the cost of their destruction. For this purpose, a Czechoslovak military delegation, which visited Saudi Arabia in late April 1991, included representatives from the defense industry and the Omnipol foreign trade association, which had been engaged in military sales in the past. Reportedly, Saudi Arabia expressed an interest in purchasing repair facilities for Czechoslovak equipment, in particular for the Tatra-815 trucks that had been delivered to Saudi Arabia during the Gulf War.[66] Also in late April 1991, Prague approved the sale of T-72 tanks and armored personnel carriers to Syria, despite the disapproval of the United States. In order to reduce the impact of negative publicity from the sale, Foreign Minister Jiri Dienstbier explained at the time that the sale was important domestically, as it would reduce economic hardships in Slovakia.[67] Finally, in addition to direct sales, the Czechoslovak defense industry has been attempting to reach agreements on joint weapons development with Western countries, including negotiations with

France over joint development of an armored personnel carrier for which the Czechoslovaks would provide the optical systems.[68]

In addition to its present attempts at cooperation with Western defense contractors, Czechoslovakia has a history of working with the Polish and Hungarian defense industries, including the joint Polish-Czechoslovak development of the OT-64 wheeled armored transport in the late 1950s and early 1960s. In addition to being a major supplier of weapons on the global market, Czechoslovakia has been an exporter of weapons to the region, including past deliveries of the SKOT armored personnel carriers to Poland and Hungary and the DANA 152 mm self-propelled howitzer to Poland. Although Czechoslovak Foreign Minister Jiri Dienstbier announced in January 1990 that Czechoslovakia would cease all arms exports forthwith,[69] joint weapons R&D projects with Poland and Hungary, as well as tripartite cooperation for large-volume joint weapons purchases from the West, are likely to continue in the future.

Czechoslovakia moved early to institutionalize security cooperation in the region. On January 21, 1991, it signed a five-year bilateral military agreement with Hungary. The agreement provides for the exchange of information on military exercises, troop movements, and redeployment along the two countries' borders, as well as the exchange of experience in the area of military training. A similar agreement was signed with the Poles on February 27 of the same year.

In addition to cooperation with Poland and Hungary, in 1990 and 1991 Czechoslovakia moved to build a strong relationship with a number of West European militaries, in particular with Italy and Germany. In November 1990, Defense Minister Lubos Dobrovsky hosted a visit by Italian Defense Minister Virginio Rognoni.[70] In the same month, the Czechoslovak and German armies signed an agreement on future cooperation.[71]

FUTURE REGIONAL INSTABILITY

For the remainder of the decade, a threat of direct military aggression against Czechoslovakia will remain largely hypothetical. Historically, only the Soviet Union and Germany posed such a threat and, between the two, only a reconstituted authoritarian Russian state may do so in the foreseeable future. On account of the internal turmoil in the former USSR, Prague has made it abundantly clear that it remains interested in the continued American military presence in Europe as the ultimate guarantee of stability and, indirectly, of Czechoslovakia's security. The Czechoslovak government's official view has been that America's interest in Czechoslovakia's independence will remain a powerful deterrent to the

Soviet successor states. As one Czechoslovak Foreign Ministry official put it, in the worst case scenario, the United States is considered by Prague as its court of last resort after all European security structures have failed to defuse pressure from the East.[72]

The likelihood of Germany constituting a direct military threat to Czechoslovakia is purely hypothetical at this point. The often-discussed issue of Sudetic Germans is highly unlikely to become a problem in German-Czechoslovak relations, and it will ultimately have a generational solution to it—that is, the total number of Germans who had been expelled from Czechoslovakia after World War II is likely to decline soon, as their generation is beginning to disappear from the scene. In addition, the history of German economic and cultural influence in Bohemia and Moravia will greatly enhance the process of building good German-Czechoslovak relations. Large-scale German investment in Czechoslovakia, such as the 1991 purchase of the Skoda automobile works by Volkswagen, is indicative of the direction of future relations between the two countries.

Relations with the Soviet Union's successor states pose a different set of problems. The Russian military in particular has come to regard the revolutions of 1989 and the subsequent disintegration of the Warsaw Pact as a most significant strategic setback to its position in Europe since 1945. In a political move symbolic of a new military relationship between Czechoslovakia and the former Soviet Union, the last Czechoslovak officer detailed to the Warsaw Pact Joint Command Headquarters had been recalled to Prague in February 1991.[73] It is likely, therefore, that relations between Czechoslovakia and the Soviet successor states will remain strained as long as the army continues to exert pressure on Moscow's foreign policy. In order to ameliorate the situation and improve the overall climate of relations, in mid-1991 the Czechoslovak Ministry of Defense approached the Soviet Ministry of Defense with a proposal to negotiate an interministerial agreement on technical cooperation, similar to the one Czechoslovakia had signed with Hungary in January 1991. The new agreement would be limited to the exchange of information on weapons maintenance, spare parts purchases, and so forth. As late as the summer of 1991 the Soviet side failed to respond to Prague's initiative. It is likely, however, that as the military reforms promised by Boris Yeltsin in the aftermath of the August 1991 failed coup are being implemented, including the purge of communist hard-liners from the military, relations between the two armed forces will improve.

Regional instability and ethnic tension at home are regarded by some Czechoslovak officials as the most immediate security threats to their country.[74] In that respect, Czechoslovakia's security is indirectly dependent on the successful transformation to democracy in Poland and Hungary, as well as on continuing liberalization in the former Soviet Union. Chaos and instability in the region might conceivably lead to the emergence of authoritarian regimes in the area, even if it remains highly unlikely that those regimes would be led by communists.

The threat of total chaos beyond Czechoslovakia's eastern border remains the gravest concern. If the newly created Commonwealth of Independent States fails to prevent the process of imperial disintegration from becoming a civil war among the Soviet successor states, Czechoslovakia could try to seal its sixty-five-mile-long eastern border, to prevent Soviet refugees from the East from entering the country, and then turn to the United Nations for assistance in dealing with the problem. Another daunting prospect is the flood of economic refugees from the East pouring into Czechoslovakia, when the Soviet successor states allow for unrestricted visa-free travel for its citizens.[75] Many in Prague fear that the country may be plunged into chaos if Czechoslovakia has to cope with masses of illegal immigrants from the East, while also struggling with its own domestic economic and social problems.

Another scenario that the Czechoslovaks have to consider is the threat of domestic subversion, which is a genuine concern in light of the rising tide of Slovak separatism and the tough economic times ahead. Moreover, it appears that the former communist establishment is stronger in Czechoslovakia than in Poland or Hungary, as evidenced by the voluntary turnout of 70,000 people in Prague for the communist-led celebration on May 1, 1991.[76] While today the communists do not constitute a serious threat to democracy in Czechoslovakia, they may exert greater influence in the future, if the economic reform program leads to high unemployment and a radical decline in the standard of living.

NOTES

1. Jiri Dienstbier, "Central Europe's Security," *Foreign Policy*, Summer 1991, p. 120.
2. Ibid.
3. *Atlas of Eastern Europe* (Washington, D.C.: Central Intelligence Agency, August 1990), p. 11.
4. *RFE/RL Daily Report*, May 2, 1991.
5. Interview with Svatopluk Buchlovsky, director of the Department of European Security, Foreign Ministry, Prague, April 30, 1991.
6. Interview with Maria Kostalova, director of the Department of International Economic Cooperation, Foreign Ministry, Prague, April 30, 1991.
7. "Press Reacts to Havel's 10 December Proposals," *FBIS-EEU-90-244*, December 19, 1990, p. 13.

8. *RFE/RL Daily Report*, May 23, 1991.

9. "Commentary Criticizes Czech Constitution Agreement," *FBIS-EEU-91-099*, May 22, 1991, p. 17.

10. "Slovak Prime Minister Carnogursky Interviewed," *FBIS-EEU-91-097*, May 20, 1991, p. 18.

11. "Carnogursky Promises Tolerant Government," *FBIS-EEU-91-100*, May 23, 1991, p. 9.

12. Ibid.

13. "Slovaks Underrepresented at Defense Ministry," *FBIS-EEU-91-098*, May 21, 1991, p. 11.

14. Ibid.

15. Interview with General Jiri Divis, deputy chief of Foreign Relations Department, General Staff of the Czechoslovak army, Prague, April 30, 1991.

16. Jan Obrman, "Interview with First Deputy Chief of the General Staff," *Report on Eastern Europe*, vol. 1, no. 29 (Munich: RFE/RL, July 20, 1990), pp. 14–16.

17. "Statement by the Deputy Prime Minister and Minister of Foreign Affairs of the Czech and Slovak Federal Republic Jiri Dienstbier in the Federal Assembly on April 9, 1991" (Prague: Ministry of Foreign Affairs, 1991), p. 3.

18. Interview with Svatopluk Buchlovsky, director of the Department of European Security, Foreign Ministry, Prague, April 30, 1991.

19. Czechoslovak diplomacy has insisted on using the term *cooperative* rather than *collective* in order to differentiate the new security policy design from the failed collective security arrangement of the interwar period and to emphasize the changed nature of international relations in Europe. See "Memorandum of the Czech and Slovak Federal Republic on European Security" (Prague: Ministry of Foreign Affairs, 1991).

20. "Havel against Treaty Clause," *Financial Times*, April 30, 1991.

21. *RFE/RL Daily Report*, January 22, 1991, and "Dobrovsky, Kolodziejczyk Sign Military Agreement," *FBIS-EEU-91-042*, March 4, 1991, p. 17.

22. "Council of Europe Delegation Arrives in Prague," *FBIS-EEU-91-025*, February 6, 1991, p. 20.

23. Interview with Svatopluk Buchlovsky, director of the Department of European Security, Foreign Ministry, Prague, April 30, 1991.

24. "Statement by the Deputy Prime Minister and Minister of Foreign Affairs of the Czech and Slovak Federal Republic Jiri Dienstbier in the Federal Assembly on April 9, 1991," p. 5.

25. "President Havel Comments on Summit, Laws, Gulf," *FBIS-EEU-91-033*, February 19, 1991, p. 23.

26. "FRG's Genscher Continues Prague Visit," *FBIS-EEU-90-214*, November 5, 1990, p. 16.

27. "Army Official Views New Military Doctrine," *FBIS-EEU-90-143*, July 25, 1990, p. 15.

28. "Military Delegation's U.S. Visit Seen Successful," *FBIS-EEU-90-149*, August 2, 1990, p. 14.

29. *RFE/RL Daily Report*, April 4, 1990.

30. "Havel Summarizes Conference Results," *FBIS-EEU-90-226*, November 23, 1990, p. 13.

31. "Dienstbier Stresses Summit Results," *FBIS-EEU-90-226*, November 23, 1990, p. 14.

32. "Havel Condemns Events in Riga; Pact Discussed," *FBIS-EEU-91-014*, January 22, 1991, p. 17.

33. "Statement by the Deputy Prime Minister and Minister of Foreign Affairs of the Czech and Slovak Federal Republic Jiri Dienstbier in the Federal Assembly on April 9, 1991," p. 5.

34. Interview with Svatopluk Buchlovsky, director of the Department of European Security, Foreign Ministry, Prague, April 30, 1991.

35. Jan Obrman, "Changing Conditions for the Army and the Police," *Report on Eastern Europe*, vol. 1, no. 26 (Munich: RFE/RL, January 26, 1990), p. 12.

36. Ibid., pp. 12–13.

37. Ibid., p. 13.

38. Jan Obrman, "Changes in the Armed Forces," *Report on Eastern Europe*, vol. 1, no. 14 (Munich: RFE/RL, April 6, 1990), pp. 10–11.

39. Ibid., p. 10.

40. "Havel Makes Personnel Changes in Army Command," *FBIS-EEU-90-215*, November 6, 1990, p. 10.

41. "Defense Minister Describes Future Army Structure," *FBIS-EEU-90-217*, November 8, 1990, p. 21.

42. Ibid.

43. "Havel, Calfa, Defense Council on Pacts," *FBIS-EEU-91-033*, February 19, 1991, p. 21.

44. "Professional Army Expected by Year 2000," *FBIS-EEU-90-218*, November 9, 1990, p. 10.

45. "Team to Make Army Professional Established," *FBIS-EEU-90-143*, July 25, 1990, p. 15.

46. Interview with General Jiri Divis, deputy chief of Foreign Relations Department, General Staff of the Czechoslovak army, Prague, April 30, 1991.

47. "Dobrovsky on Defense Bill Amendments," *FBIS-EEU-91-096*, May 17, 1991, p. 11.

48. Obrman, "Interview with First Deputy Chief of the General Staff," p. 15.

49. *Vojenska doktrina Ceske a Slovenske Federativni Republiky* (Prague: Federalne Zhromazdenie, 1991), p. 1.

50. Interview with General Jiri Divis, deputy chief of Foreign Relations Department, General Staff of the Czechoslovak army, Prague, April 30, 1991.

51. Czechoslovak Television, May 22, 1990.

52. "Havel Makes the Defense Council Appointments," *FBIS-EEU-90-029*, February 12, 1990, p. 20.

53. "Cabinet Discusses Monetary, Defense Issues," *FBIS-EEU-90-233*, December 4, 1990, p. 8.

54. "The JDW Interview with Major General Anton Slimak," *Jane's Defence Weekly*, March 24, 1990, p. 568.

55. "Defense Minister Lifts Ban on Officer Group," *FBIS-EEU-90-212*, November 1, 1990, p. 8.

56. "Spokesman on Pact Meeting, Gulf Equipment," *FBIS-EEU-91-031*, February 14, 1991, p. 17. "Euromil" has member unions in Austria, Belgium, Denmark, France, Germany, Ireland, Italy, and the Netherlands.

57. Interview with General Jiri Divis, deputy chief of Foreign Relations Department, General Staff of the Czechoslovak army, Prague, April 30, 1991.

58. "Dobrovsky Submits Army Laws to Federal Assembly," *FBIS-EEU-91-099*, May 22, 1991, p. 15.

59. *Vojenska doktrina Ceske a Slovenske Federativni Republiky,* p. 1.

60. Ibid., p. 2.

61. "Army Doctrine Outlines Major Tasks," *FBIS-EEU-91-020*, January 30, 1991, p. 15.

62. Interview with General Jiri Divis, deputy chief of Foreign Relations Department, General Staff of the Czechoslovak army, Prague, April 30, 1991.

63. "Defense Officials Meet Press on Budget Cuts," *FBIS-EEU-90-245*, December 20, 1990, p. 21.

64. *World Military Expenditures and Arms Transfers, 1987* (Washington, D.C.: U.S. Arms Control and Disarmament Agency, 1988), p. 30.

65. *RFE/RL Daily Report*, April 29, 1991.

66. *RFE/RL Daily Report*, April 30, 1991.

67. *RFE/RL Daily Report*, May 2, 1991.

68. Interview with Colonel Milan Stembera, Institute of International Relations, Prague, May 3, 1991.

69. Craig R. Whitney, "Prague Arms Trade to End, Foreign Minister Says," *New York Times*, January 25, 1990.

70. "Italian Defense Minister Rognoni Pays Visit," *FBIS-EEU-90-216*, November 7, 1990, p. 16.

71. "Army Accord on Business Trips Signed with FRG," *FBIS-EEU-90-219*, November 13, 1990, p. 33.

72. Interview with Jiri Pavlovsky, deputy director of the Planning and Analysis Department, Foreign Ministry, Prague, April 30, 1991.

73. Interview with Colonel Milan Stembera, Institute of International Relations, Prague, May 3, 1991.

74. Interview with Deputy Foreign Minister Martin Palous, Federal Ministry of Foreign Affairs, Prague, May 3, 1991.

75. "New Law May Prompt U.S. to Lift Trade Curbs," *Commercial Appeal*, May 22, 1991.

76. Czechoslovak Television, May 1, 1991.

5

HUNGARY'S ROAD TO WESTERN EUROPE

NATIONAL SECURITY POLICY

Since 1989 Hungary has viewed membership in established Western European institutions, with an eye to a future pan-European integration, as the best solution to its security needs. Hungary's policy rests on the premise that it can reasonably expect to share in the Western security system if it succeeds in postcommunist reconstruction and demonstrates to the West that it has left behind the region's ethnic and territorial squabbles. Faced with a latent threat from the former Soviet Union as well as the growing regional instability in the Balkans, especially the 1991 civil war in Yugoslavia, Hungary has been unequivocal in its goal to seek security guarantees from the West.

In 1990–1991 the notion of pan-European security remained a stated long-term goal for Hungary, but Budapest was considerably more pragmatic in its diplomacy than were Prague and Warsaw. In addition to market reform at home, in 1990–1991 Hungary pursued a series of diplomatic initiatives to negotiate bilateral treaties with its neighbors and to increase regional consultations with Western European countries in addition to the East Central European Triangle. The Hungarians were the first to claim tangible results in direct cooperation with the West, with the government of Jozsef Antall pursuing vigorously a new framework for cooperation with Austria and Italy. Budapest has actively promoted the Pentagonale cooperation agreement in the five Danubian basin countries, including Austria, Italy, Czechoslovakia, Yugoslavia, and Hungary. Largely due to Hungary's support, Poland's membership in the Pentagonale became effective in July 1991.

In 1990–1991 Hungary's strong pro-Western orientation was synonymous with the rejection of the Warsaw Pact. Budapest was the most vocal among the Triangle states in its demand for an end to the Warsaw Treaty Organization. In an interview for Hungarian television after the decisive June 7, 1990, Moscow meeting of the Warsaw Pact Political Consultative Committee, Hungarian Defense Minister Lajos Fur emphasized his government's determination to leave the Pact altogether.[1] Following the June 14–15, 1990, meeting of the WTO defense ministers in Berlin, Fur further outlined the official principles of his country's national security policy in the 1990s, including (1) close links to a European security system, (2) regional cooperation, and (3) bilateralism. Fur also disclosed that by mid-1990 it had become Hungary's official policy neither to participate in joint Warsaw Pact exercises nor to permit them on its territory. At the same time, Hungary made it known to the Soviets that it would no longer take part in joint long-term planning for Warsaw Pact combined force development and that beginning in the fall of 1990 it would withdraw its eighteen-member military staff from Moscow.[2] In short, already in the summer of 1990 Budapest was treating the Warsaw Pact as an organization that would have no place in the future Hungarian and European security system.

The Western orientation of Hungary's security policy manifested itself openly in July 1990. Although Budapest affirmed its general commitment to a pan-European security arrangement based on the CSCE structures, it showed little faith in its short-term viability. Hungarian Foreign Minister Geza Jeszenszky argued at the time that the CSCE would provide the requisite security framework only if it "could be transformed into an institution more capable of action than the United Nations, perhaps a more effective version of the UN or of its Security Council."[3] In contrast to its skepticism about the CSCE, in 1990 and 1991 Hungary repeatedly explored its prospects for association with existing Western security organizations, in particular NATO. In that respect, Hungary has been the driving influence among the Triangle states in their rejection of the Moscow axis and their search for a place in Western Europe.

PRESSURE FOR THE DISSOLUTION OF THE WARSAW PACT

The Hungarians were the first among former Soviet satellites to broach the subject of unilaterally withdrawing from the Warsaw Pact. Already in January 1990 Hungarian Socialist Party (HSP) Chairman Rezso Nyers announced that Hungary was no longer a part of the Eastern Bloc and that it was interested in promoting stronger cooperation within the zone of Central Europe, including West Germany, Czechoslovakia, Yugoslavia, and later Poland, Romania, and Bulgaria. Nyers also called on the Soviets to withdraw from Hungary as soon as possible.[4] Subsequently, Budapest negotiated an agreement for the complete withdrawal of Soviet forces by June 30, 1991, which was signed on March 10, 1990, in Moscow by the Soviet and Hungarian foreign ministers.

Throughout 1990 and 1991 Budapest was adamant in its opposition to the continuation of the Warsaw Pact in any form. In June 1990, Prime Minister Jozsef Antall suggested publicly that the Pact's military structures had to be completely eliminated at the latest by the end of 1991.[5] A month later, Hungary further announced that it intended to leave the Warsaw Pact altogether after the completion of the Soviet troop withdrawal from its territory; as such, the date for its departure from the Pact was tentatively set for December 1991.[6] The Hungarian government's actions, taken with the full approval of the parliament, reflected a broad consensus in the country that continued Soviet presence in Hungary and Moscow's overall control over the region were incompatible with Hungary's fundamental national interest to become a part of Western Europe. This implicit security policy objective put Budapest on a collision course with Moscow over the future of the Warsaw Treaty Organization.

During the critical June 7, 1990, Moscow summit of the Warsaw Pact, the Hungarians, in cooperation with the Polish and the Czecho-slovak delegations, pushed hard for the dissolution of the alliance, while reaffirming that it was not their goal to exclude the Soviet Union from the future united Europe.[7] Hungarian Prime Minister Jozsef Antall asserted that the Warsaw Pact's military organization "lost its meaning [and] it ought to be gradually eliminated by the end of 1991."[8] Next, on June 8, 1990, after talks with Soviet Defense Minister Dmitriy T. Yazov, Hungarian Defense Minister Lajos Fur announced that he had informed the Soviets of Hungary's decision not to take part in the Pact's military maneuvers scheduled for 1990. In addition, the Hungarian armed forces would no longer be subordinated to the Warsaw Pact Joint Command. Fur also made it known to the Soviets that Hungary intended to leave the Warsaw Pact even if no formula for its formal dissolution was found.[9] A Western orientation of Hungarian security policy was unmistakable. Speaking for the Hungarian delegation, Antall emphasized that Budapest supported "the idea of a single Europe and [sympathized] with the Atlantic thought, which regards the role of the United States and Canada as important from the point of view of European security."[10]

Budapest's position on the dissolution of the Warsaw Treaty Organization was reaffirmed by Defense Minister Fur a week after the Moscow summit at a press conference following a closed meeting of the Pact's defense ministers, held in Berlin between June 14 and June 15, 1990. At the time, Fur discussed briefly the Hungarian proposal concerning the procedures for the WTO's dissolution. He announced that it was Hungary's goal to leave the WTO in a negotiated fashion, that the Pact's remaining institutions should become subordinated to a new pan-European security system, that the WTO Joint High Command should be eliminated forthwith, and that the WTO member-states should welcome NATO's statement of May 1990, which declared that the Atlantic Alliance no longer regarded the WTO members as an enemy.[11] In short, Budapest's position throughout 1990–1991 was that intra-WTO negotiations could concern only the procedures for the Pact's dissolution and that the very question of whether the organization ought to be preserved in any form had already become a moot point.

While insisting that the Warsaw Pact had to go, Budapest fully appreciated the advantage of a general agreement on its dissolution over a unilateral Hungarian withdrawal. It remained very well aware throughout the 1990–1991 negotiations that a unilateral decision to leave the Warsaw Pact could generate a dangerous crisis in Hungary's relations with the Soviet Union. The most secure exit route from the WTO led through a jointly negotiated settlement, which would present the Soviets with a unified policy stance by the Triangle and the other member-states, and would force Moscow to yield on the issue. Hence, in July 1990, Hungarian Foreign Minister Geza Jeszenszky emphasized that Budapest's fundamental objective was to achieve "the Pact's dissolution by common consent, as this would be preferable to being forced to take unilateral, even if negotiated, action."[12]

Jeszenszky's attempts to find an acceptable diplomatic formula for the dissolution of the Pact notwithstanding, the Soviets viewed the Hungarian position on the Warsaw Treaty Organization as an unfriendly, if not downright hostile, act which undermined Moscow's efforts to preserve the WTO as a political organization under its continued control. Budapest's stance on the Pact's future contributed to growing tension in negotiations on the modalities of the Soviet troop withdrawal from Hungary. Frustrated in their efforts during the Moscow and Berlin talks to bring the Hungarians around to accept their policy on the WTO's future, the Soviets resorted to direct political pressure. On June 14, 1990, the Hungarian news agency MTI reported that the Soviets were now demanding from Hungary a payment of 2.7 billion rubles (50 billion forints) in compensation for the buildings left behind by the withdrawing Soviet troops. Budapest responded with a counterclaim against the USSR for 10 billion forints in compensation to Hungary for damages caused by the Soviet army to Hungarian installations and the environment. The argument over compensation became so intense that the Hungarians were beginning to fear Moscow might simply appropriate as compensation the 800 million rubles ($720 million) current account surplus that Hungary had accumulated in 1989 in its trade with the USSR.[13]

The Soviet-Hungarian quarrel over compensation for the Red Army installations in Hungary became particularly intense in early July 1990, after the commander of the Soviet Southern Group of Forces, Colonel General Matvey Burlakov, threatened publicly to suspend the withdrawal of his troops if Hungary continued to refuse payment for the buildings the Soviets would leave behind. Still, Budapest held firm. The Hungarian government responded to Burlakov's ultimatum with indignation, warning that such tactics would constitute a "grave threat" to the future relations between Hungary and the Soviet Union.[14] In order to underscore the seriousness of the situation, Prime Minister Jozsef Antall called in the Soviet ambassador to Hungary to demand an explanation of Burlakov's behavior. In turn, Moscow retaliated by reducing its oil and natural gas deliveries to Hungary and by unilaterally suspending in August 1990 an agreement on border traffic between the two countries.[15]

Ultimately, Soviet pressure in the summer of 1990 failed to change the Hungarian position on the future of the Warsaw Pact, while contributing to a considerable deterioration in relations between the two countries. After the June 1990 Berlin meeting of WTO defense ministers, Hungary remained committed to the policy of pushing for the dissolution of the Pact. In the second half of 1990, however, Budapest began to moderate its rhetoric somewhat in part due to behind-the-scenes intervention by NATO. While supporting Hungary's goal of dissolving the WTO forthwith, the United States and Western Europe feared that constant pressure from Hungary could lead to a Soviet backlash in Moscow's arms control negotiations with the West. In the summer of 1990, Defense Minister Fur openly admitted that NATO had requested Hungary not to leave the Warsaw Pact unilaterally at the time because such a move might undermine the Vienna negotiations on conventional arms reductions, which by then had entered their final phase.[16] Apparently, NATO feared that a sudden disintegration of the Pact might increase Moscow's sense of insecurity at a critical moment in East-West relations, leading to a hardening of the Soviet position on German reunification. NATO's views, undoubtedly known to Poland and Czechoslovakia as well, in part explain the Polish and Czechoslovak circumspection on the issue of the Pact's future, despite their private support for Hungary's position. Hungarian Prime Minister Antall complained after the June 1990 Moscow summit of the WTO Political Consultative Committee that during the meeting only Hungary was firm in its official demand for the complete dissolution of the Pact, while reportedly the Poles expressed their interest in maintaining the military organization for some time, with the Czechoslovaks wanting to reform the organization to emphasize its political functions.[17] The combined influence of NATO and the Soviets on the East Central Europeans helped prolong the Pact's existence for almost another year.

In order to defuse some of the tension resulting from its outspokenness on the question of leaving the Warsaw Pact, the Hungarian government moved after the June 1990 defense ministers meeting in Berlin to emphasize its overall security policy goals, such as joining a future all-European security system, developing regional cooperation, and negotiating bilateral agreements with its neighbors. Apparently, Budapest's goal was to place its decision to withdraw from the Warsaw Pact in a broader context of changes taking place in Europe as a whole and thus to deflect the charges that it had acted precipitously. During his June 1990 visit to West Germany, Prime Minister Jozsef Antall described Hungary's position on the future of the Pact as one that simply recognized the new political reality in the region. According to Antall, the reason Hungary no longer intended to remain in the WTO was not because of the country's hostility to the USSR but because under the new political conditions in the region "the military organization of the Warsaw Pact has lost its meaning."[18] Antall argued that since the Warsaw Pact could not be modernized or democratized, Hungary's insistence on its disbanding was nothing more than a logical course of action dictated by the new situation.

Budapest's policy on the future of the Warsaw Pact remained consistent throughout 1990–1991, although in 1991 Hungary no longer threatened a unilateral withdrawal and the government's rhetoric became substantially toned down after the aborted Soviet crackdown in Lithuania and Latvia in January 1991. Amidst the tension in the region generated by the killings in the Baltics, Budapest maintained a firm position on the WTO's dissolution by common consent of all member-states. It also continued to negotiate with Moscow on bilateral trade issues, a border-crossing agreement, and a future bilateral relations treaty.

Gorbachev's decision in the spring of 1991 to yield on the Warsaw Pact issue was ultimately a vindication of Hungary's position, even though Soviet-Hungarian relations remained strained. Following the March 1991 WTO summit, which led to the dissolution of the Warsaw Pact, the

Hungarians concentrated their efforts on removing the remaining vestiges of the Warsaw Treaty Organization—that is, the treaty itself—and on preventing the Soviet Union from replacing the Pact with follow-up bilateral treaty agreements that would restrict Hungary's ability to pursue independent security policy and its goal of joining Western Europe.

HUNGARIAN-SOVIET TENSION IN 1991

At the center of the tense Hungarian-Soviet relationship in 1991 lies the question of a new bilateral treaty agreement; in particular, the Soviet Union's insistence that Budapest accept a special clause prohibiting Hungary from joining any security alliance that Moscow deems hostile to its security interests. As in the case of Poland and Czechoslovakia, if accepted, the clause would undermine Hungary's national security policy and give the Soviets veto power over Hungary's future relations with the West. In the course of the 1991 round of negotiations on the future of bilateral relations between the two countries, Budapest consistently rejected the security clause as incompatible with Hungarian *raison d'état*.

Hungary's refusal to accept the clause had practical as well as symbolic implications. On the one hand, it kept open for Budapest the option of joining Western European security structures, including the Western European Union or NATO. In effect, it confirmed the basic pro-Western orientation of Budapest's foreign policy. On the other hand, it reaffirmed the country's determination to protect its newly regained sovereignty, as symbolized by the insistence on the right to develop its own national security policy based on the stated principle of equidistance between Hungary and all its neighbors. Since Hungary's ultimate foreign policy objective has been full integration with Western Europe, the rejection of the Soviet security clause as a poorly disguised attempt at the "Finlandization" of Hungary symbolized Budapest's formal refusal to accept the sphere of influence principle in European politics.

In 1991 Hungary responded to Soviet pressure on the security clause with a proposal of its own. The Hungarian formula for a workable mutual security guarantee under a bilateral treaty with the USSR rested on the principle of "negative security guarantees." Already in the fall of 1990, as the future of the Warsaw Pact was being debated, Budapest proposed that all members of the WTO sign a treaty that would commit each country not to allow its territory to be used as a launching ground for aggression against its neighbors. Budapest insisted on using specifically the term *aggression* to include subversion, political and economic pressure, as well as an all-out military attack.[19] The Hungarian proposal, which would require the former

Soviet satellites to extend a negative security guarantee to the USSR, was rejected by Moscow as inadequate, forcing a deadlock in its bilateral negotiations with the Triangle states, as Hungary's position was shared by the Poles and the Czechoslovaks. In the event, Budapest charged that the Soviet position on the regional security issue was a veiled attempt to reclaim through diplomatic channels the influence that Moscow had lost after the withdrawal of its troops from Hungarian territory. It also maintained that, if the Soviets were to succeed in forcing their security clause onto their former satellites, it would amount to the de facto restoration of the two-bloc system in Europe, marking an end to all plans for European integration.

In addition to the security clause issue, in 1991 Soviet-Hungarian relations were rocked by an escalating feud over bilateral trade. According to Hungary's International Economic Relations Minister Bela Kadar, trade turnover with the Soviet Union in 1991 was only one-seventh its level in 1988.[20] In addition to a squabble over the assets of the defunct Council for Mutual Economic Assistance (COMECON)—formally dissolved on June 28, 1991—the Soviet inability to pay for Hungarian exports severely strained relations between the two countries. As of May 1991, the Soviet Union owed approximately 1.7 billion transferable rubles to Hungary. According to Lajos Berenyi, deputy state secretary for the Hungarian Ministry of International Economic Relations, Moscow had refused to negotiate an installment repayment plan.[21] The problem of Soviet-Hungarian trade was further aggravated by Mikhail Gorbachev's ban on barter trade, which had been a direct result of the Sofia 1990 COMECON decision to conduct all trade in the region on a hard currency basis.

It was indicative of how much Soviet-Hungarian relations deteriorated between 1990 and 1991 that the first meeting of the two countries' foreign ministers took place only on May 22, 1991, a year after the new Hungarian government had taken office. Prior to Geza Jeszenszky's first official visit to Moscow in 1991, the only other high-level Hungarian-Soviet meeting had been a brief encounter between Soviet President Mikhail Gorbachev and Hungarian Prime Minister Jozsef Antall during the Warsaw Pact Political Consultative Committee meeting in Moscow in June 1990. Moreover, the 1991 Jeszenszky-Bessmertnykh Moscow round did not lead to a significant improvement in bilateral relations. In a gesture symbolic of Hungarian solidarity with the Russian republic's effort to gain autonomy from the central bureaucracy, on the first day of his visit to Moscow and before conferring with Soviet Foreign Minister Aleksandr Bessmertnykh, Jeszenszky met with the leaders of the Russian Supreme Soviet and representatives of the Russian republic's Foreign Ministry.[22] Clearly, while

Hungary was officially committed to maintaining good relations with the Soviet Union, its real foreign policy priorities lay elsewhere.

RELATIONS WITH THE WEST

Hungary's current diplomatic efforts to come closer to the West predate the 1989 revolution and the subsequent collapse of the Warsaw Pact. In 1986 the Hungarians responded to the apparent deadlock in Soviet-American arms control negotiations by becoming the first East European country to articulate the need for a new approach to security in the region as part of a future European security system. On January 14, 1987, in Prague, Hungarian Ambassador to Czechoslovakia and the dean of the diplomatic corps in Prague Bela Kovacs declared that national security was predominantly a political task. Kovacs expressed the Hungarian position that only "a universal approach to the establishment of a system of international security shows the road towards ensuring [Hungary's] national security."[23]

Hungary's search for rapprochement with the West accelerated greatly after the collapse of communism in Eastern Europe. In 1990 and 1991 Budapest sought to develop friendly relations with the rest of Western Europe, including Germany, France, Belgium, Italy, Austria, Switzerland, and Great Britain, with Germany being the primary focus of Hungarian diplomacy. During the exodus of the East Germans in 1989, Hungary kept its borders open, and it subsequently supported German reunification. Budapest's help to the East German refugees in 1989 translated into a speedy improvement in its relations with Bonn. In August 1990, Prime Minister Jozsef Antall openly welcomed German reunification, calling it "advantageous to Hungary, as a unified Germany will offer the opportunities of a good market and close cooperation. . . . It is almost certain that a united Germany will be Hungary's number one economic partner."[24] Hungary also supported Germany's continued membership in NATO. The Hungarian position on German reunification, as expressed in 1990 by Janos Matus of the Hungarian Institute of International Affairs, was that Germany's NATO membership was a preferred solution, because it would maintain the requisite stability in the transition period.[25] On account of good Hungarian-German relations, Bonn has become for Hungary not only a potential source of foreign investment but, more important, an informal channel to NATO. Germany also became a strong supporter of Hungary's eventual membership in the EEC and other Western European institutions.

Throughout 1990 and 1991, Hungary also worked to strengthen its ties with Western political and economic institutions. It was the first among the former Soviet satellites to become a member of the Council of Europe, on November 6, 1990.[26] The Hungarians have been ardent supporters of the European Bank for Reconstruction and Development (EBRD), which was created on April 15, 1991, in London with the goal of assisting the East Europeans in making the transition to a market economy. In a development symbolic of Hungary's success in building strong ties to the Western economic system, the country's former prime minister, Miklos Nemeth, was appointed one of the EBRD's deputy chairmen.[27] The EBRD will be a principal source of credits to Hungary, which the country needs to rebuild its crumbling infrastructure.

Since 1990 Hungary has pursued aggressive policies to become a full member of the European Community at the earliest possible date. On July 13, 1990, the Hungarian government formally received the credentials of Hans Beck, the first ambassador accredited to Hungary by the EC Commission.[28] Hungarian Prime Minister Jozsef Antall, during his July 1990 visit to Brussels, told EC officials that Hungary would seek associate membership in the Common Market by January 1, 1992, and full membership by 1995. Antall announced that Hungary wanted to be the first East European country to join the EC; EC Commission President Jacques Delors agreed that the associate membership deadline for Hungary was "reasonable."[29] More important, Hungary expects that its cooperation with Austria, which has expressed an interest in filing a joint application with Hungary for EEC membership, as well as its close working relations with Italy, will help it achieve the ultimate goal of full integration with Western Europe.

In addition to bringing Hungary politically closer to the West, strong relations with Western Europe have a military dimension as well. Cooperation with the West will remain essential in the foreseeable future, if the Hungarian army is to become successfully modernized. The Hungarian Ministry of Defense recognized this in 1990 when it explored the possibilities of cooperating with NATO and other Western European armed forces in the area of training and weapons acquisition. In June 1990 Colonel Gyorgy Szentesi, head of the Security Policy Department at the Ministry of Defense, disclosed that Hungary was interested in purchasing Western equipment. Szentesi announced that Hungary was trying to negotiate with West Germany, France, Sweden, and Switzerland over access to their weapons systems to be used as part of the Hungarian army's modernization program. Since the Hungarian Ministry of Defense lacked the money for direct purchases of Western weapons, Szentesi suggested that it would attempt to acquire them through co-production and barter arrangements.[30] In addition, Hungary expected to negotiate an exchange agreement that would allow a limited number of Hungarian military personnel to train in the West, with the Federal Republic of Germany again being Budapest's first choice.

A July 10, 1990, precedent-setting official visit to Hungary by West German Defense Minister Gerhard Stoltenberg indicated that the much-improved relationship between the two countries bode well for future cooperation in the area of national defense. During his visit to the head-quarters of a Hungarian armored division in Tata, in western Hungary, Stoltenberg spoke of his optimism about better future relations between the Bundeswehr and the Hungarian armed forces. The importance that Budapest attached to this visit was underscored by the fact that Stoltenberg was also received by Hungary's interim president, Arpad Goncz,[31] and held an extensive working meeting with Prime Minister Jozsef Antall and Defense Minister Lajos Fur. At a press conference after the meeting, the Hungarian and German defense ministers disclosed that they had reached an understanding on developing better relations between the two armies, including the exchange of experience between military institutes, visits by military training experts, and joint sports and cultural events.[32] In con-clusion of the visit, Fur and Stoltenberg signed a two-year military relations agreement between the Bundeswehr and the Hungarian armed forces. The official communiqué issued by the Hungarian Ministry of Defense after Stoltenberg's visit spoke of "an expressly favorable direction [in relations between West Germany and Hungary], which created ad-vantageous conditions for cooperation in security and defense policies as well. Consequently, bilateral relations between the defense ministers and armies could be further developed."[33]

Although the Hungarian Ministry of Defense was particularly interested in building a strong working relationship with the Bundeswehr, it also sought improved relations with other Western European militaries. In 1990, in addition to contacts with the West German Ministry of Defense, Hungary tried to establish similar ties with the French, Belgian, and Spanish armed forces. In the summer and fall of that year, the defense ministers of Belgium and Spain were received in Budapest by Hungarian Defense Minister Lajos Fur.[34] Subsequently, in mid-November 1990, Fur hosted Italian Defense Minister Virginio Rognoni to discuss prospects for Hungarian-Italian techni-cal military cooperation.[35] Another important step taken by the Hungarian government aimed at strengthening military cooperation with Western Europe was Fur's March 1991 trip to London and Brussels, which laid the foundation for cooperation with the United Kingdom's armed forces as well as with the British Aerospace, a major defense contractor. The visit to Brussels also served to confirm the Hungarian-Belgian military cooperation agree-ment, which had been concluded in 1989.[36]

The series of diplomatic initiatives undertaken by Budapest in 1990 and 1991 to establish ties to the Western military was aimed at securing alternative sources of weapons from Western Europe to substitute in the future for the Hungarian army's obsolete Soviet equipment. In addition, the Ministry of Defense wanted to arrange for the training of the next generation of Hungarian army officers at Western military academies. Both policies were an extension of the country's general foreign policy shift to the West. If successful, they would make the Hungarian army, its equipment, and the country's defense industry that much more compatible with NATO standards, laying the groundwork for Hungary's eventual integration with Western security institutions. In 1991, after the collapse of the Warsaw Pact and with the CSCE still an ineffective security design rather than a working system, from a Hungarian point of view NATO was the only viable security alliance in Europe.

NATO MEMBERSHIP

Hungary was the only former Soviet satellite to indicate openly in early 1990 that it was interested in becoming a member of the Atlantic Alliance. On February 20, 1990, then Hungarian Foreign Minister Gyula Horn said in a lecture at the Hungarian Political Science Association that he considered it feasible for Hungary to become within a few years a member of NATO's political structures.[37] Horn's statement was apparently a means of gauging Western reactions to the proposal. At the time, NATO rejected the idea out of hand, cautioning Hungary not to force the membership issue, as it was unacceptable to the Soviet Union and might slow down arms control.

NATO's lack of enthusiasm for Horn's "trial balloon" was in line with the West's unequivocal rejection of the principle of "alliance convergence," touted by the Soviets in early 1990 as the prerequisite to the mutual dissolution of the blocs. NATO's Secretary General Manfred Woerner responded to Horn's initiative by pointing out that it was "inconceivable for any country to be a member of both alliances."[38]

As much as they insisted in 1990 and 1991 on the dissolution of the Warsaw Pact, the Hungarians were also the most vocal among the former Soviet satellites in continuing to explore in parallel the possibility of joining NATO. On June 28, 1990, during a visit to NATO Headquarters, Hungarian Foreign Minister Geza Jeszenszky inquired about the feasibility of Hungary obtaining associate NATO membership.[39] Despite NATO's early negative response, delivered by its Secretary General Manfred Woerner and other permanent representatives of the member-countries, the Hungarians remained committed to developing close ties with the Atlantic Alliance, even if those relations were to fall short of an associate membership for the time being.

In the event, Hungary succeeded in strengthening its relations with NATO. Jeszenszky's 1990 visit to Brussels was a partial success in that it led to a public announcement by NATO Secretary General Woerner of the alliance's commitment to "seek as many links as possible with Warsaw Treaty countries, with special regard to states like Hungary that were democratic now and shared the same values as the NATO countries."[40] The Jeszenszky visit was followed shortly by an official trip to Brussels by Prime Minister Antall, on July 17–18, 1990. Although Antall's visit again failed to lead to formalized relations between Hungary and NATO, Budapest could claim some additional progress in that direction, as the two sides signed an agreement that gave the Hungarian ambassador accredited in Belgium the status of a special envoy and liaison to NATO.[41] The same offer was later extended to Poland and Czechoslovakia. In addition, Hungarian, Polish, and Czechoslovak security experts were invited to participate in NATO-sponsored conferences. For example, scholars from Poland, Czechoslovakia, and Hungary were invited to the 1991 Oslo conference on European security, sponsored by NATO, while such an invitation was not extended to other former WTO members, including the Soviet Union.[42]

In the end, even though Budapest's NATO initiative did not result in Hungary's formal association with the Atlantic Alliance, it nevertheless succeeded in making the East Central European security issue, in particular the need for a Western security guarantee, an urgent topic on the West European agenda. At first, NATO responded to pressure from Budapest by issuing general public reassurances. Secretary General Manfred Woerner, during a November 1990 visit to Hungary, told his hosts that the Atlantic Alliance would help Hungary "to overcome both economic and stabilization problems."[43] Next, in November 1990 Hungary was offered associate membership in the NATO Assembly, which was formally accepted by the Hungarian parliament on January 29, 1991.[44] By early 1991 the expression of NATO's interest in the region became explicit, leading to NATO's May 1991 statement of interest in the region's security and continued independence. Although it would be an overstatement to credit Budapest with securing NATO's security guarantee to East Central Europe, one has to recognize Hungary's contribution to placing the region's security on NATO's agenda. In effect, early Hungarian pressure for membership in NATO has initiated a special relationship between the Triangle states of East Central Europe and the North Atlantic Alliance.

Today the Hungarian government continues to regard NATO as an organization of "the highest importance and one of the main guarantees of European security" as Prime Minister Antall put it in a May 21, 1991, interview for *Le Monde*.[45] Although Antall also conceded that it would be unrealistic for former Soviet satellites to join NATO "now," he emphasized Hungary's leading role in establishing close permanent contacts with the Atlantic alliance, including his ground-breaking visit to NATO headquarters in Brussels in 1990.[46]

REGIONAL COOPERATION AND BILATERAL MILITARY AGREEMENTS

Although Hungary can influence, it cannot ultimately decide the nature and pace of its integration in the established Western institutions. Nonetheless, it has a greater opportunity to act in the area of regional cooperation. In the first instance of a successful effort at joint economic cooperation programs between developed Western democracies and postcommunist states, in 1990–1991 Hungary became a driving force behind the Pentagonale, a group of states in the Danubian basin that have agreed to collaborate in the area of trade and economic development. The group originally included Italy, Austria, Yugoslavia, and Czechoslovakia, in addition to Hungary. In July 1991 Poland was admitted to the group, thus bringing a key East Central European country into this vital regional economic cooperation arrangement and transforming the Pentagonale into the Hexagonale. The admission of Poland into the Pentagonale, agreed to on May 17, 1991, during the group's summit in Bologna, Italy, took place on Hungary's initiative.

The creation of the Pentagonale was preceded by a series of goodwill gestures on Hungary's part toward the country's neighbors. Already on September 8, 1989, Hungary announced that it intended to create the so-called zones of confidence, fifty-kilometer-deep swaths of border territory with Austria and Yugoslavia, from which between two hundred and four hundred tanks would be removed by 1990. In addition, Hungary unilaterally limited the size and extent of military exercises in those areas and invited military observers from Austria and Yugoslavia to be present during Hungarian field exercises. After the disintegration of the Warsaw Pact and in line with Hungary's new defensive doctrine, Budapest acted quickly to replace the decades of past hostility with a new spirit of cooperation.

In addition to obvious economic benefits, such as access to Italian and Austrian credits and know-how, the Pentagonale's successful progress has broader security implications. Commenting on the group's summit, held in Venice between July 31 and August 1, 1990, Hungary's Prime Minister Jozsef Antall defined the Pentagonale's role as mainly economic,[47] implying that this first case of a NATO member-country, Italy, and another highly developed Western market economy, Austria, working with former Soviet satellites augured well for Hungary's future economic integration with the West. The reorganized Pentagonale is important to the Hungarians as well as to Poland and Czechoslovakia because it proves that regional cooperation across the former East-West divide is possible. For this reason alone, the group is an important complement to the Warsaw-Prague-Budapest Triangle, serving as an underlying structure of a potentially larger future regional architecture.

The success of the Pentagonale/Hexagonale group suggests the potential viability of another direction in European economic integration, one that cuts across state boundaries and brings together mutually complementary economic regions. In the words of Ambassador Istvan Koermendy, director of the Department for Cooperation in Europe in the Hungarian Foreign Ministry, the Pentagonale is "an attempt to reestablish the traditional economic links which had been cut after the end of World War II."[48] This approach raises the intriguing possibility that in the future, once the Yugoslav civil war is over, Slovenia and Croatia may also become successfully integrated with the economies of the Hexagonale member-countries.

In addition to close consultations within the Triangle and cooperation within the Pentagonale/Hexagonale group, Hungary moved in 1991 to conclude limited military cooperation agreements with its neighbors. In November 1990, Hungary signed a limited technical military cooperation agreement with Romania. On January 21, 1991, it signed a five-year bilateral military cooperation agreement with Czechoslovakia, which covers the exchange of information on troop redeployment and the future development of the two countries' armed forces. The agreement also calls for coordination in the area of staff and field training. In March 1991, Hungary concluded a similar agreement with Poland. The Hungarian-Polish military cooperation agreement complemented a similar arrangement between the Hungarian and Polish intelligence services, signed on February 28, 1991.[49] All of the above are narrow technical military conventions falling far short of a regional security alliance structure. They concentrate on general cooperation among the three countries' ministries of defense, to include student exchanges, mutual friendly visits, sending observers to large-scale maneuvers, and sharing technical information.

The most innovative among the bilateral military cooperation treaties concluded by Hungary in 1991 was an "open skies" agreement, signed by Hungary and Romania in early May. This Hungarian-Romanian convention provides for overflights of the two countries' respective air spaces.[50] On June 28, 1991, the Romanian air force conducted the first overflight of the Hungarian territory, carried out by a Romanian plane equipped with French sensors; in turn, a specially equipped Hungarian jet overflew Romania on June 29.[51]

The "open skies" clause in the military agreement with Romania is as much a reflection of the history of hostility between Budapest and Bucharest as it is a tribute to good relations between the Hungarian and Romanian army general staffs. Paradoxically, the good working relationship between the Hungarian and the Romanian officer corps is a by-product of the past Soviet insistence that the two armies cooperate as part of the WTO's common air defense. Over the years, frequent personal contact between Romanian and Hungarian officers forged friendships that would outlast the life span of the Warsaw Treaty Organization and would serve as a foundation for regional military cooperation after 1989. Reportedly, during the Romanian uprising against the Ceausescu dictatorship, the Hungarian General Staff offered supplies and logistical assistance to the Romanians as well as assurances that it would prevent any unauthorized border crossing from Hungary into Romania. In effect, the Hungarian army assured the Romanians that, should the Warsaw Pact contemplate a military operation against Romania, Hungary would refuse to participate.[52] This capital of goodwill may prove to be priceless in the long run, as instability generated by the Yugoslav civil war threatens to spill across the country's borders and engulf the region.

Limited regional military cooperation between Hungary and its neighbors is likely to fall short of a genuine regional security alliance. The creation of such a regional pact would retard the process of East Central Europe's alignment with the West and its integration in a future common European defense system and might trigger a hostile reaction from the Soviet successor states. In purely military terms, for the time being Hungary intends to rely for its national security on its growing contacts with NATO and Western Europe, on consultations within the Triangle, and ultimately on its own reconstituted armed forces.

MILITARY REFORM

Between 1987 and 1989 the restructuring of the Hungarian People's Army followed the general reform guidelines introduced by the Soviets throughout the Warsaw Pact. Already in December 1987, Hungary announced that in the course of the year its military reform program had streamlined the army bureaucracy by eliminating 30 percent of its "leading organs," had reduced the call-up of reserves by 9 percent, and had lowered its claim on the equipment from civilian plants by 34 percent.[53] The year 1987 also saw a major change in the structure of the Hungarian armed forces. The entire army was reorganized into three corps, with one armored corps kept at a full-readiness level and the other two corps becoming training units. In 1988 the Ministry of Defense itself underwent a substantial restructuring, including a 240-men reduction in personnel. On January 1, 1989, the government forcibly retired fifty senior officers in anticipation of an announced reduction in the size of the Hungarian army. The reductions planned for 1989 included an approximately 9 percent cut in the overall troop strength, as well as the removal of obsolete equipment from the army's inventory. According to the January 31, 1989, announcement by General Ferenc Karpati, the Hungarian defense minister at the time, by the end of the year the army would be reduced by 9,300 men.[54]

The collapse of communism in Eastern Europe greatly accelerated the military reform process in Hungary. More important, by the end of 1989 the Hungarian government was beginning to make autonomous defense policy decisions. A new military oath was introduced on August 20, 1989. It no longer included the pledge of loyalty to the Communist Party and the "unconquerable ideals of socialism," but instead spoke of the soldier's obligation to his nation.[55] The Hungarian Ministry of Defense also moved to depoliticize the armed forces. On October 12, 1989, Defense Minister Colonel General Ferenc Karpati announced that he would sign an order dissolving Communist Party youth organizations in the army.[56]

On November 30, 1989, the Hungarian Council of Ministers authorized a cut in army personnel of up to 25 percent by the end of 1991. Altogether, the new round of reductions amounted to between 30,000 and 36,500 men and, according to new Hungarian Defense Minister Lajos Fur, would reduce the total size of the Hungarian army to under 90,000 by the year 1992.[57]

Like Czechoslovakia, in 1989 Hungary reformed its Border Guards units, which in the past had been subordinated to the Interior Ministry. In December 1989 the government announced that in 1990 the overall number of Border Guards would decrease by 60 percent.[58] In 1995 the strength of the reformed Border Guards units would not exceed 6,000 to 6,500 professionals especially trained for this purpose, 1,600 civilian personnel, and 2,000 to 2,500 draftees.[59]

The restructuring of the Hungarian military has proceeded in three directions. It has combined the redefinition of the nation's security needs with changes in the military doctrine and reductions in the size of the armed forces. The size of the Hungarian army went from 91,000 in 1989 to about 80,000 by the end of 1990.[60] The reform program stipulates that, in the future, the day-to-day professional management of the army will be the prerogative of the commander-in-chief, while the Ministry of Defense will concern itself mainly with the development of military policy and doctrine. The commander-in-chief of the Hungarian army has the rank of a state secretary; the position was created on December 1, 1989, with the office going to Lieutenant General Kalman Loerincz. Under the current reform program, the commander-in-chief is responsible for the implementation of military policy, as well as all personnel decisions and training programs. The commander-in-chief of the army is directly subordinated to the president of Hungary, who under the new constitution is the supreme commander of the Hungarian armed forces.

In 1990 the Hungarian government broke with the longstanding tradition of appointing a military man to the post of defense minister. Since May 16, 1990, the Hungarian Ministry of Defense has been headed by Lajos Fur, a civilian and a founding member of the Hungarian Democratic Forum.[61] Fur was selected by the new government to replace Colonel General Ferenc Karpati, a former head of the Main Political Administration and a defense minister since 1986. Fur's appointment as defense minister was followed by changes in the deployment pattern of the armed forces on Hungarian territory. During Hungary's membership in the Warsaw Pact, the bulk of its army had been deployed in the western part of the country. This had reflected Hungary's pivotal strategic importance as a springboard for Warsaw Pact offensive operations through Austria and Yugoslavia against NATO's Allied Forces Southern Europe Command. At the time, the bulk of the Hungarian army had been concentrated in the First Army with headquarters in Budapest, the Fifth Army at Szekesfehervar about thirty miles southwest of Budapest, and the Third Mechanized Corps with headquarters at Cegled about thirty-two miles southeast of Budapest.[62]

In 1990, Fur reviewed the old deployment pattern in light of the country's new defensive doctrine and ordered an increase in the number of Hungarian military units stationed along the Romanian and Soviet borders. In early 1991 the Hungarian Ministry of Defense asked the parliament for the authorization to create several new military districts.

NEW MILITARY DOCTRINE

In late 1991 the Hungarian parliament and the Ministry of Defense reached a broad consensus on the key issues of the new military doctrine. In the words of State Secretary Lieutenant General Antal Annus, an agreement was reached on the general goal of reform, that is, "the army's transformation into a force that is national and capable of an independent defense if necessary."[63] According to the new doctrine, the army can train only for defensive purposes. As in the Polish and Czechoslovak cases, the doctrine prohibits the army from operating outside of the country's territory, except for peacekeeping missions authorized by a two-thirds vote in the parliament. This restriction on the army's future deployment has been written into the Hungarian constitution.

The new Hungarian military doctrine initially called for an "all-around" defense of the country. At a press conference held in Budapest on June 20, 1990, Defense Minister Fur announced that Hungary intended to replace its former military doctrine with one that would emphasize "a concentric defense [of the country's territory] to avert a purely temporary aggression."[64] The terms *all-around* and *concentric* were subsequently dropped, for, as some in the parliament pointed out, politically they implied that Hungary was surrounded by enemies. Instead, the doctrine in its current formulation rejects all offensive operations and speaks simply of the army's duty to defend the national territory of Hungary against any potential aggression. In order to emphasize the doctrine's purely defensive character, on November 16, 1990, Defense Minister Lajos Fur announced that, in addition to the reduction in armor required by the CFE negotiations, Hungary intended to scrap all of its twenty-seven surface-to-surface missile launchers, as well as all of its 107 Frog-7 and twenty-four SCUD missiles.[65] At the same time, Hungary plans to modernize its air force and air defense forces. The Hungarian air force consists only of one air division, headquartered in Kecskemet, equipped with fifty obsolete MiG-21s and ten more modern MiG-23 aircraft.[66] In the words of Major General Bela Balogh, head of the Hungarian air force, the country is "not in a position to deter modern attack aircraft."[67]

The old structure of the armed forces, which had been divided into two services—the army (consisting of three corps) and the air defense forces—is being reshaped to accommodate the new requirements. The army, which since 1987 has been using the brigade system in place of the old division system, will be redeployed in four new military districts: (1) the Western District, (2) the Central District, (3) the Eastern District, and (4) the Budapest District. The new district system, which replaces the old

"Western Zone" and "Eastern Zone," will result in a balanced deployment of military forces throughout Hungary. In case of an attack against Hungary, the Western, Central, and Eastern Military Districts will become three army corps, while the Budapest District will remain an autonomous defense force to deal with direct threats to the nation's capital. (Budapest, with a population of about two million out of the country's total of ten million, constitutes a vital political and economic center.)

The air and air defense forces will continue to function as one unit, covering the entire territory of Hungary under one command. Hungary hopes to be able to modernize its air defenses, but due to budgetary constraints its plan will not be implemented for another five to six years. In the meantime the air force will have to make do with its obsolete equipment. As an interim solution to its equipment needs, Budapest asked the German government for the surplus MiG-29s formerly used by the GDR's air force, but Bonn did not respond to the request.

The new Hungarian military doctrine envisions the creation of a small, highly mobile army consisting of between eight and ten brigades of mechanized infantry and two to three tank brigades. All of Hungary's armor will be deployed centrally, south of Budapest.[68] In addition to the regular army, which has been targeted for 75,000 military and 15,000 civilian personnel by the year 1992,[69] the Ministry of Defense proposed that a territorial defense force be created as a home guard reserve for the regular forces. This home guard force will be equipped with small arms stored in regional depots, and it will undergo periodic retraining to maintain its requisite skill levels. The home guard will be called up every six months, and it will train in platoon- and company-size units. Including the regular force, the home guard, and the country's total manpower reserves, in a national emergency Hungary should be able to field an army of approximately 300,000 men. This will be a lightly armed force, with little armor, light mortars and artillery, antitank weapons, and no surface-to-surface missiles.

The successful implementation of a defensive military doctrine requires that the army obtain modern equipment. In 1989 Hungary removed from service the remaining World War II vintage T-34 tanks, as well as some of the obsolete T-55 models. Under present conditions of tight military budgets, however, Hungary will not be able to purchase state-of-the-art equipment to replace the old hardware any time soon. Instead, in 1990 and 1991 the government tried several schemes that would at least partially remedy the situation at an acceptable cost. For example, in 1990 the Hungarian Ministry of Defense expressed an interest in purchasing at a discount a number of the formerly East German T-72 tanks as a shortcut to equipment modernization.[70] A long-term solution to the problem, however, will depend on the country's ability to pay for imports of defense-related technologies from the West as well as on the modernization of the Hungarian defense industry.

THE DEFENSE INDUSTRY

The reform of the Hungarian defense industry presents a smaller-scale problem than the analogous task faced by Poland and Czechoslovakia, as Hungary has never developed its defense industry to the productive capacity level of the other two states. In the past, Hungary manufactured a wheeled light scout car, the FUG-75, first adopted for service in 1964. The FUG-75 was exported to Czechoslovakia, which also produced a modified version of the vehicle under license. More recently, Hungarian weapons exports have been largely limited to weapons guidance systems as well as small arms, such as AK-74-type assault rifles, pistols, and ammunition. In addition to cooperation within the Warsaw Pact, Hungary has sold weapons to several Third World countries, including Iraq, India, and Kuwait.[71]

Although the Hungarian defense industry does not face the problem of an unmanageable excess capacity, which has plagued Czechoslovakia, it needs to develop to a level necessary to assist the army's modernization program. Hungary's defense industry is small and its strength lies in communications and electronic equipment manufacturing. In 1989 military production accounted for about 1 percent of the country's total industrial output.[72] Hungary does not produce major military hardware, and in the past it purchased its tanks, heavy artillery, and aircraft mainly from the Soviet Union. On account of the 1987–1989 reductions in military budgets, by 1990 the Hungarian military industry production, which in the mid-1980s had been valued at about twenty billion forints, shrank to about half of its former size. In the process, the Hungarian army had drastically reduced its purchasing plans, leaving the defense plants saddled with a large inventory of unsold military equipment.[73]

The Hungarian defense industry, which has been struggling to cope with the annual defense budget cuts, is likely to continue to shrink, with several defense and defense-related plants going out of business altogether. In 1991 the government estimated that, from among the thirty-nine Hungarian enterprises engaged in military production, only a few will manage to survive under market conditions. Enterprises such as the Godollo Machine Plant, which in the past serviced the T-34 and T-55 tanks, are likely to go under unless they find a means of converting to civilian production. The Hungarian Ministry of Defense has no money available to save the majority of Hungarian defense industry plants from bankruptcy. As of mid-1991, the only defense plant to receive direct government assistance to facilitate a transition to the new market situation was the Esztergom Laboratory Instruments Works. In the words of Major General Karoly Janze, head of the Hungarian Ministry of Defense Economic Analysis Department, "neither at present, nor in the future will the Hungarian Army be in a situation where it can guarantee orders for the Hungarian defense industry."[74] The Hungarian military is well aware, therefore, that the only way to salvage an indigenous defense manufacturing capacity is through cooperative arrangements with Western firms, whereby the output from the Hungarian plants can become competitive on the world market.

The development of Hungary's defense industry is important not only in terms of the army's future equipment modernization program but as an essential element of the current maintenance requirements. In addition to the prospective decline of the domestic defense industry, the Hungarian army faces an immediate shortage of weapons spare parts due to the 1991 changes in trade relations with the former Soviet Union. Since the collapse of the Warsaw Pact, Hungary has tried to find an adequate source of spare parts and weapons to modernize and reequip its army. On June 20, 1990, Defense Minister Lajos Fur stressed the urgent need for equipment modernization, suggesting that the only option available at present may have to be a greater development of the indigenous defense industry.[75]

The need for spare parts for the Soviet-designed weapons used by the Hungarian army has contributed to Hungary's regional cooperation with Poland and Czechoslovakia. On account of its small defense industry, Hungary will be much less able to service its stock of Soviet-designed weapons than Poland or Czechoslovakia, and therefore these two countries will remain an important source of spare parts for Hungarian weapons systems.[76] Gradually, as the existing stock of Hungarian weapons reaches the end of its useful life, the army will replace it with hardware purchased on the world market.[77]

In the future, Hungary expects to make direct weapons purchases from the West and to license Western technology in order to modernize its domestic defense industry. The decision to look to the West for new defense technology, while being a symbol of the country's regained sovereignty, has a strictly economic dimension as well. Beginning January 1, 1991, former COMECON member-countries began trading exclusively in convertible currencies, which according to Hungarian Ministry of Defense estimates tripled the price of Soviet weapons overnight and made the price of comparable Western weapons systems competitive.[78] In 1990 and 1991 Hungary attempted to acquire German and French military equipment and technology as part of the modernization program, but it could not afford to make direct purchases. Instead, the Hungarian government has tried to negotiate co-production agreements with France and Germany. On June 21, 1991, Hungarian Chief of Staff Lieutenant General Laszlo Borsits and his French counterpart Jacques Lanxade signed in Budapest a bilateral agreement on military cooperation between the two countries. The new agreement calls for joint training of officers and frequent mutual military visits, as well as future cooperation between the French and the Hungarian defense industries.[79]

REFORM OF THE MINISTRY OF DEFENSE AND THE BUDGET

In 1989–1990 the Hungarian Ministry of Defense was reorganized with the goal of reducing its size and refocusing its duties away from the day-to-day operation of the armed forces. Today the ministry's primary concerns are defense policy, economic and personnel issues, and strategic planning. The ministry now includes six departments: (1) Military Affairs Department, (2) Economic Analysis Department, (3) Foreign Relations Department, (4) Public Relations Department, (5) Legal Affairs Department, and (6) Personnel Department.[80] The organizational reform of the ministry has resulted in a separation of the general management and policy-making functions from the day-to-day operations of the armed forces. Under the new system, the Ministry of Defense will function as a government agency responsible for the general management of the armed forces and military diplomacy (including liaisons with foreign armed forces). The overall management function will be performed by a six-member group of key ministry officials, reporting directly to the defense minister. On the other hand, the Hungarian Army Command is charged with supervising the day-to-day operations of the armed forces. In 1990 the reorganization cut the Ministry of Defense personnel by 600 and led to the replacement of Chief of Staff Lieutenant General Jozsef Pacsek with General Laszlo Borsits, who has also been given the rank of deputy commander-in-chief. As a result of the changes, the Ministry of Defense has become a policy-setting institution, more in line with a traditional Western approach. Since 1991 the Hungarian government has contemplated the creation of a national security council based on the U.S. model.

In 1990 and 1991, in addition to the debate on the new military doctrine, a central responsibility of the Hungarian Ministry of Defense was the preparation of an adequate defense budget to pay for the military reform.

According to Defense Minister Fur, in the foreseeable future Hungary could not count on spending more on defense than 3 percent of its gross national product (GNP), and it could not maintain a peacetime army larger than 0.6 to 0.8 percent of the total population.[81] At the same time, the Hungarian General Staff has recognized all too well that the successful implementation of the military reform program depends on whether or not the government will be able to provide the necessary funding. The proposed redeployment of forces, which according to the ministry's estimate would require an additional five billion forints in 1991 alone, the creation of new military districts, the repositioning of aircraft, and weapons modernization programs call for substantial additional appropriations if they are to become a reality.

The budgetary picture is likely to remain bleak for the next five years, forcing the Hungarian army to postpone all but its most essential expenditures. In fact, beginning in 1989 the parliament has consistently cut the defense appropriation, making the reduction of the size of the armed forces as much a function of economic reality as of the planned restructuring program. In 1990 the Hungarian defense budget was forty-six billion forints.[82] According to the Hungarian Ministry of Defense that amount was barely sufficient, especially in light of the growing inflationary pressures due to market reforms. In order to make up for the shortfall, the ministry was even required to raise several billion forints for its budget through direct sales of military equipment, including the 1990 sale of four MiG-21 fighter aircraft to an American entrepreneur.[83]

Since 1990 Defense Minister Lajos Fur has tried to arrest the trend toward continued reductions in defense spending. On September 5, 1990, Fur argued that the country's 1991 military budget would have to increase substantially if the ministry's planned expenditures were to keep pace with inflation.[84] The Ministry of Defense formally requested between seventy-five and seventy-nine billion forints for 1991, which allowing for the 30 percent inflation rate in Hungary, as well as the reduction in the length of compulsory military service and the need to build new garrisons in the eastern part of the country, would have kept the defense spending roughly at the 1990 level. The parliament, however, appropriated only fifty-five billion forints for 1991, which has amounted to a further reduction in money allocated for equipment maintenance and officer salaries.[85]

In addition to slowing down the Hungarian military reform program, budgetary constraints have also retarded the implementation of the promised reduction in weapons, because of the high cost of destroying military hardware. The cost of the Hungarian government's commitment to reduce the tank force to about eight hundred and to eliminate all of its

SCUD missiles has not been factored into the defense budget.[86] Most likely, the only way the Hungarian army will be able to pay for the destruction of the required number of tanks is through commercial agreements, whereby the scrap metal from destroyed armor will be valued exactly at the cost of destroying it.

In view of the steadily declining military budgets, the principal goal of the Hungarian military through the year 1995 will be economic survival under conditions of scarcity. This was implicitly recognized by Major General Lajos Kondor, cabinet secretary at the Hungarian Ministry of Defense, when he admitted that due to budgetary constraints "Hungarian defense policy will continue to be a compromise."[87]

CONTINGENCY PLANNING

Since 1991 contingency planning within the Hungarian Ministry of Defense has focused on several possible threat scenarios. The most immediate threat is that of regional instability caused by an eruption in the former Soviet Union or the escalation of fighting in Yugoslavia. Turmoil in the former USSR as the Soviet successor states emerge and, in particular, civil war in Yugoslavia in the summer and fall of 1991, prompted Major General Lajos Kondor, a ranking cabinet secretary at the Ministry of Defense, to declare that the army had to plan a response to regional instability along Hungarian borders.[88] Budapest reacted to the fighting in Croatia by calling for a political solution and supporting the CSCE efforts to mediate the conflict, while it limited its military response to the strengthening of the Border Guards and army units along its border with Yugoslavia. In the short term, Hungary is extremely unlikely to get directly involved in the Yugoslav imbroglio, even if it means failing to assist the Magyar minority living in Vojvodina in Yugoslavia.[89] However, if civil war in Yugoslavia expands to cover the entire country, the Hungarian military may come under considerable political pressure from some segments of the population to help the Yugoslav Magyars indirectly, for instance by facilitating their exodus to Hungary. Several Hungarian government officials, including Prime Minister Jozsef Antall, made statements in 1990 and 1991 that suggest that the fate of Hungarian minorities remains an important element of the country's foreign policy. Antall's notorious declaration, made in the summer of 1990, that he is "the prime minister of all Hungarians, regardless of where they live," as well as Foreign Minister Geza Jeszenszky's assertion that Hungary "cannot remain indifferent to their [the four million Hungarians living outside Hungary] unfortunately quite frequent neglect and mistreatment or the denial of their basic human rights,"[90] has been a source of concern to Hungary's neighbors.

The worst possible threat, albeit one that will remain quite remote for the rest of the decade, would be an all-out aggression against Hungary by a neighboring power. As noted by Deputy Chairman of the Defense Committee of the National Assembly Imre Mecs, the Hungarian government firmly believes that only the reconstituted Soviet Union or its authoritarian successor state built around Russia could be such a Great Power aggressor.[91] If such an attack from the East were to come, Hungary would have no chance of successfully defending itself and could only plan to fight a rear guard action, while hoping that Western Europe and NATO would come to its assistance. Hungary's search for NATO membership is a response to the perceived threat from the East.

In the 1990s Hungary will also continue to face unresolved problems in its relations with Czechoslovakia, Romania, and possibly Yugoslavia (or its successor state) over Hungarian minorities in Slovakia, Transylvania, and Vojvodina. Throughout 1990 and 1991, relations between Budapest and Bucharest remained tense, with the Hungarian side charging Romania with human rights violations in dealing with its Magyar minority in Transylvania. In private, a high-ranking Hungarian diplomat referred to Romanian policy toward the Magyars living in Transylvania as "decades of cultural genocide."[92] The Romanians have angrily rejected such charges as an unacceptable interference in their internal affairs. Relations between Hungary and Romania took a turn for the worse in mid-1991 after Bucharest accused Hungary of attempting to isolate Romania internationally. Romania has complained that its exclusion from the Triangle and Pentagonale cooperation agreements has been a deliberate Hungarian policy of building a wall between Romania and the rest of Europe. In turn, Budapest has rejected the attacks as unfounded.

In the future, the traditionally good relations between the Romanian and Hungarian military establishments could possibly pave the way to an overall settling of differences and better relations between the two countries. The rapprochement is not likely, however, to proceed unless Romania responds to Hungarian overtures with a goodwill gesture of its own and the Hungarian government stops asserting publicly its responsibility for the Magyars living outside Hungary.

Friction between Czechoslovakia and Hungary over the Magyar minority in Slovakia is unlikely to reach the intensity of the Hungarian-Romanian confrontation. In 1990 and 1991 Budapest repeatedly raised the issue of the human and civil rights of the Hungarian minority in Slovakia, and the argument became quite heated after Prime Minister Antall's assertion at the third national rally of the Hungarian Democratic Forum, on June 2, 1990, that he wished to be the "prime minister of fifteen million Hungarians," a reference to the Magyars living in neighboring countries. The confrontation was partially defused during Hungarian President Arpad Goncz's visit to Czechoslovakia in the summer of 1990, when he assured the Czechoslovaks that Budapest wanted an open dialogue about how to solve grievances on both sides.[93] The climate of the Hungarian-Czechoslovak relations improved considerably after Goncz's visit, even though Hungary's official position on the minority issue has remained largely unchanged.

Relations with Yugoslavia over a Magyar minority in Vojvodina are likely to become an issue if the crisis within the defunct Yugoslav federation results in a protracted civil war. The past record of relations between Yugoslavia and Hungary is considerably more encouraging than Hungary's relations with Romania and Czechoslovakia. Still, the relationship may deteriorate if the violence and bloodshed that has accompanied the implosion of the Yugoslav state impacts directly on the Magyar minority in Vojvodina.

The greatest danger to Hungarian security will continue to come from internal instability in the former Soviet Union. The final outcome of the Soviet crisis will have a decisive impact on the direction of Hungarian security policy as well as the overall stability in the region. Similar to the Polish and Czechoslovak concerns, Budapest fears most of all that a violent implosion of the former Soviet Union will have a chilling effect on the process of democratization in postcommunist Eastern Europe.

NOTES

1. "Fur on Pact Membership, Problems with Romania," *FBIS-EEU-90-114*, June 13, 1990, p. 42.
2. Alfred Reisch, "Hungary to Leave Military Arm of the Pact," *Report on Eastern Europe*, vol. 1, no. 26 (Munich: RFE/RL, June 29, 1990), p. 24.
3. Alfred Reisch, "Interview with Foreign Minister Geza Jeszenszky," *Report on Eastern Europe*, vol. 1, no. 30 (Munich: RFE/RL, July 27, 1990), p. 17.
4. Alfred Reisch, "The Hungarian Dilemma: After the Warsaw Pact, Neutrality or NATO," *Report on Eastern Europe*, vol. 1, no. 15 (Munich: RFE/RL, April 13, 1990), p. 16.
5. *RFE/RL Daily Report*, June 7, 1990.
6. "Envoy Views Dismantling of Warsaw Pact," *FBIS-EEU-90-141*, July 23, 1990, p. 43.
7. Douglas L. Clarke, "Warsaw Pact: The Transformation Begins," *Report on Eastern Europe*, vol. 1, no. 25 (Munich: RFE/RL, June 22, 1990), p. 35.
8. Reisch, "Hungary to Leave Military Arm of the Pact," p. 21.

9. Ibid., p. 22.

10. "Foreign Ministry Official on Moscow Pact Talks," *FBIS-EEU-90-116*, June 15, 1990, p. 32.

11. Reisch, "Hungary to Leave Military Arm of the Pact," p. 23.

12. Reisch, "Interview with Foreign Minister Geza Jeszenszky," p. 17.

13. "Discord Develops over Costs of Troop Withdrawal," *FBIS-EEU-90-116*, June 15, 1990, p. 32.

14. "Minister Fur Views Burlakov's 'Grave Threat,' " *FBIS-EEU-90-128*, July 3, 1990, p. 38.

15. "Soviets Suspend Traffic," *FBIS-EEU-90-158*, August 15, 1990, p. 20.

16. "Fur Interviewed on Warsaw Pact Membership, Queried on Plans to Leave Pact," *FBIS-EEU-91-117*, June 18, 1991, p. 42.

17. "Antall on Warsaw Pact, NATO Future," *FBIS-EEU-90-122*, June 25, 1990, p. 34.

18. "Antall Comments on German Relations, Pact," *FBIS-EEU-90-120*, June 21, 1990, p. 32.

19. Interview with Ambassador Istvan Koermendy, director of the Department for Cooperation in Europe, Hungarian Foreign Ministry, Budapest, May 10, 1991.

20. "Kadar on End of CMEA, Trade Ties with USSR," *FBIS-EEU-91-099*, May 22, 1991, p. 18.

21. "Official on Trade Problems with USSR," *FBIS-EEU-91-099*, May 22, 1991, p. 18.

22. "Hungarian Foreign Minister in Moscow for Talks," *FBIS-SOV-91-100*, May 23, 1991, p. 24.

23. "Chnoupek Addresses Diplomatic Corps Meeting," *FBIS-EEU-87-010*, January 15, 1987, p. D2.

24. "Antall: German Unification 'Advantageous,' " *FBIS-EEU-90-164*, August 23, 1990, p. 18.

25. Interview with Janos Matus, senior research fellow, Hungarian Institute of International Affairs, Budapest, May 7, 1991.

26. "Council of Europe Membership Made Official," *FBIS-EEU-91-215*, November 6, 1991, p. 17.

27. "EBRD's Nemeth on Policy Concerning Country," *FBIS-EEU-91-099*, May 22, 1991, pp. 18–19.

28. "Jozsef Antall Receives First EC Ambassador," *FBIS-EEU-90-137*, July 17, 1990, p. 39.

29. *RFE/RL Daily Report*, July 18, 1990.

30. "Interest Expressed in West's Military Expertise," *FBIS-EEU-90-118*, June 19, 1990, pp. 37–38.

31. "FRG Defense Minister Stoltenberg Meets Goncz," *FBIS-EEU-90-133*, July 11, 1990, p. 34.

32. "Antall, Stoltenberg Meet," *FBIS-EEU-90-134*, July 12, 1990, p. 35.

33. "Delegation Ends Visit," *FBIS-EEU-90-134*, July 12, 1990, p. 35.

34. "Spanish Defense Minister Serra Pays Visit," *FBIS-EEU-91-186*, September 25, 1991, pp. 34–35.

35. "Italian Defense Minister Continues Visit," *FBIS-EEU-90-221*, November 15, 1990, p. 37.

36. "Defense Minister Returns from UK, Belgium Visit," *FBIS-EEU-91-047*, March 11, 1991, p. 27.

37. Reisch, "The Hungarian Dilemma: After the Warsaw Pact, Neutrality or NATO," p. 17.

38. Ibid.

39. *RFE/RL Daily Report*, June 29, 1990.

40. "Jeszenszky Visits NATO Headquarters in Brussels," *FBIS-EEU-90-127*, July 2, 1990, p. 34.

41. "Antall Interviewed on Visit, Confirms 'Liaison' with NATO," *FBIS-EEU-90-139*, July 19, 1990, p. 31.

42. Interview with Janos Matus, senior research fellow, Hungarian Institute of International Affairs, Budapest, May 7, 1991.

43. "NATO's Woerner Continues Official Visit," *FBIS-EEU-90-227*, November 26, 1990, p. 33.

44. "National Assembly Meets in Extraordinary Session, Approves Vote on NATO Membership," *FBIS-EEU-91-020*, January 30, 1991, p. 21.

45. "Antall Interviewed on Ties with EC, NATO," *FBIS-EEU-91-099*, May 22, 1991, pp. 21–22.

46. Ibid.

47. "Antall, Jeszenszky Return from Venice Summit," *FBIS-EEU-90-149*, August 2, 1990, p. 24.

48. Interview with Ambassador Istvan Koermendy, director of the Department for Cooperation in Europe, Hungarian Foreign Ministry, Budapest, May 10, 1991.

49. "Joint Intelligence Agreement Signed with Poland," *FBIS-EEU-91-042*, March 4, 1991, p. 23.

50. Interview with Colonel Tibor Koeszegvari, director of the Defense Research Institute of the Hungarian Ministry of Defense, Budapest, May 8, 1991.

51. *RFE/RL Daily Report*, June 24, 1991.

52. Interview with Colonel Tibor Koeszegvari, director of the Defense Research Institute of the Hungarian Ministry of Defense, Budapest, May 8, 1991.

53. Reported on Hungarian Radio at 11:45 A.M. on December 11, 1987.

54. "Defense Minister Karpati Views Troop Reduction," *FBIS-EEU-89-021*, February 2, 1989, p. 34.

55. "Oath Omits Reference to Party Loyalty," *FBIS-EEU-89-160*, August 21, 1989, p. 11.

56. "Youth Organizations to Disband," *FBIS-EEU-89-198*, October 16, 1989, p. 42.

57. "Fur Comments on Country's Future Defense Policy," *FBIS-EEU-90-119*, June 20, 1990, p. 28.

58. "Government Reduces Border Guard," *FBIS-EEU-89-243*, December 20, 1989, p. 48.

59. "Border Guards Chief on Future Reorganization," *FBIS-EEU-90-248*, December 26, 1990, p. 27.

60. *The Military Balance, 1989–1990* (London: International Institute for Strategic Studies, 1989), pp. 44–48.

61. Fur, who holds a doctorate in history, was active in the 1956 Hungarian revolution and was arrested after the Soviet invasion of the country. Shortly after his release in December 1956, Fur escaped to the West and briefly settled in France. Upon his return

to Hungary, he was prohibited from following his academic career until 1964; in the meantime Fur worked as a manual laborer.

62. "Warsaw Pact Forces in Europe," *Jane's Defence Weekly*, April 4, 1987, p. 598.

63. "Military Officials Discuss Defense Issues," *FBIS-EEU-91-094*, May 15, 1991, p. 23.

64. "Fur Comments on Country's Future Defense Policy," p. 28.

65. "Defense Minister's Announcement on Arms Reduction," *FBIS-EEU-90-223*, November 19, 1990, p. 38.

66. *The Military Balance, 1989–1990*, pp. 44–48.

67. "Air Force Official Comments on Financial Problems," *FBIS-EEU-91-002*, January 3, 1991.

68. Interview with Colonel Tibor Koeszegvari, director of the Defense Research Institute of the Hungarian Ministry of Defense, Budapest, May 8, 1991.

69. "Defense Ministry Airs Future Army Issues," *FBIS-EEU-90-152*, August 7, 1990, p. 15.

70. "Ministry Official on Purchase of GDR Tanks," *FBIS-EEU-90-192*, October 3, 1990, p. 25.

71. "Army General Interviewed on Arms Trade," *FBIS-EEU-91-003*, January 4, 1991, p. 14.

72. "Hungarian Defence Industry in Crisis," *Jane's Defence Weekly*, October 28, 1989, p. 941.

73. "Defense Official on Security, Warsaw Pact," *FBIS-EEU-90-158*, August 15, 1990, p. 19.

74. "Review of Nation's Changing Defense Industry," *FBIS-EEU-91-059*, March 27, 1991, p. 22.

75. "Fur Comments on Country's Future Defense Policy," p. 28.

76. "Defense Official Queried on Upcoming Changes," *FBIS-EEU-90-147*, July 31, 1990, p. 33.

77. "Hungary's Last Soviet Deal," *Jane's Defence Weekly*, July 14, 1990, p. 46.

78. "Defense Minister Views Budget, Soviet Relations," *FBIS-EEU-90-237*, December 10, 1990, p. 31.

79. *RFE/RL Daily Report*, June 24, 1991.

80. Interview with Colonel Gabor Moricz, director of Economic Analysis Department, Hungarian Ministry of Defense, Budapest, May 9, 1991.

81. "Defense Minister Outlines New Defense Principles," *FBIS-EEU-91-058*, March 26, 1991, p. 35.

82. "Interest Expressed in West's Military Expertise," p. 37.

83. "Army Selling Military Equipment to West," *FBIS-EEU-90-120*, June 20, 1990, p. 35.

84. "Defense Ministry Budget to Increase Next Year," *FBIS-EEU-90-173*, September 6, 1990, p. 22.

85. Interview with Colonel Gabor Moricz, director of Economic Analysis Department, Hungarian Ministry of Defense, Budapest, May 9, 1991.

86. Ibid.

87. "Military Officials Discuss Defense Issues," *FBIS-EEU-91-094*, May 15, 1991, p. 21.

88. Ibid., p. 22.

89. This point was made repeatedly by several Ministry of Defense officials, although they expressed considerable concern over the fate of their countrymen living outside Hungary. For example, Colonel Endre Javor, chief of Military Policy Analysis, Ministry of Defense, interview in Budapest, May 9, 1991.

90. Reisch, "Interview with Foreign Minister Geza Jeszenszky," p. 18.

91. "Military Officials Discuss Defense Issues," p. 21.

92. Interview with Ambassador Istvan Koermendy, head of the Department for Cooperation in Europe, Hungarian Foreign Ministry, Budapest, May 10, 1991.

93. "Foreign Ministry on Relations with Slovakia," *FBIS-EEU-90-160*, August 17, 1990, p. 13.

CONCLUSION: EUROPE'S NEW
EASTERN FRONTIER

Poland, Czechoslovakia, and Hungary find themselves today on the periphery of Europe's developed northwestern core. The Triangle's integration into the West is likely to accelerate in the second half of the decade, as East Central Europe gains associate membership in the European Economic Community and continues its domestic reforms. Save for a protracted economic crisis that might undermine their internal stability, Poland, Czechoslovakia, and Hungary are firmly set to become open market economies. Their regional security and their ultimate role in a new Europe will be influenced by Western policy choices and by the course of events in the former Soviet Union, as its successor states grapple with the communist legacy. Depending in particular on future developments in the East, either the Triangle will separate Russia from Europe or it may function as a corridor that will help bring it closer to the West. Whatever the final outcome, German reunification alone has made East Central Europe an important security parameter of Western Europe.

Western discussion of the future security framework for Poland, Czechoslovakia, and Hungary has so far fallen into three general categories, including (1) a modification of the East-West divide, with NATO remaining the pivotal Western alliance, while the post–Warsaw Pact countries and the former Soviet Union continue to constitute the political "East"; (2) a collective security scenario, centered around the Conference on Security and Cooperation in Europe formula, to include all the European states as well as the United States and Canada; and (3) a pan-European integrationist vision, which would extend the Western European Union and the 1992 European unification to the postcommunist societies of the former Soviet empire, including Russia and the other Soviet successor states.[1]

In reality, such clear-cut solutions are always difficult to obtain. In the short term, the security framework in East Central Europe will likely rest on an eclectic combination of bilateral arrangements, CSCE structures, and informal ties to NATO, the Western European Union, and the EEC. It will continue to lack an explicit Western security guarantee, while being backed up instead by NATO's implicit commitment to the preservation of its independence. Provided there is no sudden explosion of civil unrest in the Soviet Union's successor states that spills across into Europe, and as long as the fighting in Yugoslavia does not spread, the above eclectic solution should constitute the underlying foundation of the emerging security system in East Central Europe for the rest of this decade.

The 1989–1991 dramatic collapse of Soviet communism notwithstanding, certain old European realities remain. Although the Soviet threat to Western Europe has all but disappeared, the specter of Russian imperialism continues to cause concern in Poland, Czechoslovakia, and Hungary. The Triangle's diplomatic efforts and military reform programs speak eloquently to the continued reality of Moscow's power. While a number of Western observers have speculated about the resurgence of German influence in the East, the former Soviet Union rather than Germany remains the principal security concern of the new democracies in the region. Anxiety about instability in the East dwarfs all thought of putative future German hegemony in East Central Europe.

The perception of the Soviet threat in East Central Europe has shifted away from direct aggression, the likelihood of which remains small, and toward the ripple effect of the current breakup of the Soviet empire. This is the point where the concern over the remaining military power available to the Soviet successor states and the fear of regional instability intersect. The real danger to East Central Europe's security in the remainder of the decade will be that of instability in the former Soviet Union, which may become translated into border confrontations and limited war on the Triangle's eastern periphery. Hence, the residual military power of the former USSR will remain a cause of great concern to governments in the region.

Poland, Czechoslovakia, and Hungary internally are cohesive enough themselves to be largely immune to interethnic conflict, even if separatism in Czechoslovakia will for some time continue to present a problem to the federal government. The real danger of regional instability lies immediately across their borders, in particular in the former Soviet Union, in Yugoslavia, and to a lesser degree in Romania. Nationalist and ethnic pressures in the countries bordering on the East Central European Triangle may ultimately require the redrawing of the frontiers and the creation of new states. This process is already under way in Yugoslavia and, if the example of the

Serbian-Croatian War of 1991 tells us anything, changing the region's map will be an inherently dangerous process. This danger will increase exponentially if the Ukraine and Byelorussia ultimately opt for independent statehood outside the new Commonwealth of Independent States.

At the same time, however, in light of the August 1991 overthrow of communist power in the Soviet Union, Poland, Czechoslovakia, and Hungary have reasons for cautious optimism. The failure of the Soviet hard-line military and party apparatchiks to return the Soviet Union to its totalitarian past has set in motion the process of the USSR's final demise, which has led to Moscow's granting independence to the Baltic states and has revolutionized the pattern of relations among the Soviet successor states. The growing diversity on the Triangle's periphery, while it is bound to revive old ethnic tensions, contains in it the seeds of a future radical remaking of East Central European security. In the long run, if the breakup and reconstruction of the former Soviet Union continue to proceed without large-scale violence, and if Russia does not revert to authoritarianism, a fundamental redefinition of the balance of power in East Central Europe is bound to occur. In the event, by the end of the decade the tension and instability of the early 1990s should be replaced with a dramatically improved security situation in the region.

In the short term, however, the prospect of continuing regional instability in the East has two major implications for the future security of Europe as a whole. First, in the next several years, Poland, Czechoslovakia, and Hungary will be facing a deteriorating security situation on their eastern borders. Second, a North-South divide separating the northwestern and north-central European states from those living farther east and south on the Continent's periphery will progressively replace the East-West divide of the Cold War period. With the immediate Soviet military threat removed, Western Europe may find it less than urgent to bring the East Central European Triangle into its security framework, leaving Poland, Czechoslovakia, and Hungary in a "grey zone," where their security is not guaranteed through formal international agreements but is shored up instead via informal ties and cooperation arrangements that implicitly affirm the West's interest in the region.

On the surface, it appears as if the region's history were about to repeat itself. As in 1918, Poland, Czechoslovakia, and Hungary are facing a period of historic opportunity for national independence because of a dramatic change in the European order. Again, as in the aftermath of World War I, Germany and Russia, the two powers that have determined European politics since the mid-nineteenth century and that are bound to influence the region heavily in the foreseeable future, are preoccupied with domestic problems.

In this decade Germany faces the monumental task of rebuilding the ruined East German economy while the Soviet successor states grapple with a myriad of domestic problems in the wake of the disintegration of the empire. And yet the present situation is different enough from the interwar period to make such a historical analogy questionable.

Today's Germany has vital interests but no hegemonic aspirations in the East, while the German state can draw upon its forty-five years of democracy to provide the necessary leadership in the region. In light of the breakup of the Soviet Union, the threat of a direct Russian imperial domination of Poland, Czechoslovakia, and Hungary may already be a thing of the past as well. While Moscow's military might is still acutely felt in East Central Europe, it is unlikely that the Soviet successor states would resort to it to restore the former empire. The latent threat to East Central Europe is a by-product of the implosion rather than expansion of Soviet power, and it may arise as a result of internal chaos spreading to the neighboring countries and not because of a calculated Russian plan.

The task of creating a stable pan-European security system is a test that Europe failed in the past. The professed permanence of the interwar settlement could not be maintained in light of strong revisionist pressures from Germany and the Soviet Union. In addition, regional cooperation and collective security arrangements were never seriously explored, while the United States' determination to remain disengaged from Europe left the Continent adrift. The situation is different today in that revisionist pressures are absent from Western Europe and remain limited in East Central Europe. Revisionism and irredentism, having been relegated to Europe's eastern and southeastern periphery, are unlikely to threaten the territorial integrity of the Triangle states. The danger of the region once again finding itself in a political vacuum and adrift because of Bonn's self-preoccupation is also greatly exaggerated. Most important for the future of East Central European security, the United States has remained firmly committed to NATO and European security. For the balance of the decade at least, the transatlantic connection is bound to remain in place.

Still, Western Europe should be concerned about regional stability in and around East Central Europe. The issue is not only whether Western Europe can export the system of liberal democracy and free markets but ultimately whether it can foster regional security without the controlling influence of an outside superpower. In order to succeed, the nascent East Central European security framework must draw upon a broader system of Western European security, including its transatlantic connection. A successful transformation of the European security system, which for over four decades rested on a bipolar design, can only occur as part of a larger

European reformulation. The West must recognize that after the implosion of the Soviet Union's power, Moscow will continue to move farther away from the center of Western European politics. The demise of the Soviet Union in December 1991 does not in itself constitute a security threat to Europe so long as the consolidation of the successor states continues to proceed in a negotiated fashion. Whatever the growing pains, the basic Western security idea is sound: with a U.S. commitment to remain engaged in Europe and with the sense of a common Western European interest present, the new framework can succeed because in practical terms pan-Europeanism means a security system centered on Western Europe and anchored in the United States via a transatlantic axis.

In addition to the collapse of the Soviet Union, the reemergence of one Germany is the most dramatic departure from the former Yalta design. It is only a matter of time for Bonn/Berlin to come to terms with the legacy of the country's historical position in Central Europe, its relationship with the East and the West, and its changing relationship with the United States.[2] The process will not be completed until 1994, when the last Soviet troops are to leave Germany and Poland. But a greater Germany in Europe today does not mean a greater level of insecurity for its historical adversaries. Over time, Germany's relations with its Eastern neighbors may come to approximate the level of cooperation that has marked German-French relations since World War II.

Moreover, depending on the final outcome of the internal crisis in the former Soviet Union, the changes now under way in East Central Europe may in the end benefit Russia more than Moscow was willing to admit in 1990–1991. If the goal of Russia's policy remains to come closer to Europe and eventually to become, together with reunited Germany, an essential part of the new European system,[3] the Triangle states may constitute a political bridge that will link Russia to the rest of Europe.

Since 1989 the states of East Central Europe have pinned their hopes for national sovereignty on the expectation that a Western-dominated collective security system is, in the long run, the best guarantee of their newly recovered independence. These high hopes must be weighed against the reality of postcommunist politics in the region. It is apparent today that, while the Warsaw Pact has disintegrated, for some time to come there will be no formal military alliance in place to bind the security of Poland, Czechoslovakia, and Hungary directly to that of Western Europe. The CSCE is still not more than a promise of collective security, and the Crisis Prevention Center in Vienna will not become an effective agency until the planned 1992 CSCE general meeting in Helsinki has underwritten its structure and authority. By contrast, NATO is a fully operational alliance, which, if modified, can offer East Central Europe a real assurance of a Western security commitment.

There were signs in late 1991 that NATO was beginning to take the necessary steps that could make the Triangle's future membership in the alliance possible. The NATO summit in Rome, November 7–8, 1991, created a new council that will enable former Warsaw Pact countries and the Baltic states to consult on a regular basis with the Atlantic Alliance. Although falling short of NATO membership requested by Poland, Czechoslovakia, and Hungary, the Rome decision was yet another landmark on the Triangle's road to Europe. NATO's new strategy, accepted at the Rome summit, reflects the dramatic decline of the direct military threat from the East and the increased instability in Europe caused by the resurgence of nationalist and ethnic passions.

From a purely practical point of view, the question of NATO membership for East Central Europe will remain a moot point until the completion of the 1994 Soviet troop withdrawal from Germany and Poland. In addition, the training, organization, and equipment of the East Central European armies are not compatible with NATO's. Even if the three plan to restructure and reequip with Western weapons, their limited resources will make this a lengthy process lasting into the next century.

Political objections to the Triangle's full membership in NATO in its present form remain. Poland, Czechoslovakia, and Hungary's full membership in NATO as it is structured today would imply that the United States' strategic nuclear umbrella would be extended to cover East Central Europe. It would also imply that NATO troops might be stationed in the region. Moscow's past vehement opposition to such a development aside, at present there is no popular support in Western Europe or the United States for such a radical reformulation of policy. Today, the political and economic costs of integrating the Triangle directly into NATO as a full member, while it remains an open issue for the future, make it an undertaking whose time has yet to come. In the aftermath of the Soviet empire's collapse, however, it may be sooner than one would think when Moscow's objections to the Triangle's membership in NATO become muted or are dropped altogether. In that case, the incorporation of Poland, Czechoslovakia, and Hungary in NATO would be a recognition of their new political alignment as well as a new balance of power in Europe.

The prospects for a regional security alliance in East Central Europe are largely circumscribed by the very limited defensive utility of such a military union. Without a firm guarantee from the West, a formal mutual assistance and security treaty among Poland, Czechoslovakia, and Hungary would not constitute a sufficient deterrent to an all-out aggression; at the same time, it would carry with it the price of possibly retarding the region's "return to Europe." Moreover, the former Soviet Union viewed such a regional bloc as a buffer hindering its access to Europe, and there is no reason to believe that the Soviet successor states should be more enthusiastic about the idea. Furthermore, Western Europe—Germany in particular—would likely consider such a regional alliance an obstacle to closer cooperation with Russia. For these reasons, although regional cooperation in East Central Europe in the 1990s is bound to increase in such areas as foreign policy coordination, economic development, and environmental protection, it will fall short of a security alliance treaty.

Since Poland, Czechoslovakia, and Hungary can do little more than what they have been doing to increase their national security, the challenge for the immediate future will be to *decrease the demand for security* in the region through political means, primarily by reducing tension with the Soviet Union's successor states.[4] The Triangle will need to focus a greater diplomatic effort than it has so far on improving its bilateral relations with its eastern neighbors, especially at the time when the collapse of Soviet communism has opened up new possibilities for balanced bilateral agreements. If Russia does not feel left out of Europe completely, it will be more apt to comply with commonly accepted European principles of cooperation. This alone will reduce considerably the residual threat Russia's power poses to its Western neighbors. Even though for the time being Europe's new Eastern frontier will run along the Bug River and the Carpatho-Ukrainian border of Czechoslovakia and Hungary, as long as it does not become a wall blocking Russia's access to the West, East Central Europe will be able to reach an accommodation with Moscow on mutually acceptable terms.

Despite the rhetoric of pan-Europeanism, the West as well as the Triangle recognizes very well that the Soviet successor states will not become a part of the new Europe any time soon. The new states' economic and political reform programs have remained virtually paralyzed by the nationalities problem, and will remain so until the question of imperial succession has been resolved. Internal turmoil in the former Soviet Union has all but eliminated the direct Soviet military threat to the West, while also reducing Moscow's ability to pressure its former satellites into policies that would restore its former control over the region. Even if the former USSR successfully reconstitutes itself into the Commonwealth of Independent States, as Yeltsin's plan for a new confederation of the successor states suggests, the new state will be a diminished power no longer capable of bringing its former weight to bear on the West; in private, the Russians admit this themselves.

If Poland, Czechoslovakia, and Hungary manage to take full advantage of the historic opportunity to rebuild their economies along the lines of the Western market system, if they attract substantial Western investment and thus create a tangible Western interest in the preservation of their new independence, and if they consolidate their democratic systems, the three countries will be able to continue on the road to full integration with Western Europe. In the process, they may turn their erstwhile vulnerability—that is, their immediate proximity to the Soviet successor states—into an asset by serving as a channel for trade between the West and the East.

The "grey zone period" in the East Central European security is likely to last until the West Europeans have reached an agreement on which institutional framework to adopt: reformed NATO, a European security system built around the Western European Union, or an all-new CSCE structure. The resolution to the regional security equation will also have to await the final outcome of the internal crisis in the former USSR. The transition period may, therefore, be one of sporadic conflicts and interstate tension. In the 1990s, Poland, Czechoslovakia, and Hungary will, by virtue of their geopolitical position, for a time straddle the reality of the old and the new Europe.

While bilateralism is the best security option open to them, Poland, Czechoslovakia, and Hungary will continue to share three broad general principles of national security: (1) cooperation with neighboring states and a search for Western security guarantees, (2) restraint and peaceful resolution of crises, and (3) active defense as a solution of last resort. The efforts by Poland, Czechoslovakia, and Hungary to obtain defense guarantees from NATO and eventually to join the Atlantic Alliance will remain at the forefront of their security policy for as long as the CSCE lacks a workable enforcement mechanism. As NATO becomes more European in character, it may eventually decide to admit new members. The complete reorganization of NATO, announced after the defense ministers' meeting in Brussels on May 28, 1991—including the creation of a British-commanded rapid deployment force by 1995, with British, German, Belgian, and Dutch units[5]—and the new defense strategy adopted during the NATO summit in Rome, November 7–8, 1991, are bound to improve the prospects of the Triangle eventually becoming a full member of the restructured alliance.

East Central Europe is in the midst of the most radical transformation since the end of World War II. In part the process has already been a success, in that Poland, Czechoslovakia, and Hungary have managed to make their goal of integrating with Western Europe a legitimate share of

Europe's future, even if the final structure of the new security system still remains unclear.

NOTES

1. For an extensive discussion of the three scenarios and their adherents, see Jan Zielonka, "Europe's Security: A Great Confusion," *International Affairs,* vol. 67, no. 1 (1991), pp. 127–137.

2. George Liska, "Between East and West: East-Central Europe's Future Past," in Michael T. Clark and Simon Serfaty, eds., *New Thinking and Old Realities: America, Europe, and Russia* (Washington, D.C.: Johns Hopkins Foreign Policy Institute, 1990), p. 163.

3. Agnieszka Magdziak-Miszewska and Jerzy Marek Nowakowski, "Droga do Rosji," *Polityka Polska*, vol. 2, no. 16 (November 1990), p. 11.

4. The decrease in the need for security has in fact been the preferred alternative for Western Europe, albeit largely because of the Western European governments' unwillingness to make the requisite expenditure to ensure their self-sufficiency in terms of security. See Josef Joffe, "After Bipolarity: Eastern and Western Europe," in *The Strategic Implications of Change in the Soviet Union* (London: International Institute for Strategic Studies, Adelphi Paper #247, Winter 1989/90), p. 70.

5. "NATO Plans Rapid Reaction Force Commanded by UK," *Financial Times*, May 29, 1991.

SELECTED BIBLIOGRAPHY

"Air Force Official Comments on Financial Problems." *FBIS-EEU-91-002*, January 3, 1991.

"Antall Comments on German Relations, Pact." *FBIS-EEU-90-120*, June 21, 1990.

"Antall: German Unification 'Advantageous.' " *FBIS-EEU-90-164*. August 23, 1990.

"Antall Interviewed on Ties with EC, NATO." *FBIS-EEU-91-099*, May 22, 1991.

"Antall Interviewed on Visit, Confirms 'Liaison' with NATO." *FBIS-EEU-90-139*, July 19, 1990.

"Antall, Jeszenszky Return from Venice Summit." *FBIS-EEU-90-149*, August 2, 1990.

"Antall on Warsaw Pact, NATO Future." *FBIS-EEU-90-122*, June 25, 1990.

"Antall, Stoltenberg Meet." *FBIS-EEU-90-134*, July 12, 1990.

"Arms Cut Details Revealed." *Jane's Defence Weekly*, February 18, 1989.

"Army Accord on Business Trips Signed with FRG." *FBIS-EEU-90-219*, November 13, 1990.

"Army General Interviewed on Arms Trade." *FBIS-EEU-91-003*, January 4, 1991.

"Army Official Views New Military Doctrine." *FBIS-EEU-90-143*, July 25, 1990.

"Army Selling Military Equipment to the West." *FBIS-EEU-90-120*, June 20, 1990.

Atlas of Eastern Europe. Washington, D.C.: Central Intelligence Agency, August 1990.

Bannan, Alfred J., and Achilles Edelenyi, eds. *Documentary History of Eastern Europe*. New York: Twayne Publishers, 1970.

Battiata, Mary. "Soviets Rebuff Poles on Troop Pullout." *Washington Post*, February 13, 1991.

Baxter, William P. *Soviet AirLand Battle Tactics*. Novato, Calif.: Presidio Press, 1986.

Bellamy, Christopher. "What the New Warsaw Pact Military Doctrine Means for the West." *Jane's Defence Weekly*, December 5, 1987.

Bender, Peter. *East Europe in Search of Security*. London: Chatto and Windus, 1972.

Bethlen, Steven, and Ivan Volgyes, eds. *Europe and the Superpowers: Political, Economic, and Military Policies in the 1980s*. Boulder, Colo., and London: Westview Press, 1985.

Bin, Xiao. "Warsaw Pact Faces Uncertain Prospects." *Beijing Review*, May 28, 1990.

"Bonn Says Polish Pact to Go Ahead." *Financial Times*, May 29, 1991.

"Border Guards Chief on Future Reorganization." *FBIS-EEU-90-248*, December 26, 1990.

Burks, R. V. *East European History: An Ethnic Approach*. Washington, D.C.: American Historical Association, 425 AHA Pamphlets, 1973.

"Cabinet Discusses Monetary, Defense Issues." *FBIS-EEU-90-233*, December 4, 1990.

"Carnogursky Promises Tolerant Government." *FBIS-EEU-91-100*, May 23, 1991.

Carnovale, Marco, and William C. Potter, eds. *Continuity and Change in Soviet–East European Relations: Implications for the West*. Boulder, Colo.: Westview Press, 1989.

Catudal, Honore M. *Soviet Nuclear Strategy from Stalin to Gorbachev: A Revolution in Soviet Military and Political Thinking*. Atlantic Highlands, N.J.: Humanities Press International, 1988.

"Changes in the Soviet Military High Command." *Jane's Defence Weekly*, October 25, 1986.

"Chnoupek Addresses Diplomatic Corps Meeting." *FBIS-EEU-87-010*, January 15, 1987.

Clarke, Douglas L. "The Conventional Armed Forces in Europe Treaty: Limits and Zones." *Report on Eastern Europe*, vol. 2, no. 2. Munich: RFE/RL, January 11, 1991.

———."The Military Implications of a Soviet Troop Withdrawal from Czechoslovakia." *Report on Eastern Europe*, vol. 1, no. 5. Munich: RFE/RL, February 2, 1990.

———. "Warsaw Pact: The Transformation Begins." *Report on Eastern Europe*, vol. 1, no. 25. Munich: RFE/RL, June 22, 1990.

Clark, Susan L., ed. *Gorbachev's Agenda: Changes in Soviet Domestic and Foreign Policy*. Boulder, Colo., San Francisco, and London: Westview Press, 1989.

"Commentary Criticizes Czech Constitution Agreement." *FBIS-EEU-91-099*, May 22, 1991.

Conditions in the Baltic States and in Other Countries of Eastern Europe: Hearings Before the Subcommittee on Europe, Committee on Foreign Affairs, House of Representatives, Eighty-Ninth U.S. Congress. Washington, D.C.: U.S. Government Printing Office, 1965.

"Council of Europe Delegation Arrives in Prague." *FBIS-EEU-91-025*, February 6, 1991.

"Council of Europe Membership Made Official." *FBIS-EEU-91-215*, November 6, 1991.

"CPSU's Musatov on Relations with East Europe." *FBIS-SOV-91-096*, May 17, 1991.

Critchley, Julian. *The North Atlantic Alliance and the Soviet Union in the 1980s*. London: Macmillan Press, 1982.

"Czechoslovakia Considering Links with NATO after Leaving the Pact." *Financial Times*, February 7, 1991.

"Czy za 'te pieniadze' mozna miec lepsza armie." *Zolnierz Wolnosci*, February 26, 1990.

"Czym sie bronic? Nasza armia znalazla sie praktycznie w slepej uliczce." *Wokanda*, May 12, 1991.

"Defense Minister Describes Future Army Structure." *FBIS-EEU-90-217*, November 8, 1990.

"Defense Minister Karpati Views Troop Reduction." *FBIS-EEU-89-021*, February 2, 1989.

"Defense Minister Lifts Ban on Officer Group." *FBIS-EEU-90-212*, November 1, 1990.

"Defense Minister Outlines New Defense Principles." *FBIS-EEU-91-058*, March 26, 1991.

"Defense Minister Returns from UK, Belgium Visit." *FBIS-EEU-91-047*, March 11, 1991.

"Defense Minister Views Budget, Soviet Relations." *FBIS-EEU-90-237*, December 10, 1990.

"Defense Minister's Announcement on Arms Reduction." *FBIS-EEU-90-223*, November 19, 1990.

"Defense Ministry Airs Future Army Issues." *FBIS-EEU-90-152*, August 7, 1990.

"Defense Ministry Budget to Increase Next Year." *FBIS-EEU-90-173*, September 6, 1990.

"Defense Official on Security, Warsaw Pact." *FBIS-EEU-90-158*, August 15, 1990.

"Defense Official Queried on Upcoming Changes." *FBIS-EEU-90-147*, July 31, 1990.

"Defense Officials Meet Press on Budget Cuts." *FBIS-EEU-90-245*, December 20, 1990.

"Deklaratsya gosudarstv-uchastnikov Varshavskogo Dogovora." *Krasnaya Zvezda*, June 8, 1990.

"Delegation Ends Visit." *FBIS-EEU-90-134*, July 12, 1990.

"Deputy Cited on Troop Withdrawal from Germany." *FBIS-SOV-91-097*, May 20, 1991.

Dienstbier, Jiri. "Central European Security." *Foreign Policy*, Summer 1991.

"Dienstbier Stresses Summit Results." *FBIS-EEU-90-226*, November 23, 1990.

"Discord Develops over Costs of Troop Withdrawal." *FBIS-EEU-90-116*, June 15, 1990.

"Dobrovsky, Kolodziejczyk Sign Military Agreement." *FBIS-EEU-91-042*, March 4, 1991.

"Dobrovsky on Defense Bill Amendments." *FBIS-EEU-91-096*, May 17, 1991.

"Dobrovsky Submits Army Laws to Federal Assembly." *FBIS-EEU-91-099*, May 22, 1991.

"Doktryna Obronna Rzeczypospolitej Polskiej." *Zolnierz Wolnosci*, February 26, 1990.

"Eastern Europe Responds to Gorbachev Cut-Backs." *Jane's Defence Weekly*, January 7, 1989.

"EBRD's Nemeth on Policy Concerning Country." *FBIS-EEU-91-099*, May 22, 1991.

"Education Reform to Boost Military Efficiency." *Jane's Defence Weekly*, January 31, 1987.

"Envoy Views Dismantling of Warsaw Pact." *FBIS-EEU-90-141*, July 23, 1990.

"First Soviet Troops to Leave Hungary Soon." *Jane's Defence Weekly*, January 21, 1989.

Fischer-Galati, Stephen, ed. *Man, State, and Society in East European History*. New York: Praeger Publishers, 1970.

"Foreign Ministry Official on Moscow Pact Talks." *FBIS-EEU-90-116*, June 15, 1990.

"Foreign Ministry Official on Warsaw Pact Session." *FBIS-EEU-91-040*, February 28, 1991.

"Foreign Ministry on Relations with Slovakia." *FBIS-EEU-90-160*, August 17, 1990.

Fouguet, David. "Hungary in Defense Plan Debates." *Jane's Defence Weekly*, January 7, 1989.

Foye, Stephen. "Soviet Army's New Political Chief on Reform of Military-Political Organs." *Report on the USSR*, vol. 2, no. 31. Munich: RFE/RL, August 3, 1990.

"FRG Defense Minister Stoltenberg Meets Goncz." *FBIS-EEU-90-133*, July 11, 1990.

"FRG's Genscher Continues Prague Visit." *FBIS-EEU-90-214*, November 5, 1990.

"Fur Comments on Country's Future Defense Policy." *FBIS-EEU-90-119*, June 20, 1990.

"Fur Interviewed on Warsaw Pact Membership, Queried on Plans to Leave Pact." *FBIS-EEU-91-117*, June 18, 1991.

"Fur on Pact Membership, Problems with Romania." *FBIS-EEU-90-114*, June 13, 1990.

Garrett, Banning N., and Bonnie S. Glaser. *War and Peace: The Views from Moscow and Beijing.* Berkeley: University of California Institute of International Studies, 1984.

Gati, Charles. *The Bloc That Failed: Soviet–East European Relations in Transition.* Bloomington and Indianapolis: Indiana University Press, 1990.

———. *Hungary and the Soviet Bloc.* Durham, N.C.: Duke University Press, 1986.

Gormley, Dennis M. *Double Zero and Soviet Military Strategy: Implications for Western Security.* London: Jane's Publishing Co., 1988.

"Government Discusses Military Service, Budget." *FBIS-EEU-90-122*, June 25, 1990.

"Government Reduces Border Guard." *FBIS-EEU-89-243*, December 20, 1989.

Griffith, William E., ed. *Central and Eastern Europe: The Opening Curtain.* Boulder, Colo.: Westview Press, 1989.

Halloway, David. *The Soviet Union and the Arms Race.* New Haven, Conn.: Yale University Press, 1987.

———. *War, Militarism, and the Soviet State.* New York: World Order Models Project Working Paper Number 17, 1981.

"Havel against Treaty Clause." *Financial Times*, April 30, 1991.

"Havel, Calfa, Defense Council on Pacts." *FBIS-EEU-91-033*, February 19, 1991.

"Havel Condemns Events in Riga; Pact Discussed." *FBIS-EEU-91-014*, January 22, 1991.

"Havel Makes Personnel Changes in Army Command." *FBIS-EEU-90-215*, November 6, 1990.

"Havel Makes the Defense Council Appointments." *FBIS-EEU-90-029*, February 12, 1990.

"Havel Summarizes Conference Results." *FBIS-EEU-90-226*, November 23, 1990.

"Hungarian Defence Industry in Crisis." *Jane's Defence Weekly*, October 28, 1989.

"Hungarian Foreign Minister in Moscow for Talks." *FBIS-SOV-91-100*, May 23, 1991.

"Hungary's Last Soviet Deal." *Jane's Defence Weekly*, July 14, 1990.

"Interest Expressed in West's Military Expertise." *FBIS-EEU-90-118*, June 19, 1990.

Ionescu, Ghita. *The Break-up of the Soviet Empire in Eastern Europe.* Baltimore, Md.: Penguin Books, 1965.

Isby, David. *Weapons and Tactics of the Soviet Army.* London: Jane's Publishing Co., 1988.

"Italian Defense Minister Continues Visit." *FBIS-EEU-90-221*, November 15, 1990.

"Italian Defense Minister Rognoni Pays Visit." *FBIS-EEU-90-216*, November 7, 1990.

"The JDW Interview with Major General Anton Slimak." *Jane's Defence Weekly*, March 24, 1990.

"Jeden dzien z Januszem Onyszkiewiczem." *Zolnierz Rzeczypospolitej*, June 1–3, 1990.

"Jeszenszky Discusses Relations with Romania." *FBIS-EEU-90-160*, August 17, 1990.

"Jeszenszky Visits NATO Headquarters in Brussels." *FBIS-EEU-90-127*, July 2, 1990.

"Joint Intelligence Agreement Signed with Poland." *FBIS-EEU-91-042*, March 4, 1991.

Jones, Christopher D. *Soviet Influence in Eastern Europe: Political Autonomy and the Warsaw Pact.* New York: Praeger Publishers, 1981.

"Jozsef Antall Receives First EC Ambassador." *FBIS-EEU-90-137*, July 17, 1990.

"Kaczynski Walks out of Defense Meeting." *FBIS-EEU-91-100*, May 23, 1991.

"Kadar on End of CMEA, Trade Ties with USSR." *FBIS-EEU-91-099*, May 22, 1991.

Kaufman, Michael T. "Soviet Proposes Major Troop Reductions in Europe." *New York Times*, June 12, 1986.

Klein, George, and Milan J. Reban, eds. *The Politics of Ethnicity in Eastern Europe.* New York: Columbia University Press, 1981.

Kolodziejczyk, Admiral Piotr. "Model lat 90-tych." *Polska Zbrojna*, November 16–18, 1990.

"Kommyunike zasedaniya komiteta ministrov oborony gosudarstv-uchastnikov Varshavskogo Dogovora." *Krasnaya Zvezda*, June 16, 1990.

"Kontrowersje w sprawie KON." *Zycie Warszawy*, April 23, 1991.

Kovrig, Bennett. *The Myth of Liberation: East-Central Europe in US Diplomacy and Politics since 1941.* Baltimore, Md., and London: Johns Hopkins University Press, 1973.

Koziej, Colonel Stanislaw. "Problem strategii wojskowej: polityczno-militarna przyszlosc Europy." *Polska Zbrojna*, December 11, 1990.

Kvitsinskiy, Yuliy A. "Vostochnaya Evropa: Chto gryadet za peremenami." *Pravda*, March 18, 1991.

Lambeth, Benjamin S. *Has Soviet Nuclear Strategy Changed?* Santa Monica, Calif.: The Rand Corporation P-7181, 1985.

Liska, George. "Between East and West: East-Central Europe's Future Past." In Michael T. Clark and Simon Serfaty, eds. *New Thinking and Old Realities: America, Europe, and Russia.* Washington, D.C.: Johns Hopkins Foreign Policy Institute, 1990.

Lushev, General Pyotr G. "Edinstvo oboronnykh usiliy stran Varshavskogo Dogovora— faktor nadezhnoy zashchity sotsializma." *Voyennaya Mysl'*, January 1990.

———. "Security Versus Dogma." *World Marxist Review*, vol. 32, December 1989.

———. "Varshavskiy Dogovor: istoriya i sovremennost'." *Voyennaya Mysl'*, May 1990.

———. "Varshavskomu dogovoru—35 let." *Krasnaya Zvezda*, May 13, 1990.

Macartney, C. A., and A. W. Palmer. *Independent Eastern Europe: A History.* London: Macmillan and Co., 1962.

MccGwire, Michael. *Military Objectives in Soviet Foreign Policy.* Washington, D.C.: The Brookings Institution, 1987.

———. *Perestroika and Soviet National Security.* Washington, D.C.: The Brookings Institution, 1991.

McNeill, William H. *Europe's Steppe Frontier, 1500–1800.* Chicago and London: University of Chicago Press, 1964.

Magdziak-Miszewska, Agnieszka, and Jerzy Marek Nowakowski. "Droga do Rosji." *Polityka Polska*, vol. 2, no. 16, November 1990.

Medvedev, Zhores. "Before the Coup: The Plot inside the Kremlin." *Washington Post*, September 1, 1991.

Mellor, Roy E. H. *Eastern Europe: A Geography of the Comecon Countries.* New York: Columbia University Press, 1975.

The Military Balance, 1988–1989. London: International Institute for Strategic Studies, 1988.

The Military Balance, 1989–1990. London: International Institute for Strategic Studies, 1989.

"Military Delegation's U.S. Visit Seen Successful." *FBIS-EEU-90-149*, August 2, 1990.

"Military Officials Discuss Defense Issues." FBIS-EEU-91-094, May 15, 1991.

"Minister Fur Views Burlakov's 'Grave Threat.' " FBIS-EEU-90-128, July 3, 1990.

"Ministry Official on Purchase of GDR Tanks." FBIS-EEU-90-192, October 3, 1990.

Moiseyev, General Mikhail A. "S positsiy oboronitel'noy doktriny." Krasnaya Zvezda, February 10, 1989.

———. "Voyennaya reforma: deystvitel'nost' i perspektivy." Krasnaya Zvezda, November 18, 1990.

Musatov, Valeriy. "Vostochnaya Evropa: Tayfun peremen." Pravda, March 13, 1991.

"Nadszedl czas, aby Europa przeszla do tworzenia konkretow wspolpracy." Zolnierz Wolnosci, January 31, 1991.

"National Assembly Meets in Extraordinary Session, Approves Vote on NATO Membership." FBIS-EEU-91-020, January 30, 1991.

"NATO Plans Rapid Reaction Force Commanded by UK." Financial Times, May 29, 1991.

"NATO's Woerner Continues Official Visit." FBIS-EEU-90-227, November 26, 1990.

Nelson, Daniel N., ed. Soviet Allies: The Warsaw Pact and the Issue of Reliability. Boulder, Colo., and London: Westview Press, 1984.

"New Law May Prompt the U.S. to Lift Trade Curbs." Commercial Appeal, May 22, 1991.

"Nowi wiceministrowie obrony narodowej." Zolnierz Rzeczypospolitej, April 4, 1990.

"Oath Omits Reference to Party Loyalty." FBIS-EEU-89-160, August 21, 1989.

Obrman, Jan. "Changes in the Armed Forces." Report on Eastern Europe, vol. 1, no. 14. Munich: RFE/RL, April 6, 1990.

———. "Changing Conditions for the Army and the Police." Report on Eastern Europe, vol. 1, no. 26. Munich: RFE/RL, January 26, 1990.

———. "Interview with First Deputy Chief of the General Staff." Report on Eastern Europe, vol. 1, no. 29. Munich: RFE/RL, July 20, 1990.

"Official on Trade Problems with USSR." FBIS-EEU-91-099, May 22, 1991.

Okey, Robin. Eastern Europe 1740–1985: Feudalism to Communism. Minneapolis: University of Minnesota Press, 1986.

"Pact Military Doctrine." FBIS-SOV-87-104, June 1, 1987.

"Pact's Future Pondered on 36th Anniversary." FBIS-SOV-91-097, May 20, 1991.

Papuga, Jerzy. "Temat: Nowa Polska w Europie." Konfrontacje, May 1991.

Piotrowski, Waldemar. "Wojska NATO w Polsce." Zycie Warszawy, June 1, 1990.

"Poland Neutral." Financial Times, February 7, 1991.

"Poles Plan 4% Spending Cut." Jane's Defence Weekly, January 14, 1989.

Polish Army: Facts and Figures. Warsaw: Ministry of Defense, 1990.

"Polish Minister Details Forces Cuts." Jane's Defence Weekly, March 18, 1989.

Polonsky, Antony. The Little Dictators: The History of Eastern Europe since 1918. London and Boston: Routledge & Kegan Paul, 1975.

"Polska i RFN podpisaly traktat o potwierdzeniu istniejacej miedzy nimi granicy." Polska Zbrojna, November 15, 1990.

"Polski przemysl zbrojeniowy: czolgiem do Europy." Gazeta Bankowa, April 14–20, 1991.

"Powstanie nowa sluzba wychowawcza WP." Zolnierz Wolnosci, March 16–18, 1990.

"President Havel Comments on Summit, Laws, Gulf." FBIS-EEU-91-033, February 19, 1991.

"Press Reacts to Havel's 10 December Proposals." *FBIS-EEU-90-244*, December 19, 1990.

"Problems Facing Polish Army." *Jane's Defence Weekly*, February 11, 1989.

"Professional Army Expected by Year 2000." *FBIS-EEU-90-218*, November 9, 1990.

"Przemiany w Wojsku Polskim: Rozmowa z czlonkiem Biura Politycznego KC PZPR, Ministrem Obrony Narodowej, gen. armii Florianem Siwickim." *Trybuna Ludu*, January 4, 1989.

Puchala, General Franciszek. "Zmiana dyslokacji jednostek WP: to wynika z naszej racji stanu." *Polska Zbrojna*, December 12, 1990.

"Rabochiy vizit G. Kola." *Krasnaya Zvezda*, July 17, 1990.

Rakowska-Harmstone, Teresa, Christopher Jones, and Ivan Sylvain. *Warsaw Pact: The Question of Cohesion. Phase II*. Vol. 2. *Poland, German Democratic Republic, and Romania*. Ottawa: ORAE Extra-Mural Paper No. 33, November 1984.

Ransom, Charles. *The European Community and Eastern Europe*. London: Butterworths, 1973.

Reisch, Alfred. "The Hungarian Dilemma: After the Warsaw Pact, Neutrality or NATO." *Report on Eastern Europe*, vol. 1, no. 15. Munich: RFE/RL, April 13, 1990.

————. "Hungary to Leave Military Arm of the Pact." *Report on Eastern Europe*, vol. 1, no. 26. Munich: RFE/RL, June 29, 1990.

————. "Interview with Foreign Minister Geza Jeszenszky." *Report on Eastern Europe*, vol. 1, no. 30. Munich: RFE/RL, July 27, 1990.

Remnick, David. "The Hard-Liners' Bad Boy Challenges Gorbachev." *Washington Post*, February 8, 1991.

"Review of Nation's Changing Defense Industry." *FBIS-EEU-91-059*, March 27, 1991.

RFE/RL Daily Report. Munich: Radio Free Europe/Radio Liberty Research Institute, January 22, 1991.

RFE/RL Situation Report: Czechoslovakia. December–January 1989.

Rice, Condoleezza. *The Soviet Union and the Czechoslovak Army, 1948–1983: Uncertain Alliance*. Princeton, N.J.: Princeton University Press, 1984.

Roberts, Henry L. *Eastern Europe: Politics, Revolution, and Diplomacy*. New York: Alfred A. Knopf, 1970.

Rollo, J. M. C. *The New Eastern Europe: Western Responses*. New York: Council on Foreign Relations Press, 1990. Published in North America for the Royal Institute of International Affairs.

Rothschild, Joseph. *East Central Europe between the Two World Wars*. Seattle and London: University of Washington Press, 1974.

————. *Return to Diversity: A Political History of East Central Europe since World War II*. New York and Oxford: Oxford University Press, 1989.

"Rozmowy Skubiszewski-Szewardnadze." *Polska Zbrojna*, October 12–14, 1990.

Rychlowski, Bogumil. *Niestabilnosc Europy Wschodniej i Problemy Bezpieczenstwa Miedzynarodowego*. Warsaw: PISM, 1991.

Schopflin, George, ed. *The Soviet Union and Eastern Europe*. New York and Oxford: Facts on File Publications and Muller, Blond, and White, 1986.

Scott, Harriet Fast, and William F. Scott. *Soviet Military Doctrine: Continuity, Formulation, and Dissemination*. Boulder, Colo., and London: Westview Press, 1988.

"Sie taten morgen kommen wolle." *Der Spiegel*, January 7, 1991.

Simon, Jeffrey. *Warsaw Pact Forces: Problems of Command and Control*. Boulder, Colo.: Westview Press, 1985.

Simon, Jeffrey, and Trond Gilberg, eds. *Security Implications of Nationalism in Eastern Europe*. Boulder, Colo., and London: Westview Press, 1986.

"Skubiszewski on Entry into 'Pentagonal Group.' " *FBIS-EEU-91-097*, May 20, 1991.

"Slovak Prime Minister Carnogursky Interviewed." *FBIS-EEU-91-097*, May 20, 1991.

"Slovaks Underrepresented at Defense Ministry." *FBIS-EEU-91-098*, May 21, 1991.

Snow, Donald M., ed. *Soviet-American Security Relations in the 1990s*. Lexington, Mass.: Lexington Books, 1989.

"Sondaze Centrum Badania Opinii Spolecznej." *Rzeczpospolita*, April 15, 1991.

"Soviet View of Future War after Arms Cuts." *Jane's Defence Weekly*, January 28, 1989.

"Soviets Suspend Traffic." *FBIS-EEU-90-158*, August 15, 1990.

"Spanish Defense Minister Serra Pays Visit." *FBIS-EEU-91-186*, September 25, 1991.

"Spokesman on Pact Meeting, Gulf, Equipment." *FBIS-EEU-91-031*, February 14, 1991.

Staar, Richard F., ed. *United States–East European Relations in the 1990s*. New York: Crane Russak, 1989.

"Statement by the Deputy Prime Minister and Minister of Foreign Affairs of the Czech and Slovak Federal Republic Jiri Dienstbier in the Federal Assembly on April 9, 1991." Prague: Ministry of Foreign Affairs, 1991.

Stelmaszuk, General Zdzislaw. "Jakie zmiany w WP." *Polska Zbrojna*, November 16–18, 1990.

———. "Nowy model armii." *Polska Zbrojna*, November 22, 1990.

The Strategic Implications of Change in the Soviet Union. London: International Institute for Strategic Studies, Adelphi Paper #247, Winter 1989/90.

"Struktury cywilne i wojskowe: prace nad nowym ksztaltem systemu obronnosci panstwa." *Zycie Warszawy*, April 16, 1991.

Sukiennicki, Wiktor. *East-Central Europe during World War I: From Foreign Domination to National Independence*. New York: Columbia University Press, 1984.

Szymanderski, Jacek. "Sprawa armii jest sprawa niezwyklej wagi." *Zolnierz Wolnosci*, February 13, 1990.

"Tank Unit Withdrawals Revealed." *Jane's Defence Weekly*, March 18, 1989.

"Team to Make Army Professional Established." *FBIS-EEU-90-143*, July 25, 1990.

"Temat: Nowa Polska w Europie. Z ministrem obrony narodowej wiceadmiralem Piotrem Kolodziejczykiem rozmawia Jerzy Papuga." *Konfrontacje*, May 1991.

Terry, Sarah Meiklejohn, ed. *Soviet Policy in Eastern Europe*. New Haven, Conn., and London: Yale University Press, 1984.

"2 Million Volga Germans Pose Settlement Issue for Bonn, Moscow." *Washington Post*, February 4, 1991.

Vojenska doktrina Ceske a Slovenske Federativni Republiky. Prague: Federalne Zhromazdenie, 1991.

"Vojenske stavebni kapacity." *Rude Pravo*, August 5, 1989.

Volgyes, Ivan. "The Warsaw Pact: Changes in Structure and Functions." *Armed Forces and Society*, vol. 15, no. 4, Summer 1989.

"Voyennaya reforma: opyt, problemy, perspektivy—'krugloy stol.' " *Voyennaya Mysl'*, April 1990.

Walters, Garrison E. *The Other Europe: Eastern Europe to 1945*. Syracuse, N.Y.: Syracuse University Press, 1988.

Wardak, Ghulam Dastagir, and Graham Hall Turbinville, Jr., eds. *The Voroshilov Lectures: Materials from the Soviet General Staff Academy.* 2 vols. Washington, D.C.: National Defense University Press, 1989.

"Warsaw and Bonn Agree to Goodwill Treaty." *Financial Times*, May 3, 1991.

"Warsaw Pact Forces in Europe." *Jane's Defence Weekly*, April 4, 1987.

Whitney, Craig R. "Prague Arms Trade to End, Foreign Minister Says." *New York Times*, January 25, 1991.

"Wielkie Zmiany." *Sztandar Mlodych*, April 19–21, 1991.

World Military Expenditures and Arms Transfers, 1987. Washington, D.C.: U.S. Arms Control and Disarmament Agency, 1988.

"Wychowawczy to znaczy jaki." *Zolnierz Wolnosci*, February 19, 1990.

"Youth Organizations to Disband." *FBIS-EEU-89-198*, October 16, 1989.

"Zadania Ukraincow." *Rzeczpospolita*, March 22, 1991.

"Zasadniczo przebudowujemy armie akcentujac jej obronny charakter." *Zolnierz Wolnosci*, January 5–7, 1990.

Zielonka, Jan. "Europe's Security: A Great Confusion." *International Affairs*, vol. 67, no. 1, 1991.

"Zmeny v armade." *Rude Pravo*, July 12, 1989.

"ZSRR gotow do rozmow na temat wycofania swoich wojsk z terytorium Polski." *Zolnierz Wolnosci*, February 12, 1990.

INDEX

ABOUT THE AUTHOR

ANDREW A. MICHTA is Assistant Professor of International Studies at Rhodes College in Memphis, Tennessee, where he holds the Mertie Willigar Buckman Chair of International Studies. Dr. Michta is the author of *Red Eagle: The Army in Polish Politics, 1944–1988*, and a number of articles on Soviet and East European politics.